AGENTS, ROVERS AND CRICKET LOVING OWNERS

by

Michael Blackburn

Grosvenor House
Publishing Limited

This book is published by
Grosvenor House Publishing Ltd
28-30 High Street, Guildford, Surrey, GU1 3EL.
www.grosvenorhousepublishing.co.uk

A CIP record for this book
is available from the British Library

ISBN 978-1-78148-544-6

Contents

Acknowledgements

First of all I would like to thank Phil Lloyd for the many hours he has spent proof reading and editing the original draft copy of *Agents, Rovers and Cricket Loving Owners.* Not only has it been great to have the help of somebody who is far better at spelling than me (I think the first draft broke the world record for most foreign names spelt wrong in one place!) but more importantly it has been an absolute godsend to be able to talk through the book with another passionate Rovers fan and proud local man. Thank you for all your help, Phil.

Many thanks to Tom McGrath for the design work on the Rovertaken logo, book cover and promotional stationary. A truly talented guy and absolute pleasure to work with – check out his website at www.spikedmcgrath.com. Thank you to Allan Scott for the www.rovertaken.co.uk website. If you are looking for affordable web design and development www.allanscott.co.uk comes recommended. I would like to thank Corrina, Ruth, Paul, Kim and all at Grosvenor House Publishing for all their help getting the book out there. I am hoping I can repay your efforts in book sales! Thank you also to Christine and Janet at Eanam Wharf and Cara at BTC.

I would like to thank the hundreds of Rovers fans home and abroad who have offered me messages of support and encouragement since details of the book were first announced. We all want the same thing and if we stick together we will get it. Special thanks go to the administrators and members of BRFCS, BRFC Action Group, The Fans' Forum, BRSIT, Bleeds Blue 'n' White, Vital Blackburn, 4,000 Holes, RoversMAD, Roverstruth and Roversfans.co.uk.

Most of all I would like to thank my beautiful wife. She doesn't like football and without her patience, love and understanding throughout the last nine months there is no way this book would have ever got off the ground. I am looking forward to finally putting the laptop away so we can enjoy the good things in life - not least our perfect little boy.

Thank you to the Lancashire Telegraph. This is the point where I would have liked to have thanked all the people involved in football and Blackburn Rovers Football Club for their help trying to piece this story together. Unfortunately, despite numerous attempts on my behalf, it proved an almost impossible task trying to engage members of the football world in meaningful two-way dialogue regarding the goings-on at Blackburn Rovers. The questions have been asked and until they are answered I don't see them going away. I would like to thank all those in the media that have reported this story honestly and fairly and from the heart. Not all people in the media are numpties and the work done by the cream of the profession is truly appreciated by Rovers fans. As well as the websites and publications referenced in the text, Atomic Soda, Wikipedia, YouTube and transfermarkt.co.uk have been great resources. Anybody I have not mentioned, please accept my sincere apologies and get in touch at michael.blackburn@live.co.uk

I may not be Shakespeare; I may not be Sherlock Holmes but I have gone to the verge of insanity to get this book out. I am not doing this for profit and I don't want a medal or a chat show. Like thousands of other Rovers fans, I just want to be able to walk out of my front door on a Saturday afternoon and feel the buzz of going to Rovers games again. Come on you Blues!

CHAPTER 1

Champions League Dreams

"I'm Kean to put us in the Champions League," read the latest instalment of the comedy hit painfully unfolding down at Ewood Park. The Rovers fan in me tried to picture Xavi and Messi stepping out at the Nou Camp ready to pit their wits against Vince Grella and Jason Roberts. All I could see was tabloid-reading Britain belly laughing into their cornflakes at my club's expense. There was a kind of innocent charm when Del Boy used to tell Rodney, "This time next year we'll be millionaires, Rodders" and eventually the scriptwriters did make them millionaires but somehow this felt more like the middle-aged village idiot on *X-Factor* who says he is going to be a pop star. It had become embarrassing. As my 2011/12 season ticket renewal form sat on top of the microwave with the rest of my unwanted mail it was becoming more and more difficult to summon up the strength to fill it in. Suddenly a life of DIY began to hold more appeal than the thought of watching another season of the shambles that had become Blackburn Rovers Football Club.

I had witnessed bad times at Rovers – Graham Le Saux rabbit punching David Batty in the head live on ITV, Ashley Ward making Crewe Alexandra's goalkeeper look like Dino Zoff, George Courtney awarding the most scandalous penalty ever seen to end our Play-off dreams back in 1989. I am sure fans older than me had witnessed far worse but I was really struggling to remember anything that came close to the catalogue of bad decisions being made by the owners and management at Blackburn Rovers over the summer of 2011. In the space of little over eight weeks, despite making several big early summer promises, our best player had been sold to Manchester United in what appeared to be a low bid auction; a laughable bid had been made for global superstar Raul; a series of underwhelming new signings had been unveiled; the financial position of the club continued to be a source of much speculation; the club had failed in the search for a commercial shirt sponsor; the pre-season visit to India had been cancelled and members of the club's playing staff had starred in an advert for chicken nuggets that almost made Pele's erectile dysfunction advert seem cool. It was no wonder that our odds for relegation were shortening by the hour and our fans were getting angrier by the minute – and the season hadn't even started.

I had been very lucky. Having just turned 30, my years supporting Rovers had been filled with unimaginable joy and success. Still one of only four clubs to have won the Premier League (Manchester City have just made it five), we had also won the

League Cup, the Full Members Cup, two promotions to the top division, been in countless semi-finals, never lost a game to our nearest rivals Burnley, competed in the UEFA Champions League and played numerous times in Europe. If you take into account both legs of a League Cup semi-final, I counted up that I had been to watch Rovers in 10 major domestic semi-final games. To put it in to perspective, when Manchester City got in to the League Cup semi-final in January 2010 it was the first time they had been in a major domestic cup semi-final for nearly 30 years.

When I first stood in the Blackburn End as a kid towards the end of the 1980s, the pursuit of major silverware was the last thing on anybody's mind. If you wanted trophies, turn on your television and watch Liverpool. Down at Ewood Park, it was all about getting promotion to the top flight and maybe a big name in the FA Cup. The town almost came to a standstill when we drew Liverpool in the FA Cup in January 1991. We would have beaten them that day as well if they hadn't equalised in the last minute. Famously, Jimmy Hill blamed the ball girl for throwing the ball back to Liverpool too quickly. In fairness, it wasn't the ball girl who stuck one in her own net 30 seconds later – that dubious honour had to go to Mark Atkins. We got battered 3-0 in the replay and barring this all-too-brief flirtation with "success" I don't remember once thinking one day I will be watching Blackburn Rovers challenging and beating the biggest clubs in the world. My love of Rovers and my love of football were like two unrelated things. On reflection, even then, we weren't actually that bad. Players like Scot Sellars, Simon

Garner and Frank Stapleton would have little problem getting in the current Rovers team in their prime. We regularly finished towards the top of the old Second Division and in the main played an exciting brand of good attacking football. It is easy to look at the past through rose-tinted spectacles but it is these games from the late 1980s that I actually find most entertaining when I watch old Rovers videos back. I loved the atmosphere down at Ewood Park. It has become a cliché, but the smell of fag smoke and pies will be forever etched in to the memory of every football fan. I didn't mind being caged in as it meant you could stand on the little wall at the front and hold on to the bars for the best view in the ground. When someone like Andy Kennedy rocked back to pull the trigger you instinctively knew to jump back on to the floor or the vibrations of the ball striking the fence would zap you to the ground like a fly. I stood and marvelled at the new electronic score board at the Darwen End for at least a season – and I wasn't alone. Grown men used to wait for the little Space Invaders-style graphic to shoot a goal through the square thing that I think was meant to be a net – and they would cheer louder than the actual goal that had just gone in. It wasn't that people who lived in Blackburn were simple; it really was fun. Throughout this time, however, in my eight-year-old mind there always remained a clear line between the Blackburn Rovers football that I watched in real life and the other type of football I watched good teams play on television.

By the time I was 25, I was sat in a pub in Amsterdam waiting to get a train to Feyenoord to watch the same club compete in Europe for the sixth season in just over a decade (we had one more final flirtation with Europe the following season) – taking it all for granted really, as if it was just another away day. It showed how far we had come. It had been a long road from the little wall at the front of the old Blackburn End to the bright lights of Amsterdam. It all started in the autumn of 1991 with the arrival of King Kenny. I remember clearly the buzz around Ewood Park when Kenny Dalglish first rolled in to town on 12 October 1991. Earlier that year multi-millionaire steel magnate and life-long Rovers fan Jack Walker had taken full control of Blackburn Rovers. Jack Walker had a dream to turn Rovers in to the best team around. It is now widely acknowledged that he had been throwing bits of money in to the coffers since the mid-1980s - ever wondered why World Cup winner Ossie Ardiles and Barcelona's Steve Archibald signed for Second Division Blackburn Rovers? Only when Uncle Jack lured King Kenny to Ewood Park did the rest of the football world really sit up and take note. Rovers beat Plymouth Argyle 5-2 that day and all the national press and television news crews were there to watch. This was to be the start of a four-year adventure that didn't slow down until Dalglish stepped upstairs shortly after we won the league in 1995. It was a great time to be a Rovers fan. When Tina Turner sang out "You're Simply the Best" after every home game she really meant it. Not only was going to Ewood Park still a laugh, but now we were actually good and not just good – the best. Even people who didn't like football started turning up for their fortnightly fix. Forget big away games – you had more chance of finding a ticket to visit *Willy Wonka's Chocolate Factory*.

Everything goes in circles and nobody at Blackburn Rovers expected the heady days of the early to mid-1990s to last forever, and they didn't. After winning the league in 1995 the next four years, were a steady slide, culminating in relegation from the Premier League in 1999. Even the so-called slide was still one of the most successful periods in the club's history. We continued to regularly feature in the top half of the Premier League and even looked like making another push for the title for a brief spell under future England manager Roy Hodgson. None of the managers brought in after 1995 could recreate the Dalglish magic however, and by the time we eventually got relegated in 1999 it had started to look a little bit inevitable.

The saddest thing about our relegation in 1999 was that it was to be the last time Jack Walker would see his beloved Blackburn Rovers play in the top flight of English football. He had taken Rovers on an unbelievable journey – one that anyone who was with him will never forget. Towards the end of the 1990s, as the fair-weather fans drifted away and the Premier League winning team of 1995 all moved on, Jack Walker remained as passionate about Blackburn Rovers as the day he first walked into the club. I will never accept that our achievements were somehow cheapened because they were funded by Jack Walker's millions, to me that is just jealously and the self-appointed elite trying to protect their monopoly on success. Don't kid yourselves that other clubs weren't spending big at the same time, Rovers were just better at it. The same year that Spurs spent £5 million on Teddy Sheringham and Darren Anderton; we paid £4.6 for Alan Shearer and Tim Sherwood. Two years later Spurs spent £8.5 million on Jurgen Klinsmann; Gheorghe Popescu, Ilie Dumitrescu and Ronny Rosenthal; they came seventh in the league and some fans hailed it a golden era for the club. We spent the same amount on Chris Sutton and Jeff Kenna and won the Premier League. You can't just buy success and for certain people to suggest that floating your club on the stock market and selling as many replica kits as you can is the only authentic way to achieve it is laughable. When I see the way some clubs fund their success, or lack of it, sorry to gloat, but I think being funded by a life-long proper fan, in it for nothing more than his love of the club, is as good as it gets. Jack Walker was truly a one-off. It became common to hear that rival clubs were "searching the world for a Jack Walker". It makes me laugh. You can find a lot of things down at the bottom of a Middle East oil well or on the trading floor of the New York Stock Exchange but you won't find a Jack Walker. Blackburn Rovers found Jack Walker in the Blackburn End – shoulder to shoulder with his fellow Rovers fans.

Thanks to the legacy that Jack Walker meticulously put into place prior to his death, the years that followed the turn of the millennium proved to be another great time to be a Rovers fan. We didn't have the open chequebook of the previous decade but what we did have was a great stadium; a state of the art training complex; one of the best academies in football and a regular flow of extra money courtesy of the Walker Trust. Success can have seductive powers but the fans expectations were re-tuned to match our financial position and people like Chief Executive John Williams and managers Graeme Souness and Mark Hughes ensured that these expectations were exceeded and then some. After a decade of being the big money club everyone wanted to take down I enjoyed returning the role of unfashionable overachievers. We quickly got ourselves back into the top flight and once we were there we set about showing the big talkers that we weren't just there to make up the numbers. I will never understand the small minority of fans that still allow Souness' one bad season to overshadow the three great seasons that preceded it. The fact is he took at team that was struggling in The Championship to a sixth place finish in the Premier League, playing some of the best football I can remember Rovers ever playing. There was also the small matter of winning the League Cup in-between. Yes, he made some bad buys towards the end but his development of existing talent like David Dunn, Matt Jansen and Damien Duff, plus bargain-buys Brad Friedel, Tugay, David Thompson, Steven Reid, Brett Emerton and Morten Gamst Pedersen more than made up for that in my eyes. By the time Hughes took over from Souness it was time for a new man in charge. Football was changing and, in Hughes we had a manager that could roll with the times. Although we could no longer compete with the big boys in the transfer market, Hughes always made sure no stone was left unturned when it came down to competing where it mattered. Regular qualification for Europe almost became a given.

Burnley fans love to point out our defeat to Swedish part-timers Trelleborgs on our first foray into Europe back in 1994, and yes, our European record isn't the best. The very fact that Burnley fans judge Rovers by our European record and we judge them by the number of great consolation goals they have scored at Ewood Park best illustrates the gulf between the two clubs. My European trips were limited to Feyenoord and a four-hour coach journey to Glasgow to watch Rovers take on Celtic at Parkhead. More dedicated and financially astute Rovers fans than me have been much further afield – France, Germany, Austria, Russia, Greece, Bulgaria, Poland, Sweden, Turkey. Our record in Europe is pretty ordinary but to see Blackburn Rovers compete in major European competition in all these different countries really was reward enough. Much lamented in the media for our attendances, strangely, there was little reporting of the 5,000 fans we took to Amsterdam for the Feyenoord trip. We might have been supporting a club that was as unfashionable as a shell suit but there wasn't a Rovers fan in town who would have swapped the 15 years we had just had.

So when did it all start to go wrong? On the playing side the current downward slide had started as far back as the end of the Hughes days as far as I was concerned. Hughes had performed miracles at Rovers on a shoestring budget, but by the end of his reign the Walker Trust cash had been chronically diluted by the massive amounts of money at other clubs and it was getting noticeably more difficult, even for well run clubs such as Blackburn Rovers, to compete for anything more than a mid-table place. No doubt this played a major part in the Walker Trust's eventual decision to sell up. We gave the 2007-08 campaign everything and still missed out on a European place to richer clubs with bigger squads paying bigger wages. I was pretty philosophical about it all – as we got stronger in the 1990s other teams got weaker and now the same thing was happening to us, only in reverse. There was so much money within the top handful of clubs that without major financial investment, barring a good cup run, realistically even that last UEFA Cup place that the smaller clubs had always been able to strive for was starting to look beyond our means. Look at Stoke City; they are considered the epitome of how to run a Premier League club on a tight budget. They have spent a small fortune and are still to finish a Premier League season in the top 10. Combine the fact that the league was getting tougher with the hapless stewardship of Paul Ince and a pretty bleak period of consolidation under Sam Allardyce and I think most Rovers fans were well aware that our Premier League status could no longer be taken for granted.

The unrest that has since boiled over at Ewood Park is not the result of a collective fear of relegation however and by the end of the 2011/12 season I think football fans were starting to realise that. Any Rovers fan over 18 has experienced The Championship, any Rovers fan over 30 has experienced the prospect of long term non-achievement; any fan over 40 has probably watched us play league games against Halifax Town. If we were just in it for the glory we could all be at Old Trafford in under an hour. No fan at Blackburn Rovers thinks they are too good to watch football outside of the Premier League and the prospect of going down has never been the thread with which true fans hang their support. The problems Rovers fans have been crying out about run deeper than dropping down a division. The majority of Rovers fans I know were brought up on football in the second tier and good times they were too.

The real problems for Rovers fans started on the eve of the 2010/11 season. By this stage the club had been for sale for over two years and there had been little talk of anyone willing to meet the owner's £25 million asking price. When Bahrain-based businessman Ahsan Ali Syed came in with a high profile takeover attempt it was clear that whatever happened next, times were about to change forever at Ewood Park. Syed's takeover was ultimately unsuccessful but reports were that other interested parties were waiting in the wings. On 19 November 2010, Venky's London Limited completed their purchase of Blackburn Rovers Football Club. I certainly had never heard of Venky's prior to their involvement at Blackburn Rovers but in fairness I had never heard of Roman Abramovich before he got involved at Chelsea so not a great deal could be gauged from that. Rovers' fans everywhere rushed to the Internet to see what we could find out about our new owners. A quick scan of the World Wide Web painted an interesting picture. Since setting out back in the 1970s, the Venky family had become quite a force in the Indian poultry market. They didn't appear to be billionaires, maybe not in pounds anyway, and their website wasn't really what I would expect of a multi-million pound international company but there was little to suggest that Venky's didn't have more than enough money to keep things ticking over nicely at Ewood Park. Established by Dr B.V. Rao, control of papa Venky's empire had since passed down to his children – Venky's Chairwoman Anuradha Desai (Mrs Desai from this point on!) and Managing Directors Venkatesh Rao and Balaji Rao. Mrs Desai is the one that looks like a female version of brother Venkatesh and Balaji is the one that looks more like 1970s Walrus of Love Barry White than either of his siblings. It wasn't entirely clear why a family from India with no obvious passion for football had bought our club and Rovers fans had to accept that this was more likely a business transaction than a labour of love. Mrs Desai told the *Indian Express* shortly after the takeover, "I had never watched a single football match in my life. Cricket, yes; hockey, sometimes; but never football." I didn't expect the new owners to be lifelong Rovers fans but I did find Mrs Desai's comments slightly disturbing. Understandably there were doubts but all the noises coming from the Walker Trust and the Rovers board were positive. Rovers' fans had little reason not to back the outgoing owner's judgement. Venky's were welcomed to Ewood Park as warmly as any new manager or big signing. The fans wanted Venky's to succeed and it was all about what they could now do for Blackburn Rovers Football Club; not what people feared or thought they might do.

Two decades earlier Jack Walker had made the football world sit up and take note by replacing unknown Don MacKay with big name Kenny Dalglish. Venky's decided to do it the other way round – out went Sam Allardyce and in came Steve Kean. Many of the Blackburn Rovers board followed Allardyce out of the door and a combination of questionable early personnel changes and cringe worthy declarations to the media ensured that Venky's enjoyed a lively start to life in the Premier League. "Yes, we were trying to get Beckham much earlier. Then we went lax on it as we were pursuing Ronaldinho," Balaji Rao told *The Times of India*. Add Venky's penchant for an embarrassing sound bite to the fact that they had made their fortune in the Indian poultry market and seemingly overnight their involvement with Blackburn Rovers had become a tabloid writer's dream. The constant chicken references in the media were lost on me. Everyone has to make their money somehow. After the initial chuckle that Venky's had made their money by breeding and frying chickens I didn't really see why chickens were that much funnier than steel or oil or however else people decided to make their fortune. I seemed to be in a minority of one on that one though, and chicken jokes have become part of the furniture at Ewood Park. One fan even came to a game with a live chicken stuffed up his jacket – well before the now world famous Ewood chicken met Yakubu in 2012. The fan waited for a quiet passage in play and then just released it on to the pitch. Why? I really don't know. I just dread to think what he had in his pocket for the West Ham game.

Whilst Venky's media appearances quickly became a source of great mirth for anyone outside of Blackburn I still remained pretty confident that it wouldn't be long before someone at the club just pulled them to one side and told them to cool it with the interviews and that would be problem solved. Of more concern at this time were stories about the involvement of football agent Jerome Anderson at the club. The media flocked round Ewood Park like seagulls round the proverbial trawler and reporting football matters wasn't always their priority. Towards the end of the 2010/11 season as media speculation grew the problem for Rovers fans was that we had started to get sucked in to a relegation battle. Despite unhappy murmurings from large sections of Rovers' support it was widely acknowledged that any public protests were likely to seriously compromise our Premier League safety. A handful of kids danced around the Jack Walker statue after one particular defeat but the overwhelming majority of fans were still prepared to give the owners and manager time. Football fans are fed on rumours and half stories and, the truth is, unless we are there or know somebody that is the information we get is all just Chinese whispers. Such was the media battering of Rovers off-field activities at the time it was difficult to know if some of it wasn't motivated by other clubs trying to see off one of their relegation rivals. A fear of affecting performances on the pitch and feelings of paranoia towards the media possibly saved Venky's a much tougher ride during their first six months. Rovers managed to avoid relegation that first season, but within the space of six months following Blackburn Rovers had become like watching a soap opera. Everybody appeared to love it except Rovers fans. It wasn't even a soap opera about football. This soap opera focussed very much on business. I don't like soap operas and I have no real interest in the world of business. If I did I would just plough all my season ticket money in to shares and sit and read the *Financial Times* every Saturday at three o'clock.

By the eve of the 2011/12 season, once the time did eventually come to fill in my season ticket renewal form, I did it, but in truth it felt like I was handing over my soul. Like I said, I had no superiority complex about dropping down to The Championship or a fear of losing games I just struggled to come to terms with the sudden transformation from football club to business. Football used to be a laugh. It used to be about more than just profit and loss, chasing contracts and the pursuit of individual gain. In September 2011 Kean told reporters,

> "You can measure results in different ways – your points, your improvement, or the price that everyone

is worth. And we have a squad worth more money than it was six months ago."

This wasn't the sort of thing I wanted to be hearing. Money may have played a significant part at the club for 20 years but the primary function of Jack Walker's money hadn't been to make individuals rich; it had been used to make our club great. I didn't mind Alan Shearer getting rich from football or even hard-working professionals churning out a comfortable living from the game, but do people really deserve to become rich for being around to facilitate the transfer of a mid-table squad player? I wasn't so naive to think that football's hopeless addiction to money had just happened overnight but at least the previous regime kept it out of your face and used a large part of any incoming money to keep things ticking over on the field. I no longer recognised the club I had followed from being a boy. It got much worse during Venky's first full season in charge. I used to wake up at 4 am the night before Tranmere away because I was too excited to sleep and that is when I was 20 years old. There were times during the 2011/12 season where I could barely muster the enthusiasm to make the 15 minute walk from my house to Ewood Park to watch some of the best players in the world – such was the detachment I felt from Blackburn Rovers Football Club and the parallel world of Premier League football. Friends would talk about their weekend watching Accrington Stanley and I would be secretly jealous. Stanley have their fair share of off-field dramas and I don't want to sound like the lottery winner that decided he wanted his old life back but Stanley seemed to have something that had been lost from the money-chasing wacky-race world of the Premier League. There were times when I contemplated giving Ewood Park a wide berth and going off to watch Darwen play non-league football but why should I? Blackburn Rovers is my club. Why should Rovers fans lose out? There may not be millions of us and those fans that we have are strangely attacked for the fans we don't have. We are not customers to a business we are members of a club and this is where we needed to show it. Following Rovers had never been about getting in to the UEFA Champions League for me. Nor had it been about playing cheerleader to millionaires. The more I thought about it, following Rovers hadn't even been about success. Yes, I will never forget singing *Rocking All Over The World* at The Millennium Stadium or sitting on a phone box to get a view of the play-off winners outside Blackburn Town Hall, but by the same token I will never forget standing outside a Working Men's Club having a laugh on the way to Charlton; stopping off in Thirsk on the way to Middlesbrough; four-man pitch invasions at Stockport County or 20 man pile-ups at the front of the Walkersteel Stand. These were the times that made following my club great. So much has changed in the town of Blackburn even in my lifetime and not always for the better. I do sometimes wonder whether there will be anything left of the town except for houses and pound shops by the time my son turns 18. Rovers' fans have shown a great spirit throughout Venky's controversial reign. There are clubs that can fill their ground twice over every league game; there are clubs that need to re-stock the club shop on the hour every hour. Blackburn Rovers is not one of those clubs but that doesn't mean that we are a club that is void of spirit and passion – far from it.

I began to resent the fact that the only way of defending the reputation of the club I had supported from a boy was futile exchanges on Internet message boards. I don't have the energy to sit on the Internet for hours every time a television expert decides to stick the boot in. Everybody in the story seemed to have a voice – the owners had a voice, the manager had a voice, the players had a voice, ex-pros, pundits, journalists, reporters – even agents suddenly had a viable forum to publicly express their views. You can say the protest gave the fans a voice but it was so poorly reported that in the end it became no more than a tool for the television sofa monkeys. For me the final straw came when a concerned Rovers fan called Jason Roberts on *Five Live* following Rovers' shambolic surrender to Wolves on the opening day of the 2011/12 season. The caller made a lot of sense but I felt that Roberts and co-presenter Darren Fletcher were actually quite dismissive of a man who made a number of valid points about the state of the club. Rovers fans deserve a voice in this story. Jason Roberts has already made his money and gone and the rest will soon follow. Rovers fans will be here until the end. I don't claim to speak for every Rovers fan. I am sure there are those that will disagree with my views on Allardyce, Williams, the Walker Trust, Kean and the many other names that feature in this story. Just because we are part of a club doesn't mean we all have to think the same about everything but when all is said and done, the one thing we do all agree on is that we want the best for our football club. Events at Blackburn Rovers over the last

18 months have actually been very sad and although many in the media changed sides when it was too late, I feel that the overall coverage of what has been happening hasn't always been particularly well balanced or indeed very accurate. Blackburn Rovers Football Club is more than just a business to its thousands of followers and after 18 months of listening to everyone else's version of events I feel that it is important to redress the balance.

CHAPTER 2

Who Cares?

It is easy to see why Rovers fans care about the future of Blackburn Rovers Football Club. It may be easy to see why Burnley fans don't care about the future of Blackburn Rovers Football Club. What is not so easy to understand is why anyone else should care either way. It is a long time since Blackburn Rovers have held much appeal to the neutral supporter. Blackburn is hardly Monte Carlo, the type of football we play is hit and miss, we rarely fill our ground and our fans are viewed by many as being ungrateful and uneducated. Even if we could meet the moneymen's basic criteria of what makes a worthwhile football club it is debatable how many people would care anyway. Football fans are renowned for not caring about other clubs.

When Blackpool fans sang "Kean Out" during their play-off victory over Birmingham in May 2012 it was a real first but it was a gesture that Rovers' fans are unlikely to forget. The fact is, to show empathy towards another club's misfortune is just not how it is done. Touching shows of solidarity between opposing fans are few and far between, so why should I expect anything to change just because it is my club that has sailed in to stormy waters? Blackburn Rovers aren't the first club to be run by owners that don't meet the basic standards set by the fans. There have been high profile campaigns by the supporters of both Liverpool and Manchester United to remove their respective owners. In both cases, there was little involvement from fans of other clubs. Those connected with Liverpool managed to see off Hicks and Gillett just before off-field problems did any real long term damage and whilst I understand the reasons behind Manchester United's on-going anti-Glazer campaign, unrest amongst the fans about how the club is run off the pitch is yet to manifest itself in any major weakening of the team on the pitch.

The fans of Portsmouth FC have not been quite so fortunate. Most football fans are well aware of Portsmouth's story. When Milan Mandaric sold his share of the club to French businessman Alexandre Gaydamak in 2006 it all started well enough. Portsmouth became big players in the transfer market and manager Harry Redknapp was given the funds to totally transform the team. The club went on to secure their highest ever Premier League finish in 2007 and followed this up by winning the FA Cup in 2008. The good times were short lived and over the course of the 2008/09 season Portsmouth's financial problems began to unravel. Although they managed to avoid relegation in 2008/09, with debts well in excess of £100 million the writing was on the wall and the following season Portsmouth were predictably relegated. Between winning the FA Cup in May 2008 and playing their last game in the Premier League in May 2010, Portsmouth had four different owners; four different managers and the old adage that it is the fans that suffer when everything goes wrong could not be more true. Millionaire Harry Redknapp didn't hang around to work for free. He shot of to Spurs almost as quickly as he had shot off to Southampton three years earlier. Many of Portsmouth's expensively assembled squad were re-united with Redknapp and the rest of his backroom staff at White Hart Lane; agents filled their boots in the fire sale and the businessmen who many fans blamed for the problems found themselves at the top end of the long list of creditors. Local businesses and charities received a fraction of what they were owed and the fans were left to face up to the very real prospect that their club could be banished to the pages of history at any moment.

I don't know much about the fans of Portsmouth but what I do know I like. In 2008 I found myself reading *Up Pompey* by Chuck Culpepper. Culpepper is a self-confessed clueless American sportswriter who decides to learn more about England's love of football by adopting an unfashionable team to support. He ends up adopting Portsmouth and the book charts his journey through the 2006/07 season following his new club. It was a entertaining book and it was hard not to warm to Portsmouth fans after reading it. My one and only trip to Fratton Park came two seasons later to see Paul Ince pit his wits against Tony Adams. I needed a few beers to prepare myself for this clash of brain cells so I thought I would chance my arm in one of the pubs just outside the ground. I don't know what the pub was called but it was about two minutes walk from the away end, had really big windows and a carpet that looked like it had been recovered from the Titanic. I was expecting the usual "Home Fans Only" greeting at the door but there was none of that. The Pompey fans were more than happy to welcome Rovers fans inside for a pre-match beverage. Rovers fans were in good spirits but most of the Pompey fans were still cursing the one that had got away. Three days earlier they had thrown away a two-goal lead at home to AC Milan. I suppose it showed how far Portsmouth had come in such a short space of time but let's not kid ourselves that it didn't come at a cost. Even then, I think Portsmouth fans were well aware that they had just hit the summit and it was all downhill from here on in. You had to feel for them. These were good people who didn't deserve what came next. The Portsmouth band banged away regardless. Everybody knows about the band of all-singing, all-dancing travelling nutcases Portsmouth bring along to every game. There aren't thousands of them but what they lack in numbers they certainly make up for in noise. The racket they make is relentless and whether it is a league game, cup game, good game, bad game the noise they make never seems to dip below loud and lively. I could only say good things about the fans of Portsmouth FC yet when their club's off-field troubles really began to unravel in the months that followed my visit to Fratton Park, the truth is I quietly celebrated one less relegation place and watched on as if I was watching an episode of *Eastenders*. A worrying pattern has emerged amongst football fans. Facilitated by the increasing role of social media in our everyday lives and actively encouraged by the powerful influence of television the dominant trend these days seems to be to not only dislike our traditional rivals but to show zero concern towards the troubles of any club other than our own. It is fine to film the car crash just don't be caught ringing the ambulance. Whilst the real enemy wreak havoc with our game, somewhere along the line football fans have been duped into believing that every other club is a rival and our fellow football fan is the enemy.

I enjoy a good bit of banter with opposing fans as much as the next man. I don't want to see Liverpool and Manchester United fans holding hands in the Stretford End singing *Kumbaya* together like they do in rugby. It is one of the things that makes football what it is. Rivalry in football is not a new thing; it goes back through the history of the game. Rovers rivalry with Burnley can be traced right back to 1879. The obvious root of this rivalry, and indeed most big rivalries in football, is the close proximity of the two clubs geographically but this is not the only factor – there are also social and historical reasons behind Blackburn and Burnley's dislike of one another. Burnley fans love to moan about the Martin Olsson dive at Turf Moor that helped send them down in 2010. If they check the history books they will see that it was Burnley who started the cheating way back in 1890 by fielding illegal numbers of Scottish players – so it's swings and roundabouts really. A bit of banter with our nearest rivals is all part and parcel of the game and the truth is both sets of fans quite enjoy it. Some of the best moments as a fan are the bits of banter you have with opposing fans. It's difficult to think of examples, it's just the day-to-day Mickey taking that goes on – reminding the giddy Blackpool fan that the nearest his club has been to Europe is that Micky Mellon free kick that was heading for the Irish Sea or breaking it to the Everton fan that they have no money for players this season because *Woodison Park* has just been varnished. Arsenal fans giving it *We've Only Got One Song* for the entire first half as Arsenal's Alex Song ran rings round a bewildered Rovers is a recent one that springs to mind. The impressive Song started the second half not so impressively. His own goal proved to be the catalyst for an unlikely Rovers victory and the Blackburn End's taunts of *You've Only Got One Song* became true on so many levels as Arsenal fans were stunned in to silence by their team's second half implosion. We're not talking the pinnacle of comedy here but sometimes it's the little things that crack you up. *Did you cry at Ewood Park?* always gets a good laugh when Newcastle United turn up for their annual East Lancashire knees up. It's now 15 years since boyhood Newcastle fan Graham Fenton came off the bench for Rovers and snatched two late goals to end Newcastle's title dreams and leave dozens of beer bellied Geordies crying their eyes out in the Darwen End. Time's a great healer and even most of the Geordies have a little chuckle at that one these days. It works both ways – I didn't realise I had a big nose until 500 Birmingham fans started singing *Sit down Pinocchio* in my direction one night at St. Andrews. If I had a pound for every time I have had to take stick about Rovers' attendances, the Riverside Stand or the population of sheep in Blackburn I'd be able to cover Vince Grella's wages for a full week. You may even find the occasional dig at other clubs within the pages of this book. With the exception of the odd comment, in the main it's just tongue in cheek stuff.

I apologise in advance Leeds fans for the gentle ribbing about your attendances at the start of Chapter Six but in my defence I was provoked by 90 minutes of relentless abuse about the three empty seats next to me at Elland Road. I didn't mind, it was a good laugh, and that is the spirit I hope you will take my response in because that is how it is meant.

I don't have a problem with genuine rivalry and a bit of banter but I do think it's time football fans woke up and got wise to what is happening to our national game. I will hold my hands up and admit I did absolutely nothing to help the fans of Portsmouth when things started to go wrong there. When Liverpool and Manchester United fans first started to express concern about the direction their club was going my initial reaction was to ask how much they were whingeing when they signed Fernando Torres and Wayne Rooney. I accept now that I was wrong. When your club is refinanced to never-before-seen levels and the cost of watching your team continues to rise, signing a few star names may appease a coach load of tourists but it does little to allay the fears of your typical supporter. When you see fans of the two most successful clubs in British football protesting against their club's owners it should start to register that something is not right here. It wasn't until football's problems landed at my club's door however that it hit home how rotten top-level English football has become. There is so much easy money to be had that football now seems to play second fiddle to making money and things are only going to get worse. There are so many different ways these people can make money why would they stop now?

First of all there is the television money. From 2010, through television money alone, even a mid-table Premier League team could expect to receive in excess of £100 million over three seasons. The 2013-16 Sky television deal is set to increase even further but more about that deal later The domestic Premier League television deal for 2010-2013 was worth £1.782 billion. This money is shared out amongst the 20 teams in the Premier League, with some put a-side for relegated clubs. As explained by the BBC in March 2010, "each place in the Premier League table is worth around £750,000 with a £13.9 million payment to each club and 'facility fees' of £480,000 for each televised match (with a minimum of 10 per club)." Add to this the overseas television rights deal, worth more than £1 billion, and each club receives an extra £7-8 million for each season they are in the Premier League. It is common knowledge that even relegation from the Premier League triggers another big payday. Clubs relegated from the Premier League now receive £48 million over four seasons. We are always told that most of this television money is accounted for in wages. This may well be the case but don't kid yourself that all that money is going on your playing staff. There will be more than a few handsomely paid *pigs* in suits that have no intention of taking their head out of the trough just because they can't kick a football.

Then there are the huge amounts of money that can be generated on a match day. I can't grumble too much about the price of a ticket down at Ewood Park but some of the prices charged at away grounds are well in excess of what I am prepared to pay to watch a 90 minute game of football. A lot of these big grounds have just become tourist attractions. You look around and it is the same people that you see when you go out for a day to a theme park. Key rings, hot dogs, DVD's, magazines, underpants – it's like going to a massive pound shop but nothing costs a pound – in fact coins will get you nowhere in this shop – you need notes. Certain grounds you go to and you will just see rows and rows of faceless consumers brain washed in to buying £50 nylon t-shirts made by sweatshop workers. Who are these morons you see filming throw-ins on their mobile phone? To me they are the lowest form of football supporter – they are even worse than the prawn sandwich brigade. Are they doing it to prove that they have actually attended a game? Not only would nobody on earth want to watch mobile phone footage of pretty much any throw-in that has ever been taken, but the game is usually on television being filmed by a professional film crew anyway. It is not just the odd two or three doing it, I swear there are thousands of them. What do they do with it? Do they save it on their phone to watch when they are feeling down or do they casually drop it in to conversation the next day at work, "Hi, I went to a big football ground yesterday and I took a film of a celebrity full back taking a throw-in, would you like to see it?" I'm sorry but if anyone EVER comes up to me and asks me to watch anyone taking a throw-in on their mobile phone I swear I will become Rory Delap and their phone will become a Mitre Delta. I urge any real fan that can afford a season ticket to do the same.

Still one of the most lucrative ways for football's money men to make big easy cash has to be the vast array of money-making opportunities available to them in the transfer market. For the agents, players, staff, owners, management, advisors, corporate partners and even the media the money making opportunities from transfer activity are too long to list. For the clubs, money-making in the transfer market can be anything from buying a player, watching him improve and then selling him on at a profit to a whole host of much more colourful practices. Hence the ever increasing numbers of parasites and hangers on that attach themselves to every pre-pubescent boy who can do 50 keep-ups. If you want to make real big money, just spend money you don't have and then when it comes to paying it all back, make sure that your company tops the list of creditors. Insufficient regulation is the key but football fans' total apathy towards the problems of any other club certainly makes life so much easier for these people. It is almost as if football fans have been fooled in to believing that the prospect of other clubs struggling off the field just adds to the drama of the show. It is easy to see how people have been lead to this conclusion but the reality is far from it. There are communities in Britain that are held together by their football club and for me it is not good enough to say it's all part and parcel of the game.

The games influential bodies don't appear to be in any rush for change. The Premier League isn't a charity. Generating revenue is a major part of what it is all about. If a club like Blackburn Rovers is replaced by a West Ham United or a Southampton, the other 19 shareholders in the corporation don't make any less money. In fact, there is a fair chance that they stand to make a whole lot more. I don't have a problem with the Premier League making money but do I really get excited every time I am told how much money those at the top end of the pyramid are making? Not particularly – in fact not at all. Whilst those at the top are feasting handsomely it is quite clear that the rest of football is slowly dying of starvation and it is no longer healthy for the game. Sorry for not wetting my pants with excitement every time Sky's Jim White tells me transfer deadline day is on its way.

Yawn. There are people who like to make out that prior to the inception of the Premier League, English football was just a load of sub-standard English players hoofing it up field whilst a handful of lager louts stood behind cages and had a fight. It is a lie. Football has always been great. The new money may have created a buzz for a while but in my opinion, any feel-good factor that came from the launch of the Premier League had well gone by the turn of the millennium. Yeah, it was exciting to see the best players in the world play on your doorstep at first but once the novelty wears off I can honestly say that I wasn't really bothered whether Brazil's number nine scored the winning goal for Rovers or the local postman scored it. As for anything Sky coverage has added to our enjoyment, watching four games a weekend is nice but I came up with the same idea when I was five years old. There are people in the Sky studio who are getting paid seven figure salaries and still patting themselves on the back for being able to talk about football. It was widely reported that former Sky TV presenter Andy Gray was paid £1.7 million a year before he was dismissed in 2011 but there are dozens of others on similarly crazy salaries.

You might argue that it is a bit rich a Rovers fan whingeing about the Premier League now the milk has turned sour, but the truth is, I don't feel my club has actually benefited that much from the Premier League anyway. Our achievements in the 1990s were down to Jack Walker's money more than anything the Premier League gave us. Jack Walker built our team and our ground and if the Premier League hadn't been formed, we would have won the old First Division instead. Other than listening to the odd away game on the radio rather than watching on television, it would have felt no different to winning the Premier League. Once the Walker money dried up the main function of the Premier League money seemed to be to service the freakishly high wages that the Premier League money helped create in the first place. By 2009 a staggering 91% of Rovers annual turnover was being used to cover the club's wage commitments. Although 91% was amongst the highest in the Premier League, there were many other clubs with exactly the same problem. How was this helping anybody outside football's well established circle of financial power? Do people really believe that the squad players who get paid £30,000 a week to sit on the bench at a mid-table Premier League club are that much better than the squad players that were around 20 years ago?

By the start of the 2011/12 season, the Government didn't seem to be in too much of a rush for change. Why would they be? Perhaps when the football bubble bursts they will introduce a tax on season tickets to ensure all those five-year contracts are honoured. There are organisations such as the Football Association and UEFA. I don't even know what these organisations do. I don't know if they answer to us or we answer to them or if our paths even cross other than when we enter in to one of their sponsored cup competitions. I have seen how easily UEFA have turned the European Cup in to a mid-week three hour advert and how the Football Association try to squeeze every last penny out of England games and the FA Cup. Don't try telling me that these two organisations haven't built up some rather expensive habits over the years. Then you hear people referring to FIFA as the "Football Family". Do me a favour. The real football family are the millions of people who spend all their spare cash following their club year after year. We are the lifeblood of the game as we know it. The fact is without us our national league would be no more than a load of grown men playing in the park. It is our spirit and loyalty that the moneymen are making their fortunes out of yet we chose to turn it on each other. I'm not one of those people that believe you are only a real fan if you go and watch your team play live either. I have come across too many numpties in football grounds and enough genuinely passionate armchair fans to swallow that popular misconception. Take for example the old bloke who sits near me at Rovers. I am convinced his family just buy him a season ticket because it is cheaper than sticking him in care for the afternoon. Such is his ignorance of anything that goes on outside of his own mental bubble I don't even think he realises Rovers play away games and cup games in between the obligatory 19 home games he gets with his season ticket. He turns up with his butty box five minutes before kick-off; tuts all the way to his seat and doesn't shut up moaning until he slopes off home about 20 minutes in to the second half. He gets annoyed when Rovers score because it undermines all his whingeing. Fair enough, he is a season ticket holder but this man is living proof that attending games really isn't the barometer true support should ever be measured. I have spoke to loads of football supporters who don't go to games but can more than hold their own when it comes to football. Take for example David Somerto Jacobsen from Norway. Although he is yet to visit Ewood Park the guy eats, sleeps and breathes Blackburn Rovers. Having adopted Rovers as his team following the signing of Henning Berg his love of Blackburn Rovers has continued right through the current day. There have been as many highs as lows since Berg lifted the Premier League trophy back in 1995 and the thought of this Norwegian Rover trawling the bars of Oslo to find a pub showing Rovers versus Burnley is the mark of a true fan for me. When it comes to Rovers, he has got more passion in his little finger than the old guy who sits near me at Ewood Park has got in his entire body.

In many ways I am lucky. I happen to live 15 minutes walk from my chosen club's home ground and at £225 Rovers season tickets are amongst the cheapest openly available adult season ticket in the entire top four divisions. Getting a season ticket is a no-brainer for me – or at least it used to be. Away games are not so simple. There was a time when I would go to as many away games as home games, if not more because season tickets were dearer and away games were a better laugh anyway. When I lived on my own I was more than happy to eat crisp butties for a week so that I had a spare £100 for 10 cans of lager, a fry-up, mid-afternoon bag of chips, money for a bet, a match ticket and return coach travel to Norwich or whoever we happened to be playing. Unfortunately, it is just not that simple to impose the one-week crisp butty diet on the wife and child because you have had a look at the fixture list and you fancy another booze-up in Norwich. This means every other Saturday I become the armchair fanatic that regular game-goers such as me supposedly detest. Let me tell you now, I am speaking from experience here, when I tell you the rigmarole the non-game attending fan has to go through in order to follow their team puts season ticket holders like me to shame. Is the game on Sky? No. Is it on *Five Live*? Don't be stupid. Is it on local radio? Can I get a decent reception in the house? Do I try and find a pub that will be showing it? Which pub? How do I get there? Will it definitely be on? Can I get it on the Internet? Will I have to pay? Will they sign me up for a yearly subscription? Will my computer end up with incurable viruses? Why is the commentary in Arabic? What a palaver. Home games, I just open the fridge, drink a few cans, watch a bit of pre-match build-up and stroll down to the ground about 15 minutes before kick-off. It's a comparative doddle. I wouldn't have the nerve to suggest that someone who goes through my away day routine every game is somehow any less a Rovers supporter than I am. Season-ticket fans, home and away game fans, never-miss-a-game fans, good-time fans, part-time fans, television fans, armchair fans, internet fans, trawling the bars of Oslo fans, whatever you are- as long as you are truly passionate about your club you are all part of the real football family as far as I am concerned.

Anyone who has seen the seventies cult film *The Warriors* will know that it starts with the leader of the most powerful gang in New York, a guy called Cyrus, calling on all other gangs in the city to unite to form a super-power that can go out and take on the authorities. Now, I don't want to sound like Cyrus from *The Warriors*, not least because he got shot dead half way through explaining his idea to all the other gangs, but I do believe that there is a bigger enemy in football than the local mob down the road and if football fans get wise to what is happening and channel our efforts as one we can defeat that enemy. First of all we have to overcome the barriers that have traditionally kept us apart. The spirit I am trying to capture is best summed up by this message left on the *Lancashire Telegraph* website by Internet poster Houseclaret around 12 months into Venky's reign at Ewood Park.

> I have been following this with interest and, originally, a certain amount of amusement but I have to say not any longer. I am of course a lifelong Claret and have no love for your club but, on reading the posts (hundreds of them) I am now beginning to realise the scale of what is happening at your club and may I say (if you don't mind the opinions of a "dingle") that I believe what is happening there is nothing short of disgraceful and I really would not wish it on any football fan. I really do believe that at this point you should have the whole-hearted support of all football fans because, no matter what we may think of each other, we are all the same at heart. I will make no more fun of your plight and wish you all the best, I really do.

Once we have accepted that football fans are all the same at heart we need to identify the real enemy. This is easy enough – it is anybody who puts the pursuit of money before football. I am talking about mercenary footballers who show no loyalty to their club; managers who behave no better than their players; agents who cream millions from the game; television networks who use the game as an advertising tool; pundits who don't really care as long as they are getting paid; owners with no passion for the game; chairmen who take from the poor to give to the rich and governing bodies who fail to regulate this shambles because they are too scared to turn down a payday. No matter how many eggheads with degrees in corporate speak try to turn football in to a brand I will never accept it. Football is not a brand. *Tampax* is a brand. Football is a passion – a way of life. I am not asking the losers who video throw-in's to understand what I am saying or to sympathise with the troubles of Blackburn Rovers Football Club, but if I can convince one proper fan to read this book from the perspective of a football fan rather than the fan of a rival club surely that is the first step towards claiming back our beloved game.

I don't claim to be Rovers number one fan. Nor do I claim to be some sort of investigative journalist who has the key to the Venky's safe. I am just a normal bloke from Blackburn who loves Blackburn Rovers and hates seeing what is happening to our game and my town team. If you want to know who scores the best goals in training or what your favourite players' preferred pizza topping is you are probably reading the wrong book. This book is my attempt to piece together what I have read in newspapers, seen at games, watched on television and heard around Ewood Park since Venky's first took a hold of Blackburn Rovers Football Club in

November 2010. Blackburn Rovers is the glue that holds Blackburn together. This time it was my club; next time it could be your club.

I want my Rovers back! Pompey want their Portsmouth back! Reds want their United back! WE WANT OUR FOOTBALL BACK!!!

CHAPTER 3

The Takeover

When Jack Walker lost his battle with cancer in August 2000, it marked the end of an era for Blackburn Rovers Football Club. Born on the cobbled streets of Blackburn in 1929, Uncle Jack and his brother Fred helped turn their father's backstreet scrap metal business into the largest steel stockholder in Britain. Armed with a strong work ethic and a shrewd business brain, by the mid-1990s Jack Walker sat level with Paul McCartney on *The Sunday Times Rich List* with a personal fortune approaching £600 million. He may have set up home in Jersey (and who can blame him!) but Uncle Jack never forgot his Blackburn roots. Whilst others were happy to schmooze in boardrooms playing at being a fan, Uncle Jack really was the real deal. Forget the comparisons with Abramovich at Chelsea or that Sheikh bloke at Manchester City. The only way I can describe Uncle Jack to fans who don't really know what he was all about is imagine your club's biggest fan is also a self-made multi-millionaire with not an ounce of pretension about him; one day he comes along and promises to turn your Second Division club into the best team in Britain – and then does it. That is Jack Walker. Uncle Jack's place in the history of Blackburn Rovers can never be understated. He wasn't just a wealthy benefactor he was, as the plaque next to his statue reads, "Rovers Greatest Supporter." Following his death there was a huge out-pouring of public sadness and it was hard to argue with this fitting tribute from Blackburn's MP and then Home Secretary Jack Straw.

> "Jack Walker did more than any other individual in the last century to enhance the self-confidence and the prosperity of his home town. He was completely committed to the town and its people. Blackburn Rovers was in many ways the love of his life. His contribution to the club was enormous but that was based in turn on the prosperity he created through his astonishing development of Walkersteel and of many other investments in the area. He was a great local hero."

Uncle Jack was always going to be some act to follow. At the time of his passing, the club that Jack built found itself back in the second tier of English football and very much at a crossroads. Rovers had been the Premier League's sixth highest spenders on wages (behind only Manchester United, Liverpool, Chelsea, Newcastle United and Arsenal) the year we were relegated. A withdrawal of funds at this stage would have undoubtedly have had catastrophic consequences for the club. The fans knew the heady days of the 1990s were over but what lay in store for our club next? More great days in the Premier League or more of the mid-table Championship dross we had witnessed in 1999/2000? If outsiders had been in any doubt how much Blackburn Rovers meant to Jack Walker they would have got all the answers they needed when he gave this interview with the *Lancashire Telegraph* shortly after being diagnosed with cancer early in 2000.

> "A number of years ago I put in place a family trust structure to own my various business interests, including Blackburn Rovers. This structure ensures continuity of management and provides the necessary financial support for all my businesses for the foreseeable future. I have made known my wishes to my colleagues, who I am confident will carry forward the policies necessary to promote and enlarge all my business interests."

Following Jack Walkers' death, ownership of the company that owned his shares in Blackburn Rovers transferred to the Walker Trust. Chairman of the Walker Trust, Jersey based solicitor Paul-Egerton Vernon was quick to put Rovers fans at ease about the situation,

> "The future is safe. There seems to be a bit of a misunderstanding that there is an ever-shrinking pot of money that is available. That is not the case. There are other businesses apart from the club, which generate profits which are available. The fans need not be concerned in any way. The club is provided for for the foreseeable future. Jack was not

> a short-term man. We have complete confidence in the board and the management and their objective of getting Rovers back into the Premiership."

The exact terms of the trust were not made public but Egerton-Vernon explained that Rovers would be subsidised by other assets in the Walker portfolio, which included property and the Jersey-based airline, Flybe. Uncle Jack's association with Blackburn Rovers wasn't just a bit of retirement fun it was a passion he took with him to the grave and beyond.

Shortly after Uncle Jack's death his colleague and long-standing confidante David Brown was appointed to the Blackburn Rovers board. It would be Brown's responsibility to liaise between the Walker Trust and members of the board. At the time of the appointment the *Lancashire Telegraph* reported,

> "Brown's links with Walker stretch back over 30 years during which time he was finance director of C. Walker and Sons Ltd until the company was sold to British Steel in 1990.
>
> Since then, he has been an adviser and consultant to Walker across a whole range of business affairs. He is also an adviser to Walker's trusts, including BRFC Investments - the company set up Walker by to control and administer his major shareholding in Rovers and ensure its financial stability. The Blackburn-based businessman is a long-time Rovers supporter who has held a season ticket at Ewood for the last 10 years and he is delighted to be taking up the post with a mandate to ensure Walker's legacy lives on."

The Walker Trust era got off to a great start and Rovers were back in the Premier League within a year. Rovers' fans had grown used to Jack Walker being the public face behind Blackburn Rovers but it was totally different with the trust. Few Rovers fans knew what the Walker Trust's football background was. Neither did most know whether or not the trust's members had taken an interest in Blackburn Rovers prior to its formation. We didn't know who they were and in the main still don't. The Walker Trust had now become shareholders in Blackburn Rovers but that was about as much as your regular fan knew. From the outset, Rovers' fans were worried that members of the trust may come to see the club as a drain on the resources of their other business interests and were keen to know who was actually running the club. In response to fan's concerns, Paul Vernon-Egerton told the *Lancashire Telegraph*,

> "The people who are running the club are John Williams, Rob Coar, the other members of the board and the manager, Graeme Souness. The role of the shareholders is not to run the club. The role of the shareholders is to ensure that the objectives the board sets themselves can be met."

To me the clue was in the title – "The Walker Trust". Jack Walker had never let Blackburn Rovers down before and I didn't envisage he was about to do so now. Whilst we continued to flourish on the pitch, albeit under different financial circumstances than the big-spending 1990s, the vast majority of Rovers fans remained respectful of the Walker Trust's desire to stay out of the spotlight. The Walker Trust continued to back the team and Rovers enjoyed three great years of success under Souness, including promotion to the Premier League, winning the League Cup and qualification for Europe through a sixth place league finish.

In January 2004 the full extent of the Walker Trust's contribution to Blackburn Rovers was revealed for the first time. Those in attendance at Rovers Annual General Meeting were told that the trust fund had given the club £3 million per year since Jack Walker's death as well as a £14 million interest free loan. John Williams emphasised the importance of this regular £3 million in helping bridge the gap between Rovers and our big city rivals. A resolution was passed at the 2006 AGM that saw a £14m loan from the Walker Trust capitalised into shares, a move that effectively wiped £14m of debt off the balance sheet. By this point the Walker Trust had been involved with Blackburn Rovers for six years. It had been an on-going battle to balance the books and keep pace with the best clubs in the country but somehow Rovers had managed it. The days of competing with the big boys in the transfer market were well gone but it was difficult to name a football club that was better run than Blackburn Rovers. The Walker Trust remained very much in the background, preferring to leave the day-to-day running of the club to John Williams, the board and the manager. Although Souness' final season had not gone to plan, Mark Hughes had come in and proved an excellent replacement for the departing Souness.

Football was changing at lightning speed and there was only so much Rovers could achieve through careful planning and team spirit alone. £10 million may have got you Alan Shearer, Tim Sherwood and a new stand 15 years earlier but by 2007 you were as likely to land a complete turkey with £10 million as you were to sign someone who might play two seasons in the first team. Owning a football club was a totally different proposition from the early days of Jack Walker and millionaires had made way for billionaires. The £3 million the Walker Trust threw in to the coffers every season was now doing little more than servicing the wages of those sat on subs bench. Jack Walker's ultimate aim for the club, beyond the silverware and success, was for Blackburn Rovers to be self-sufficient. John Williams had told us as much in 2000 after our first full season in The Championship.

> "Jack Walker's ambition is that he wants the club to be self sufficient and the best way of doing that is to return to the Premiership. But at the end of the day Jack Walker the fan always comes through. He always puts football considerations before financial."

Jack Walker had held our hand for the past 15 years but by 2007 the Walker Trust saw the time for the financial relationship between the Walker family and Blackburn Rovers to come to an end. By the time the Walker Trust had appointed the investment bank Rothschild to find a buyer for the club, Walker investment in Blackburn Rovers had reached £97 million. With a new television deal bringing fresh money in to the club, the Walker Trust stopped the £3 million yearly payment and although further funds were released for new managers Paul Ince and his successor Sam Allardyce, the emphasis was now very much on finding a buyer who could invest heavily enough to move the club forward.

Once the club had been put on the market there was no stampede of billionaires looking to buy Blackburn Rovers. The truth was a quick look at the profit and loss figures for 2005 to 2009 showed that the risks were high and without the vast sums of money being generated by outgoing transfers the potential for long term profit was negligible.

BLACKBURN ROVERS PROFIT & LOSS ACCOUNT

£ Millions	**2005**	**2006**	**2007**	**2008**	**2009**
Match Day	7.4	7.1	9.0	6.2	6.8
Television	21.5	25.7	23.9	41.3	35.4
Commercial	12.5	10.7	10.5	9.0	8.8
Turnover	**41.3**	**43.4**	**43.3**	**56.4**	**50.9**
Wages & Salaries	(31.3)	(33.4)	(36.7)	(39.7)	(46.1)
Administrative Expenses	(9.0)	(9.4)	(9.9)	(10.7)	(11.3)
Expenses	**(40.3)**	**(42.7)**	**(46.6)**	**(49.8)**	**(57.4)**
Operating Profit/(Loss)	**1.0**	**0.7**	**(3.3)**	**6.6**	**(6.5)**
Player Amortisation	(6.9)	(6.2)	(5.6)	(7.8)	(8.0)
Profit/(Loss) on Player Sales	1.4	(0.6)	6.5	5.8	19.0
Player Tading	**(5.5)**	**(6.8)**	**0.9**	**(2.0)**	**10.9**
Net Interest Payable	**(0.5)**	**(0.7)**	**(1.0)**	**(1.6)**	**(0.8)**
Profit/(Loss) before taxation	**(5.0)**	**(6.9)**	**(3.4)**	**3.0**	**3.6**

There was the odd report of interest from various different businessmen and JJB Sports supremo Chris Ronnie, American-based tycoon Daniel Williams and South African billionaire Johann Rupert were all mentioned at various points. In February 2009 *The Guardian*'s Andy Hunter reported the challenges Rovers faced finding a buyer after John Williams confirmed the Walker Trust were still not close to finding a buyer.

> "It is not the greatest time. It seems to me, the current fashion is moving towards the only deals being super rich deals with super rich people. I don't really think anyone is going to buy into Blackburn Rovers looking for a return on their investment. Maybe for capital growth in the medium to long term, but to maintain the club in the Premier League it would seem to be difficult to do that and make a short term return on investment. That doesn't mean that the acquisition of Rovers as a Premier League club with relatively small debts does not present a tremendous opportunity for the right person. The credit crunch has made it very difficult for people to invest in football clubs to make money. It was difficult enough in a more favourable climate."

It was slow going but in the summer of 2010 the search for a new owner finally started to gather pace. In June 2010 it was reported that Mumbai businessman Saurin Shah had expressed an interest in buying Blackburn Rovers. At the time, most Rovers fans weren't aware that football agent Jerome Anderson had taken on the task of finding Rovers an investor – if you were anything like me, you had still probably never heard of the guy. Saurin Shah's interest signalled the start of the public's association between Blackburn Rovers and the Indian business world. Although ultimately no takeover came from Saurin Shah's enquiries, it wasn't long before a Rovers spokesperson felt the need to publicly address the issue of the club's impending sale.

> "The club has been for sale for some time and, for it to remain competitive in one of the world's toughest sporting competitions, we accept that new investment is required. Equally, the trustees of the late Jack Walker, who are being professionally advised, and the club's board of directors are acutely aware of the responsibility involved in passing the club to a new owner. We are custodians of a club with a proud heritage dating back to 1875."

On 17 August 2010, the tenth anniversary of Jack Walker's death, it was revealed that head of Bahrain based investment company Western Gulf Advisory, Ahsan Ali Syed, had been involved in a "cordial and productive meeting" with senor figures at Blackburn Rovers. Syed was given a four-week period of exclusivity to check through the accounts and all the talk in the press was that a substantial bid was about to follow. Headlines like "Blackburn edge closer to joining the financial elite" and "Allardyce to lead Rovers revolution", gave an early indication of the role the media would come to play in the Rovers story. The BBC declared, "Syed Pledges £100 million war chest to Blackburn." Few fans at Rovers could be bought with big headlines but at least something was happening. Syed's plans for the club appeared sound enough. In an interview with *The Guardian* in August 2010, he said,

> "The first step is to maintain Premier League status, enhance the capabilities of the academy, see if there lies potential to increase the seating of the stadium, help Big Sam with the transfer budget and to market the club properly in other parts of the world, specifically in India, the Far East and Middle East."

The key issue for me was how did Syed plan to fund this takeover? Syed was an elusive figure and it wasn't immediately obvious where he had made his self-proclaimed fortune. In August 2010 Syed told the BBC*'s Five Live,* "My family has been into business for 180-odd years, mine is the ninth generation into finance. Until now we have not run out." How re-assuring. In the interview with *The Guardian* Syed added, "I own more than 130 companies and publicly my assets are worth more than £8bn." His company Western Gulf Advisory appeared to make money by offering massive loans to high-end business clients. According to the company's website, "The loan amount can be as low as USD 25 million and as high as half a billion USD." If there are people out there who are prepared to pay 7% interest on a half a billion dollar loan then fair play to whoever is collecting the returns but anyone can have a website and a big idea. What Rovers fans now wanted to see was something that indicated that Ahsan Ali Syed was the real deal. For me, this never really came. There was the comical news clip showing a fleet of blacked out cars turning up outside the club shop but this proved absolutely nothing. I thought the new car wash contractors were being unveiled. I started to worry about where all this was heading. The board at Rovers had been keen to emphasise that the calibre of the buyer was as important as the actual sale itself. Had something changed? Syed confirmed that he had never been to Blackburn but was ready to pump £300 million in to a project he described as "an emotional vehicle for myself." He went on to add, "If my finances allow and his intentions are positive then I would love to take Beckham." It was only when Syed's financial past was exposed in a BBC documentary that talk of his takeover started to cool. *Five Live Investigates*, originally broadcast on 5 September 2010, exposed a trail of UK debt left by Syed between 2001 and 2005 as well as posing serious questions about the strength of some of his other businesses. All in all, the documentary didn't paint Syed in a very positive light. Lawyers representing one of Syed's companies responded to the programme by claiming,

> "The BBC's report contained a number of false and misleading allegations. In particular, there is no basis for the suggestion that Mr Ali had a questionable track record in business and a 'colourful financial history' such that he is unsuitable to take over Blackburn Rovers Football Club."

From this point on Syed's bid appeared damaged beyond repair. He remained in the background but on 1 November 2010 it was finally announced that he had withdrawn his interest in Blackburn Rovers. Syed did still honour donations totaling £65,000 that he had promised to a local homeless charity and the Blackburn Cathedral choir appeal. Syed wasn't out of the limelight long and he quickly turned his attention to Spain. In January 2011, he took over at Racing Santander, where he immediately fired the boss and made a series of big transfer promises. Relegation and administration followed, Syed went missing and it wasn't long before Interpol wanted to speak with him. In 2011, Pete Jenson of the *Daily Mail* offered a fascinating insight in to Syed's time at Racing. Despite the big transfer promises, in reality, he had delivered little. Many of his business clients could sympathise. Minority shareholder at Racing Miguel Angel Rivella said of one of Syed's trips to the director's box,

> "He had never been to a match in his life. I am by his side in the director's box and I am dying with laughter. A defender gives the ball back to the keeper and he applauds like a maniac. He doesn't know anything about football."

A clueless owner who doesn't know the first thing about football – who brought this guy to our club? Things were changing at Rovers. Ultimately, Blackburn Rovers Football Club was the Walker Trust's to do with what they liked, but was the trust really that keen to sell that they would court interest from a man of Syed's reputation?

Around this time media interest in Blackburn Rovers grew at lightning speed. By the time Ahsan Ali Syed's takeover attempt had fizzled out another high profile takeover attempt was already underway. Again, it was interest from India and again it was a company that your average English football fan was unlikely to have ever heard of. On 16 October 2010 the *Lancashire Telegraph* revealed that Indian company Venky's was considering putting a deal together to buy the club. I had already given up hope that Rovers would attract interest from the sort of business that I would describe as a household name and when details of the proposed new interest was announced the word Venky's meant absolutely nothing your average Rovers fan. Alan Nixon of the *Daily Mirror* seemed to know more than most fans when he wrote,

> "The V H Group are known throughout Asia as leaders in the poultry business but they want to crack European markets and see Premier League football as a base for their expansion. Known locally as Venky's – short for Venkateshwara Hatcheries – they have amassed a great fortune in the past few decades and have the money to buy out the late Jack Walker's Trustees with no borrowing."

The Indian poultry market wasn't an obvious starting point for owning a Premier League football club but anyone who thought this was about football rather than business probably needed to carry on playing with their sticker album. In the month prior to the purchase Venky's Chairman Mrs Desai, had already told the Indian press,

> "People are crazy about football. In all these markets that I am talking about, southeast market, Middle East market and even in the European market, it is a very famous game and I feel that the Venkys brand

> will get an immediate recognition if we take over this club. This is the main reason, why we are doing this."

At the time, I wasn't a big reader of the Indian newspapers and I had to go on the information that was available to me in my own local newsagents. My initial thought was that at least Venky's had an actual business that you could see with your own eyes. This had to be considered an improvement on the vague investment portfolio of Ahsan Syed Ali. Having seen that Venky's were big in Indian chicken circles; I wanted to know what kind of money they had. According to one report the collective turnover of the V H Group in 2010 was approaching £1 billion with profits of £100 million. How true this was we would find out in due course. At this point I was happy to accept that Venky's fell in to the bracket of comfortable and most importantly they had more than enough money to fund any takeover they were planning. When asked about Rovers potential new owners, Indian finance and stock advisor Vikram Kapoor told leading Rovers' website *BRFCS,*

> "The worry for Blackburn fans should be: how much of a role is Anuradha Desai going to take? If she is hands-on, then you will see your club grow and progress as she has the business acumen to take this type of project forward positively. The uncertainty will come if she decides not to be hands-on with this venture and leaves her brothers to run this – the jury is very much out on their ability to drive forward a business."

Kapoor got the first bit right but I am not too sure about the rest. On the playing side manager Sam Allardyce did his best to ensure that football matters remained at forefront of everybody's mind but even he had to concede that it was difficult to totally ignore all the takeover talk.

> "The club has always been for sale from the day I first walked in and the Chairman told me that. Because recently there has been some interested parties doing some due diligence you do think a little bit more about it."

As newspaper speculation increased about Venky's proposed takeover, by the end of October it started to look more and more likely that Venky's would become the new owners of Blackburn Rovers Football Club. A new subsidiary of the V H Group, Venky's London Limited, was created and Rovers Chairman John Williams told reporters,

> "A series of meetings, including discussions with the Premier League, have followed an extensive diligence process. Both parties are hopeful that the transaction will be completed in November."

Allardyce was happy with the prospect of new owners and he quickly went on record as saying so. "The sooner the club changes hands the better. New investment is needed for football clubs and we have not had it for a long time. Without it a business will crumble and fall." As a fan it was difficult to make too much of a judgment call based on the limited information that was available. We just had to hope that this was a "Mark Hughes moment" rather than another decision like the one that had landed us with Paul Ince. Over the next few weeks we were drip-fed more details about Venky's and increasing media speculation about their wider plans. Bar one seemingly groundless report in the *Daily Star* that claimed Allardyce could be handed a £40 million nest egg for new signings, most newspapers were reporting a much more low key approach from Venky's. "We don't expect to be in the top five of the Premier League. We will be happy to be in the top 10-12," Mrs Desai told the *Economic Times of India*. Part of me felt that we could get this with the Walker Trust but the other part welcomed Mrs Desai's realistic outlook. Mrs Desai added,

> "We will do the best by the fans and by the club and it is very important to continue the traditions of the club. We are going to be good, responsible owners and we want to make the club stronger. There are a lot of marketing plans but nothing is certain yet. The possibility of allowing sponsorship will be investigated. There will be £5m put in straight away to buy players. But, of course, there will be much, much more than £5m. We want fans to know we are fully committed to Blackburn. There is a new generation of boys aged between 10 and 17 in India that are football mad, but lots of them support Chelsea. My dream is to make Blackburn Rovers an even bigger brand in India than Venky's."

In truth a fair proportion of what Mrs Desai said prior to the takeover made some amount of sense. £5 million per transfer window was hardly going to have Manchester City quaking in their boots but it was more than we had been getting from the Walker Trust in the years leading up to the sale. If the growth of the Premier League in India was as substantial as we were initially led to believe I also thought that it was pretty logical to try and increase Rovers popularity on the sub-continent. Provided we weren't about to compromise the club's good name for a few rupees I saw no harm in trying to promote Blackburn Rovers abroad. If a kid in India wants to support a team from the Premier League they may as well support Rovers than Chelsea. As for re-naming Ewood Park I have never been too precious about what the official name for a ground is. The Riverside Stand has had more names than I care to remember but I am still to see anyone arrested for calling it the wrong one. There were reports of a new approach to transfers that slipped pretty much under the radar at the time. The headline "Indian buyer wants to turn Blackburn in to a Market Stall" in October 2010 gave the first real insight in to the new owner's transfer plans. Again it was Alan Nixon of the *Daily Mirror* who seemed to be the first to report the story. According to Nixon,

> "V H are tied up with top football agency Kentaro, who will try to bring in some of their best young clients and give Rovers a stream of talent to use - and eventually sell at big prices."

I am not too sure what was wrong with the old way but at the time the story didn't seem too big a deal. At least were planning on actually signing some players. From what I could see, Venky's weren't perfect but for me they ticked more boxes than Ahsan Ali Syed and I actually started to find their mid-table declarations quite comforting. There is nothing to say that you can't push for more once you have met your initial target.

On 19th November 2010 Venky's London Ltd completed the purchase of Blackburn Rovers Football Club for a reported figure of £23 million. Venky's also took on the club's debt which at that stage was around £20 million. There was no public statement about the handling of the club's debt but Venkatesh Rao did offer these words of reassurance regarding the club's finances,

> "We are all truly honoured to be working with such an historic club and are committed to creating a long-term financial platform which the club can use to realise its obvious potential on and off the field."

There was the predictable round of back-slapping and compliments once the deal had been closed. David Brown resigned from his position on the Rovers board but the rest of the existing board and management remained in place. As far as outsiders were led to believe, they would remain in place this would continue to be the case after the sale. The new owners said they were "delighted, proud and humbled" and vowed to "absolutely respect Jack Walker's legacy" and to make Rovers a "truly global brand." Chairman of the Walker Trust Paul Egerton-Vernon responded by saying,

> "We have been impressed with their (Venky's) enthusiasm for the club and their plans and ideas for

> future investment to develop it further as well as their wish and commitment to preserve the legacy of Jack Walker."

It turned out to be a prosperous end to 2010 for the Walker Trust. Three weeks later and the trust sold 21 per cent of its shares in Flybe as the airline completed a £215 million floatation on to the stock market. The deal netted the trust around £45 million.

Back at Rovers and the fans reaction to the takeover was mixed. When the *Lancashire Telegraph* posed the question "Is the Venky's takeover of Blackburn Rovers a good thing?" 52% of those polled answered yes and 48% answered no. I was quite phlegmatic about it all. It had been clear for some time that the Walker Trust was ready to end its financial relationship with the club and most Rovers fans had long since accepted the inevitability of their departure. Whether the Walker Trust was right or wrong to sell the club was a sticking point amongst fans and a lot depended on how the new owners performed. Venky's came in with fresh enthusiasm, a believable plan for the future and gave hope of new investment in the team. Importantly they also had the endorsement of the existing Blackburn Rovers board. As an all round package they appeared to be the best option available. If the Walker Trust felt they could not commit any more than they had already pumped in to the club then, with the information that was on-hand to the average Rovers fan, it was difficult to argue that Venky's did not represent a viable way forward from here on in. I was glad it was all sorted so that we could just get on with playing football. All the new owners had to do now was let the football people get on with it. As long as they kept us in the Premier League, from what I could see, there was no reason why Rovers and Venky's couldn't continue to flourish both on and off the pitch. Although we knew relatively little about them, even at this early stage, we already knew more about them than we knew about the Walker Trust. It seems so naive now, but I wasn't the only one who just expected Venky's to sign off the cheques and let the existing board and management team get on with it.

When Venkatesh and Balaji Rao were paraded in front of the Ewood Park crowd the day after the takeover any doubts Rovers fans may have had towards the new owners were quickly put to one side. Ushered onto the pitch by the club's press officer Paul Agnew, the two brothers were given a rapturous reception in the build up to the Premier League clash with Aston Villa. For every fan that was unsure about Venky's there was another who was more than ready to embrace the change. Based on the information that had dripped through via the media in England, Venky's had been quite impressive leading up to the takeover. I was not so sure how much they knew about football but again, how much did the Walker Trust know about football? Venky's didn't appear to court publicity, a fair proportion what they said seemed logical and their business appeared to be financially sound. Even the media coverage of it all didn't seem too over the top at this point. There was a noticeable increase in column inches but in the main, barring really the *Daily Mirror* that was still one step ahead of the pack in terms of news, it was just the same story in every national newspaper with a different chicken pun. I don't know about regurgitated chicken – a lot of the national newspapers still seemed to be regurgitating the previous night's *Lancashire Telegraph.* The general mood in the press appeared to be one of intrigue and even mild excitement. 18 months on, I can see why they were so excited.

Having been impressively low key up to this point, not long after the Aston Villa team bus rolled out of Ewood Park on 20 November 2010, the football world soon became increasingly familiar with Blackburn Rovers' new owners. Mrs Desai suddenly had some big opinions about a sport that she had previously ranked behind cricket and hockey. The week following the impressive 2-0 victory over Aston Villa, in a telephone interview from her base in Pune, Mrs Desai told the *Lancashire Telegraph,*

> "I am going to speak to the manager soon and tell him the fans' opinions are very important. We should go up in the rankings but playing well is not just about winning. I am going to convey that to him. The way we play is vital."

At this point Mrs Desai was still to watch a first team game at Ewood Park. I don't even know whether she had actually been to Ewood Park or even Blackburn. Mrs Desai's conversion from cricket to football was still all pretty recent. "I am now becoming a big football fan. I was a hardcore cricket fan but that is all changing. My view has changed overnight."

Fans had been frustrated with Allardyce's style of football but if anything needed to be said it needed to be said to Allardyce's face in the privacy of the boardroom – not via long distance telephone calls with the local newspaper. Worringly for Allardyce, Mrs Desai went on to add, "We are not going to make any hasty decisions about the management of the club." Where had this come from? The Walker era was over and Venky's had arrived.

Chapter 4

Allardyce Out; Kean In

Throughout the takeover one topic continued to dominate conversation across Blackburn pubs, clubs, message boards and forums. It wasn't Venky's and it wasn't chicken. The subject that had provoked debate and divided opinion amongst Rovers fans since the summer of 2008 was Sam Allardyce. On the face of it Allardyce was one of the hottest managers in the game. As well as successful spells at Notts County and Blackpool, he had turned Bolton Wanderers from mid-table second flight strugglers to a team that regularly challenged for European qualification. Allardyce had also been instrumental in putting Rovers back on track following the ill-fated stewardship of Paul Ince. There had been a couple of flirtations with relegation, but in the main, Allardyce always had the wherewithal to pull us away from the pack when it mattered. His hotchpotch squad of solid signings and players bought by other managers was well drilled and disciplined. Most of the players appeared to like him and, whether they did or they didn't, there were few who came out and questioned his authority publicly. The guy had a sense of humour too. With Rovers sitting 14th in the Premier League four games in to the 2010/11 season Allardyce famously told reporters,

> "I'm not suited to Bolton or Blackburn. I would be more suited to Inter Milan or Real Madrid. It wouldn't be a problem for me to go and manage those clubs. I would win the double or the league every time. Give me Manchester United or Chelsea, it would be the same, no problem."

So why was it, with so much going for Allardyce by the time Venky's took over, he was disliked by so many Rovers fans, not least me? With all that has gone on since Venky's arrival it is easy to forget that for a significant period of Allardyce's time at the club he was not actually that popular with large sections of the Rovers crowd. Nothing has done more for his legacy than memories of the manager that went before him and the monumental failings of the manager that followed. Not only are fans more inclined to acknowledge all the good things Allardyce brought to the table but even his harshest of critics, of which I include myself, would have him back in a flash over his successor. As difficult as it is to accept now, that wasn't necessarily the case for a lot of fans at the start of the 2010/11 season. Some people have tried to re-write history by suggesting Allardyce was always well thought of amongst fans. He wasn't. There are no official records of conversations in the stands but anybody who is in any doubt about how unpopular

Allardyce was during his final year at Rovers would benefit from reading the thousands of comments left about him on the Internet over the course of 2010.

I was delighted when Allardyce was appointed Rovers manager in December 2008. I couldn't understand why he hadn't got the job in the summer. There had been rumours that an Internet smear campaign had originally put John Williams off. Both Williams and Allardyce were quick to dispel such talk. John Williams told the *Lancashire Telegraph*,

> "He was actually very close to getting the job in the summer. He made the short list and in the end it was him who withdrew from the process. We have never turned him down."

When Allardyce was finally unveiled to as the new Rovers manager at the end of 2008, he received as warm an Ewood Park welcome as any manager I can remember. Any feelings of uncertainty that had greeted his links to the club in the summer appeared to have subsided. Allardyce had polled a measly 10% when 1,000 Rovers fans were asked six months earlier who they would like to see installed as the next manager. Following the departure of Ince, Allardyce topped the same poll with a whopping 46% of the vote – more than twice as many as second placed Roberto Mancini – and this faith seemed well founded as Allardyce took over with the team six points adrift of safety. The new manager injected some much needed steel in to the team and straight away Rovers went on a nine-game unbeaten run that saw us climb out of the relegation zone and also progress nicely in the FA Cup.

At this point, the *Anti-Allardyce Brigade,* as they became affectionately known, had little vocal presence at games and seemed to be no more than a handful of keyboard bashers trying to stir up bad feeling on the Internet. There were a number of reasons they gave for not liking Allardyce – the obvious one being his Bolton connections. A contentious El-Hadji Diouf penalty at Ewood back in 2005 didn't help matters much either. While playing for Bolton, El-Hadji Diouf had tripped himself up in the box and fooled the referee in to awarding a penalty. Brad Friedel saved but El-Hadji Diouf tapped in the rebound to steal all three points. When interviewed about the dive after the game, Allardyce refused to condemn his player, enraging Rovers fans. As frustrating as it was, it was no different to Graeme Souness and Mark Hughes standing by Rovers players when hand-ball winners at St. James' Park became a yearly pleasure. Big Sam was one of us now and so was his partner in crime El-Hadji Diouf. There were grumblings about the 2006 BBC *Panorama* documentary *Undercover: Football's Dirty Secrets* and also a few groans about ugly football. The *Panorama* documentary had been dealt with by *The Stevens Report* in 2007 and the prospect of ugly football didn't bother me too much. Hughes' Rovers team had supposedly played ugly football. It was an unfair tag and the major reason why we finished bottom of the fair play league season after season. We didn't play like Arsenal but so what? Hughes had found a way of squeezing every last bit of talent out of a group of players that, as individuals were often inferior to the opposition. Football can be played in many different ways. Although the casual television observer may like to see

Van Persie and Fabregas pass it round in pretty triangles, I loved nothing more than watching someone like Paul Dickov chase down every little scrap or Andy Todd putting his face where others were too scared to put their feet. It made for a great atmosphere at games and Rovers fans loved it. That is the sort of energy and passion that had been lacking under Ince and in Allardyce I was glad we had someone who could replicate this kind of spirit.

Rovers continued to accumulate points throughout the second half of the 2008/09 season and our Premier League survival was secured with two games to go. This was no mean feat considering the position we found ourselves in at the end of 2008. At this point, Allardyce remained popular with the majority of fans but the first early signs of the ways that would see his popularity wane had begun to surface. Allardyce described keeping Rovers in the Premier League as his greatest achievement in management - somewhat surprising considering this was the man who had led Bolton Wanderers into Europe. I thought Mike Ashley had put the trumpet back in its box. Rovers were poor under Ince but essentially Allardyce inherited the core of a squad that had finished the previous three seasons seventh, tenth and sixth. Having spent the best part of a week's wage on away trips to Anfield and The Emirates, I didn't really enjoy watching fringe players get turned over by Liverpool and Arsenal either. Fair enough, putting weakened teams out for the early rounds of the League Cup but not Saturday afternoons in the Premier League. In Allardyce's defence when we came up against the teams around us we did look that little bit sharper. If this is what it took to stay up, I was happy enough to see our key players wrapped in cotton wool for games we had little chance of winning and Paul Robinson smashing 60 yard balls over our relegation rivals straight in to the path of our new striker Chris Samba. Over that first six months Allardyce quickly proved himself to have one major quality that set him apart from his peers – the likes of Mick McCarthy and Steve Bruce – and that was the ability to win football matches regardless of the quality of performance. The Spurs match at Ewood Park in April 2009 is a game that illustrates this point better than any. How we won that game still astonishes me. We were awful, but win it we did and this became a regular feature of Allardyce's time at the club. I was quickly learning that the ugly football played under Hughes and the ugly football played under Allardyce were two totally different animals. There had been a sort of unconventional beauty about the football played under Hughes that had lazily been tagged ugly. Make no mistake the stuff we were playing under Allardyce was not, by anybody's definition, beautiful. It was ugly – seriously ugly – ugly in a way that would have made the Elephant Man's mother wince. Some fans were happy just to be picking up points but equally there were large sections of Rovers fans who did struggle with Allardyce's style. There are very few football snobs amongst Rovers fans. We have enjoyed all kinds of different types of football over the years. Most fans appreciate that the club's financial position makes it difficult for us to play like Barcelona but this version of the game was difficult to come to terms with. We may have been playing at a higher level and for bigger stakes but there were few that could argue that it was as fun as football used to be. I am sure Newcastle and West Ham fans will back me up on this one but at times it was like watching a sort of bizarre cross between Gaelic Football, Rugby Union and a never-ending corner kick. It was a stop-start form of the game I had only ever witnessed before in penalty shoot-outs. This was more a sort of general set-piece shoot out – throw-ins, free-kicks, corners, even goal-kicks became a more viable route to goal than good old pass and move. A great believer in sports science and statistics Allardyce delighted in telling us that statistically this was the most effective way to play the game. When his results were compared to those of Ince it was difficult to argue otherwise. We had come a long way since the late 1980s and, even once we had secured our Premier League status, it appeared that winning was now the sole form of entertainment.

Herein began the complex and often fractious relationship between a large proportion of Blackburn Rovers fans and Allardyce. At a time when most fans were expecting the club to build on the momentum we had gained from staying in the Premier League, Allardyce's Plan A was about to be unveiled as his plan A all the way through to Z. Not only this but the summer of 2009 was about to prove a bit of a wash out in the transfer market. Yes, the fans were aware that there were financial constraints at the club – but there had been for some time. All most wanted to see was a little less chat about it and a real effort to get the team back up to the levels that we had seen under Hughes. Unfortunately, if *Sky Sports News* had been looking for a man to fill the broadcasting void left by Jose Mourinho's defection from Chelsea two years earlier in

Allardyce they had finally found their man. This guy liked to talk. Over the summer I started to get used to his regular slot on the hourly *Sky Sports News* loop and having liked how he had come across in the media up to this point, I wasn't overly enamoured with much of what he now had to say.

> "We know we are not going to score a lot of goals in the Premier League because we don't spend the money on strikers like everyone else does. That usually determines what position you finish in the league."

For me, this became typical Allardyce. On the face of it, a fair point, that was no doubt backed up by overpaid ex-pros across the land. As a Rovers fan, however, I felt that Allardyce's media transfer groans quickly became a little too regular and were somewhat flawed seeing as Hughes had managed to finish in the top half of the Premier League three seasons in a row under equally difficult financial constraints. I know football was changing but I don't think it was changing that fast that we suddenly had to be content with dropping eight places down the league. Allardyce pointed out that even free transfers cost a fortune these days but you can't have a massive backroom team, top wages and an unlimited transfer budget at Blackburn Rovers. I am not sure what purpose it served to keep bringing these issues up. Rather than moaning about lack of money, Hughes had used what little transfer funds he did have to set him apart from his big-spending rivals. I thought Allardyce would have relished the challenge of trying to emulate, or even surpass, the benchmark set by his predecessor – particularly as he came with such a big reputation for uncovering cut-price diamonds. We did sell a lot of players during Allardyce's time at Rovers (notably Matt Derbyshire, Benni McCarthy, Andre Oojer, Paul Gallagher and Aaron Mokoena) and Tugay retired but if you look down the list of players that left you would say Roque Santa Cruz and Stephen Warnock were missed but anyone else who left under Allardyce was unlikely to feature in his first choice starting 11 anyway. The Walker Trust had made no bones about their desire to sell the club but Allardyce was still given the best part of £15 million pounds and a sizable wage fund to replace departing players – as well as having the core of a decent squad left over from previous managers. "Just get on with it" was the call from the fans. Of the players Allardyce brought in I would say his transfer dealings were good. How involved Allardyce's successor came to be in transfers is still cause for much debate but during Allardyce's time in the hot seat I was very much under the impression that it was the manager who was calling the shots. Givet was an excellent buy, El-Hadji Doiuf made a difference, Salgado turned out to be a quality addition and the uncovering of Steven Nzonzi made up for stinkers like Goulon, Linganzi, Basturk and Chimbonda. If these had been Allardyce's only buys he no doubt would have been considered a real success in the transfer market. The one thing that did blot Allardyce's transfer record, however, was his constant struggle to sign a decent striker. Allardyce often bemoaned Rovers lack of a quality goal scorer and made no qualms about stating that this was the main reason he wasn't able to achieve more at the club. I see his point about the lack of a quality striker but I think Allardyce has to shoulder a fair amount of the blame here. Allardyce started the search for a 15-goal a season striker in 2009 and 18 months later he still hadn't found one that could get near double figures in the Premier League – despite spending a sizeable chunk of money on Nikola Kalinic and almost as much again on four full-backs in Chimbonda, Givet, Jacobsen and Salgado. It may sound harsh but Allardyce was more than happy to regularly remind people of the signings he did get right (does anybody realise that he signed Jay Jay Okocha?) and appeared equally happy to use the media to advertise the fact that he would be more suited to a bigger club. It's really obvious but if you need a 15-goal a season striker don't blow the budget on four full-backs and an untried 21-year-old. Allardyce was quick to give himself a big pat on the back for the loan capture of Franco Di Santo and Mama Biram Diouf but soon started moaning about lack of transfer funds again when neither could hit a barn door with a banjo.

This period signalled the start of my falling out of love with football. I used to genuinely love going to Rovers. Not because we were winning or playing against the biggest teams. I just loved the buzz of going to Rovers. I am a football fan. I have pulled out of family functions to watch Rovers. I have gone hungry to watch Rovers. I have skived off school to watch Rovers. As sad as it sounds I have literally found myself rubbing my hands together with glee because I was about to go to Wrexham to watch Rovers play in a friendly. I just didn't feel that excitement anymore. The truth is I just went now because it is what I had always done. I was just going out of habit. There were loads of reasons why I had fallen out of love with football but Allardyce was one of them. I continued to attend home games and fully back the team but I wasn't going to fork out too much more money to watch weakened sides at big away grounds. Nor was I going to spend half my weekend watching the more winnable games turned in to dog-fights. The plain fact is it was absolutely boring. This is from somebody who stays up until 1 am to watch Japanese football and actively campaigned for Allardyce to be named as Rovers manager. As I have said, fans of other clubs may not understand but I have no doubt whatsoever that fans of West Ham and Newcastle will know exactly what I am talking about. Even when we did put out our best 11 I found a lot of these games difficult to watch live so I wasn't going to go out of my way to follow away games. It was all about the result and I could find the result out in two seconds at full time. I had seen enough of Allardyce's Rovers to fill in the gaps. The key to ugly-win-at-all-costs football is that, in the main, people will tolerate it for as long as the team is getting results. The big problem is that as soon as you start losing games you would normally expect to win, the manager is going to be on the receiving end of some pretty stiff criticism. That is inevitably what happened in the case of Allardyce. At the end of 2009, Rovers went on a nine game winless streak in the league that was rounded off with an utterly toothless 4-1 defeat away at Manchester City live on Sky. It was during this period that some of the Internet big mouths and concourse grumblers became increasingly vocal at games and the pent up frustration towards Allardyce was no longer confined to the silent minority. It was nothing compared to the fury that would be unleashed on his successor but Big Sam became Fat Sam; football became hoof-ball and the Blackburn End adopted a new anthem to the tune of *Ere we go* that went "4-4-2, 4-4-2, 4-4-2". An obvious dig at Allardyce's continual refusal to play two up front, it was hardly *You'll Never Walk Alone* but what it was, was a clear indication that Rovers fans were becoming more than a little bit tired of Allardyce's negative brand of anti-football. By now, Rovers were three points from the relegation zone, and having played more games than most of our rivals, speculation was growing that Allardyce had two games to save his job. Allardyce is not a man who is prone to back tracking and true to form, rather than using this warning as an opportunity to tweak the methods that had undoubtedly cast a black shadow over his entire career, not only did he start name-dropping his pal "Sir Alex" even more but he actually started taking public digs at the fans of the club that employed him. "I don't know why they booed. Fans seem to think they are much bigger experts than ever before" was Allardyce's take on a pretty feeble 1-0 defeat to Aston Villa in the first leg of the League Cup semi final in January 2010. "If you are a lover of football, how much of the dirge that is being served up at Ewood can someone stand" was one of the more printable comments left by an angry fan after the same game.

Allardyce was back for round two a week later when he was apparently stunned that only 1500 tickets had been taken up by Rovers fans for the second leg at Aston Villa. "If the fans aren't as excited as we are then it's hard luck. They'll be moaning when we get to the final and they can't get a ticket" was Allardyce's charming taunt towards his own fans. I wonder if he talked to "Sir Alex" like that. Personally, I was surprised that we had sold 1500 tickets. I don't want to sound blasé about getting to a domestic cup semi final but let's get real for a minute. Getting to the League Cup semi final (less glamorously translated – beating Nottingham Forest and Peterborough – Allardyce was in hospital when we beat Chelsea in the Quarter Finals) may have gone straight on to the Allardyce CV but, despite playing reasonably well in the first half, any Rovers fan who missed the opportunity to spend £50 watching Rovers get pulverised 7-4 on aggregate on a freezing cold night in Birmingham, three weeks after Christmas, especially considering our precarious position in the league and Allardyce's growing reputation for fielding weakened teams for games we were unlikely to win, hardly missed out on a golden night in the history of Blackburn Rovers Football Club.

Famous himself for boycotting the BBC, it was around this time that I imposed my own personal media ban on Allardyce. For me, football had been losing touch with the common man for years and Allardyce had become the embodiment of football's transcendence into the world of new money. This isn't jealousy by the way – just an honest personal opinion. As is true of most of the highly paid non-playing staff employed within football, I just didn't buy in to the fairy tale that bigger wages were still getting us better quality. For me, take away the zeros in his salary and Allardyce was just a modern day version of Big Ron and Harry Bassett. Don't get me wrong, Allardyce was not a bad manager – unlike the manager that followed him! He got a lot of things right and had one or two real qualities. I can't think of a manager in football who keeps his players as well disciplined as Allardyce and keeping a squad of 20 or so new millionaires in check is some achievement. Barring his struggle at Rovers to find a 15-goal a season striker I actually think that he was pretty good in the transfer market too. On the flipside, no matter how many times he tried to cover it up with Opta Stats the football we played was so bad it was verging on being another sport, I didn't like the way Allardyce came across in public and despite keeping us safe from relegation for two seasons I still wanted to see more. I look forward to seeing how Allardyce fares with West Ham over the next couple of seasons now they are back in the Premier League. When times got tough, Allardyce was never short of people in the media ready to massage his ego and tell him he was doing well just to keep us in the Premier League. This may have been true when he started out at Bolton Wanderers but when he took the job at Blackburn Rovers we had no inferiority complex about mixing at the top table. Are you trying to tell me that Blackburn Rovers shouldn't back themselves to compete against Birmingham, Fulham, Stoke, Wigan, West Ham, Bolton, Portsmouth, Burnley, Hull and Wolves? And equally all these teams should back themselves to compete against us. It is complete fiction that you have got to beat the likes of Manchester United, Chelsea, Arsenal and Liverpool every week to make it in the Premier League.

In true Allardyce style, after antagonising so many Rovers fans, he then went on a run that saw us take

29 points from the final 17 games and finish the season in an impressive tenth in the Premier League. That was the frustrating anomaly of the man. Just when you thought you could take no more he would pull out a string of results that would leave you lost for words. Allardyce would argue that these results were a consequence of his much-derided methods; Rovers fans would argue that you shouldn't have to play Gaelic football to beat Wigan at home.

By the time Venky's took over, the relationship between Allardyce and the fans was very much a marriage of convenience. Both parties had long since given up on the idea of true love but the fact was Rovers were able to give Allardyce the big stage he thrived on and in return he was able to keep us in the Premier League. Although Allardyce may have been dreaming of practising corners at the San Siro, and Rovers fans were dreaming of the ball touching the grass, the reality was Inter Milan seemed happy enough with Jose Mourinho and there were hardly a host of great managers banging down the door for the Rovers job. It was an unconventional relationship but one that Allardyce and the fans both seemed to understand. Some fans liked him, some fans didn't, some fans shouted about it and some fans just let him get on with it. There was always that feeling that Allardyce was open to offers and by the same token, a lot of Rovers fans wouldn't be shedding too many tears if he were replaced by somebody better. In the mean time as long as we kept Allardyce in the spotlight and he kept us in the Premier League, the current arrangement more than suited both parties. Maybe finance had been the problem and now we would see Allardyce flourish.

Allardyce had his fair share of faults but the players all seemed happy enough, most of the players he did sign were good value for money and the team continued to pick up points when it mattered.

On 13 December 2010 it was announced that Venky's would be relieving Allardyce of his duties at Blackburn Rovers with immediate effect. At the time, I thought that Venky's had picked up on the underlying current of bad feeling towards Allardyce, put two and two together, made five and seen this as their time to act. The football world was aghast, Rovers fans were bemused and Allardyce was as close to lost for words as I have seen him.

> "I am very shocked and disappointed to be leaving Blackburn. I am extremely proud to have managed this club and I enjoyed a fantastic relationship with the players, my staff and the supporters during my time in charge. I now wish them and the football club every success for the future."

I had been waiting 18 months for this sort of humility and he goes and saves it for his leaving speech! Despite Allardyce's increasing unpopularity with significant sections of Rovers support even the *Anti-Allardyce Brigade* were struggling to get their heads around this one. The sentiment of Venky's decision may have been something they agreed with but the truth was, unless there was a massive name waiting in the wings, the timing of it was totally bizarre. For his many faults, everyone knew that Allardyce specialised in home victories against teams outside the top four. Already on 21 points, with home games coming up against West

Ham, Stoke, West Brom, Newcastle and Blackpool we would have been safe by the end of March. If Venky's then wanted to bring in their own man I think everybody involved would have understood. Why rock the boat two weeks before Christmas?

Up until this point, the media had gone pretty easy on Venky's but once the departure of Allardyce was announced the tone quickly changed. "Sam sacking is a Clucking Disgrace" exclaimed the *The Sun*: "Superman is needed to save Rovers from this mess" cried *The Daily Express*. A host of senior players, including Ryan Nelsen, Chris Samba and Michel Salgado, quickly came out to publicly question the decision to dispose of Allardyce.

"I've never heard of such a stupid decision in all my life, it's absolutely ridiculous" was Alex Ferguson's take on it all. Cue a whole host of ex-pros and desperados chipping in with their two pence worth. I was too busy drawing up names for the now vacant manager's position to take too much of an interest in what the *Sky Sports* sound-bite posse had to say. Early favorites in the betting were Martin Jol, Martin O'Neill, Chris Hughton and Alan Shearer.

In the meantime Venky's placed first-team coach Steve Kean in temporary charge. Kean had been appointed first team coach by Allardyce the previous season. His only other taste of the big time had been as Chris Coleman's assistant manager. To my shame, when I saw the porky bald bloke jogging up the steps at Brockhall on *Sky Sports News* I don't think I had ever seen him before in my life. At this point I would have still maintained that the position of Blackburn Rovers manager was one of the most attractive jobs in football.

It may have been a constant struggle to keep attendances around the 25,000 mark and Blackburn is not what you would describe as a millionaire's playground but if you look past these two frequently highlighted drawbacks this was quite an opportunity. Rovers were a well established Premier League team with realistic expectations and an excellent infrastructure and support network for any new manager. Steve Kean wasn't a name I was aware of at the time so I wanted to know whether there was anything about his achievements in the game that suggested he was a serious candidate for the job. Over the next few days I familiarised myself with Kean's achievements in football and while there was little to suggest that he wouldn't be capable of holding the fort for a couple of weeks, I didn't see anything about his time in the game that suggested he was a serious candidate to replace Allardyce. When Rovers fans went looking for a bit of background on Kean many found themselves drawn to his Wikipedia page. Unfortunately, and this is by no means the fault of Kean, whoever had been updating the Wikipedia page of the largely unknown first team coach of Blackburn Rovers, appeared to be somewhat of a fantasist. We now know that the mildly credible playing career involving the Portuguese football league, something that Kean himself talked about in 2008 when linked with the role of Phil Scolari's assistant at Chelsea, was something quite different in reality. Now that the people at Wikipedia have verified Kean's playing achievements against official records his Wikipedia page has undergone quite a make-over (or make-under). The truth was, by the end of 2010, I think Kean had actually done pretty well to well to have found himself in the position of first team coach at a Premier League football club. Kean's playing career had been limited to four games in the old fourth division, a game for Alloa and a few years in Portugal – even Kean himself has given different information exactly how many. When asked about his football background in an interview with the *BRFCS* website in September 2011, Kean told the site's chief reporter,

> "I spent five years at Celtic as a young player but it was very hard to establish myself and get in the first team so I then left Celtic and went to play abroad. I played in Portugal for five years with Academica which is a team in the top division in a city called Coimbra and I played for a club called Naval for two years as well so that was a time when I saw a different side to football because it was a different style it was very technical the Portuguese always produced really flair players different from the Scottish style and the English style."

It all sounds quite impressive if you say it quickly enough but having looked in to the standard of football Kean was referring to – Portuguese Second and Third Division at the turn of the 1990s – I am confident that I could probably walk in to the local pub and find somebody that had played football at a higher level than Kean. Academia may be in the top division now but they weren't when Kean played his 12 games for them and neither were Naval. As for the technical style it probably owed as much to playing on Astroturf as it did to the innate footballing flair of the Portuguese. Not playing at the highest level is no crime, look at Jose Mourinho, but anybody who was only hearing the words Celtic and Portugal wasn't really getting an accurate picture of what Kean's playing career was all about.

> "Then after I left Portugal I went back to Reading because the manager of Reading at the time was Mark McGhee and I had played with Mark at Celtic and I went there and then I finished at Reading with a dislocated ankle broken tibia and fibula and started coaching in the centre of excellence as it was then, in the evenings with the young kids and then worked my way up until I was Academy director at Reading."

Kean never played a game at Reading and I am not too sure what his subsequent role at the club involved but in an interview in The People in 2011, Kean told Alan Nixon,

> "When I was at Reading, I was youth coach, goalkeeping coach, club taxi driver, estate agent, groundsman and even translator. Our keeper Bobby Mihailov, who wore a wig, was Bulgarian and didn't speak English, but he had played in Portugal like me so we spoke Portuguese."

It sounds like the role of a dogsbody to me and by the time Kean took up the role of Youth Academy Director at Fulham in 2000 his achievements in top level football were still negligible. Kean's real big break came in 2003. With Fulham manager John Tigana's contract coming to an end, owner of the club Mohammed Al Fayed terminated Tigana's employment and asked Chris Coleman to fill the role of caretaker manager. Youth Academy Director Kean was asked to work alongside him. At the time Fulham were still in danger of relegation from the Premier League but Coleman and Kean helped steer the club safety. This was a quality Fulham squad that included players like Edwin van der Saar, Louis Saha, Luis Boa Morte and Lee Clark. Coleman was given the job of manager full time and with Kean filling the position of assistant manager, Fulham ended the following season ninth in the Premier League. The club's better players were eventually sold on and over the next few seasons Fulham struggled to push on. There were a few mid-table finishes for Coleman and Kean but from this point on their record as a management team is ordinary at best. With Fulham hovering just four points above the relegation zone, Coleman and Kean were sacked by Fulham in 2007. The following season they turned up at Real Sociedad, with Kean again filling the role of assistant manager to Coleman. Real Sociedad had competed in the UEFA Champions League in 2003/04 but by the start of 2007/08 they were actually in the second tier of Spanish football. After just six months at the club Coleman resigned and Kean followed. Kean has said that he was offered the position of manager at the time but he chose to turn it down out of loyalty to Coleman. Coleman and Kean's next job in management was at Coventry City but after starting well at Fulham their star was rapidly fading. Coventry finished the 2008/09 season 17th in The Championship and Coleman and Kean parted ways. Coleman stayed on at the club and was quick to dispel any talk of a bust-up between him and Kean. Coleman was sacked the following season after overseeing Coventry's lowest league finish for 45 years. In summary, with the exception of a couple of good seasons at Fulham even Kean's more notable achievements in football weren't actually that remarkable and at the time of his appointment of caretaker at Rovers I didn't think it would take Venky's too long to find a host of better qualified managers. Of the unknown Kean, Mrs Desai told *Five Live*, "This is a guy who is hard-working, who loves the team and is very motivated." Aren't we all? If these were the qualities Venky's were looking for it looked like the local milkman was in with a shout. The tabloid speculators went in to overdrive and some big names were linked the position of Rovers manager. Rafa Benitez, Gareth Southgate, Sven Goran Eriksson and even Maradona got a mention.

"Our thinking now is that it will be a British manager, but we are open if there is an outstanding candidate: someone who would be really, really good for the club," Mrs Desai told the *Lancashire Telegraph*. I was more than a little concerned that, having sacked Allardyce, Venky's didn't appear to have a high profile replacement ready to step straight in to the job. It was a baffling development but Rovers fans just had to back the new owners' judgement. Venky's came with the endorsement of a board we trusted and what real power did we have to do anything but back them? It is a total myth that we didn't give Venky's support – if anything we gave them too much support when we perhaps should have been protesting from day one. Either way, the fans couldn't win.

On 22 December 2010, after an unimpressive home draw against bottom of the table West Ham, it was announced that caretaker manager Steve Kean would become Blackburn Rovers permanent manager. I'm sure I wasn't the only Rovers fan to get that horrible sinking feeling. Either Venky's knew something we didn't or Rovers were back in a relegation dog-fight.

Chapter 5

Kentaro and SEM

Rovers fans wanted to know why, less than a month after Venky's had bought our club, Sam Allardyce had been replaced by Steve Kean. Allardyce's methods may have divided opinion but even his harshest critics were struggling to fathom Venky's decision to replace him with first team coach Kean. Allardyce was a proven Premier League manager. At the time of his sacking he had managed over 700 games in English football – many of them in the Premier League. Kean was yet to manage a professional team in his life. There was little about his modest achievements in the game to suggest he was worthy of his unexpected promotion. On the occasion that Allardyce had taken time away from his post it had been his assistant Neil McDonald who had managed the team. Why was the third in command now suddenly in charge? In the days that followed Allardyce's sacking, Mrs Desai told the *Lancashire Telegraph,*

> "We want good football and Blackburn to be fourth or fifth in the league or even better. The fans should trust us because this is in the best interests of the club. We wanted the games to be interesting and of course wanted to win and to have good players."

No Rovers fan had a problem with Venky's aiming high (although it was a noticeable departure from the mid-table talk of the previous month); what your typical fan wanted to know was how Kean was better qualified than Allardyce to actually achieve these ambitious new goals.

Shortly after his departure, Allardyce told *Sky Sports*, "Having never really met the new owners and had little dialogue, somebody somewhere has obviously said something derogatory to get me out of this job." Venky's gave their own reasons for the removal of Allardyce. They said that Allardyce didn't fit in, he didn't share their vision, he wasn't positive enough and also questioned how successful he had been in the transfer market. Mrs Desai told the BBC,

> "My father once told me that out of 10 decisions you must get at least seven right – you can get two or three wrong, we're not gods. But to get nine or 10 wrong is not good and things have been going wrong with transfers – that's a fact."

I don't know where Mrs Desai was getting her facts from but I had to disagree with her on this one. Rovers had made millions from player trading over the previous 10 seasons and to suggest that Allardyce had got nine of his previous 10 transfer decisions wrong was far from being a fact. As a Rovers fan, it was difficult not to get angry. What did Mrs Desai know about how successful Allardyce's signings had been? This is the same woman that told *BBC Radio Lancashire*, "The impression is I've never watched a football match. I've not watched in a stadium but I have been watching the World Cup in India." Whatever. Venky's were being advised on football matters by Kentaro and The Sport Entertainment and Media Group (SEM). What fans wanted to know was who were Kentaro and SEM and how had they come to hold such apparent influence at our football club?

Blackburn Rovers had been up for sale for two years when Rothschild, the investment bank working on behalf of the Walker Trust, contacted agents to search global markets for potential suitors. Although the name Kentaro meant little to the average Rovers fan, the company was well known in football circles and it was hoped that their vast network of high-end business contacts could significantly speed up the takeover process. Launched in 2003 by Philipp Grothe and Philippe Huber, Kentaro had quickly established itself as one of Europe's leading sports rights agencies. Prior to the formation of Kentaro, Grothe and Huber had been working for IMG, a global sports and media business. IMG was founded by Mark McCormack, an American lawyer who spotted the potential for athletes to make large incomes from endorsement way back in the 1960s. He signed golfer Arnold Palmer as his first client in 1960 and IMG went on to represent sportsmen including Jack Nicklaus, Bjorn Borg and Pete Sampras. Following the death of McCormack in 2003, Grothe and Huber decided to set up on their own. They naturally gravitated towards football and by 2009 the company had significant involvement in a whole host of fields including event management, sponsorships, talent management and consulting on football investment. Although Grothe and Huber had a passion for football, from the outset this was clearly a serious corporate business venture. In the corporate world football is a market, teams are properties, properties represent opportunities, games are "delivered", crowds are ticket revenue, viewers are advertising audiences, brand development is pivotal and ultimately markets are there to be exploited. Phillip Grothe embraced corporate attitudes in sport,

> "You can only market and exploit a sport when you understand it; and I wouldn't say I'm a big expert in, say, golf or tennis. I wouldn't say we have a natural competence in those things. That doesn't mean we don't look into opportunities. But, in the foreseeable future, Kentaro will be a football agency; especially as long as there is so much to develop."

Kentaro's development of international friendly matches was a major feature of their rapid growth. I had spent a lifetime wondering why there were so many seemingly pointless international friendlies. Having seen what a money spinner these games were I now had a better idea. Organisers of the "Gillette Brazil World Tour," in which the Brazilian national team played international friendlies around the world, to give an idea how lucrative this "market" was, Kentaro were once able to sell 80,000 tickets in a day just to watch Brazil train. Having built up an impressive list of contacts from their many years in sport it wasn't long before Kentaro had secured important contracts with various clubs and football associations around the world, including Liverpool, Chelsea, Arsenal and the English Football Association.

In January 2009, in an effort to increase their activity in the player management business, Kentaro became corporate partners with Jerome Anderson's SEM. At the time, many Rovers fans were still counting the cost of Christmas and an FA Cup trip to Blyth Spartans. Kentaro and SEM were living in a different financial world. The closing of the deal was celebrated with a dinner held at Arsenal's Emirates Stadium prior to the international friendly between Brazil and Italy - a match that was managed, promoted and marketed by Kentaro. Already successful companies in their own right, the corporate partnership between Kentaro and SEM made them quite a force in football.

Born in 1958, SEM Chairman and Chief Executive Jerome Anderson was a boyhood Arsenal fan and having landed the gig as the stadium announcer at Highbury in the 1980s he quickly established himself as a leading football agent. In 1984, he formed the company SEM and early clients included Arsenal players Charlie Nicholas and the late David Rocastle. With the formation of the Premier League just around the corner this was a great time for any budding football agent to be establishing himself in the game. Jerome Anderson shared close personal links with Arsenal vice-chairman David Dein and went on to represent Arsenal players Dennis Bergkamp, David Seaman and, now part of the Kentaro senior management team, Emmanuel Petit. David Dein's son

Darren Dein worked with SEM and the relationship between Arsenal, the Dein family and SEM has come under no small amount of media scrutiny over the years. When questioned about this by the *Sunday Mirror's* Paul Smith in 2004, Jerome Anderson's response was,

> "Let's make this clear once and for all. Darren Dein is a qualified lawyer, and competitors and respected companies like IMG employ several lawyers to oversee contracts. Darren's role is very simple. He is a qualified lawyer who works with us as a legal consultant overseeing various commercial contracts."

By 2009, SEM represented over 150 professional footballers. High profile players under their management included Cesc Fabregas, Rio Ferdinand, Alex Song, Micah Richards and Thierry Henry. They also represented Premier League managers Owen Coyle and Tony Pulis. Players with Rovers links managed by SEM include Paul Robinson, David Bentley and Stephen Warnock. SEM's media operations came to be as important to the story as their involvement in football. Media personalities represented by SEM included Ian Wright, Glen Hoddle, Matt Le Tissier and Charlie Nicholas. As well as providing middle-aged men to talk about football on Sky, SEM were able to set a number of their clients up in major advertising campaigns. Several SEM clients also have columns in newspapers and in some cases they have even starred in their own television shows. Who knows if one-off classics like *Rio's World Cup*

Wind-ups and *The Cesc Show* ever would have got off the ground without SEM?

Most football fans understand the need to take the everyday stresses out of a sportsman's life in order to allow them to focus on the area they excel in; many would also acknowledge that it is important that any young person entering into contract negotiations with massive multi-million pound organisations has some form of representation. I would even agree with the view point that football agents are a necessary part of the game. This being the case, why is it that football agents are so widely disliked by regular football fans? In my case, the answer is pretty simple – in the main they are grossly overpaid for what they do. The role of the modern day football agent is to identify "talented individuals" and then take care of their contract negotiations, commercial management, image rights, financial and wealth management and career planning. The skills involved would be unlikely to warrant too high a salary in most other lines of work, yet the financial rewards for the modern day football agent operating in and around the Premier League are massive – in many cases obscene. Some would argue that you are as good as what people are prepared to pay you but in the case of the grossly under regulated free-for-all of the Premier League I would argue that this doesn't really apply. In June 2008, the Premier League agreed that from 2009 onwards each club would publish the total amount it paid to authorised agents for the period 1 October the previous year to 30 September that year. Here are the figures for the 15 clubs that were in the Premier League for all of the first three seasons after this agreement was made.

MONEY SPENT BY PREMIER LEAGUE CLUB'S ON AUTHORISED AGENTS

	2008/09	2009/10	2010/11
Arsenal	£4.7m	£3.6m	£4.6m
Aston Villa	£1.7m	£2.2m	£3.1m
Blackburn Rovers	£1.6m	£1.6m	£4.2m
Bolton Wanderers	£3.6m	£3.5m	£1.9m
Chelsea	£9.9m	£9.2m	£6.4m
Everton	£2.0m	£3.5m	£2.9m
Fulham	£1.4m	£2.0m	£0.9m
Liverpool	£6.6m	£9.0m	£7.0m
Manchester City	£12.8m	£5.9m	£9.6m
Manchester United	£1.5m	£2.3m	£4.4m
Stoke City	£0.7m	£2.1m	£2.2m
Sunderland	£2.0m	£4.4m	£3.7m
Spurs	£6.0m	£5.3m	£7.5m
Wigan	£3.5m	£2.4m	£0.6m
Wolves	£1.2m	£1.2m	£1.1m

Although Blackburn Rovers had been the first club to pay a player £10,000 a week wages when we signed Chris Sutton from Norwich in 1994, I would argue all day long that the Premier League's subsequent problems had little to do with anything that came out of Jack Walker's pocket. For me the financial lunacy that was endemic across top level English football had far more to do with lack of regulation; foreign investment; television money; the Bosman ruling and the emergence of a general 'greed is good' attitude. Football agents played a massive part in this. Including the other clubs that spent time in the Premier League between 2008 and 2011, the total figure spent by Premier League club's on agents in this period is a mind-boggling £209,699,302.64 - an average of just under £70 million per season. When former Rovers player Mike Newell spoke out about the role of agents in football in 2006 he alleged that not all money made by football agents makes it on to official records. Speaking under the banner of the Association of Football Agents, Jerome Anderson publicly condemned Newell's comments and he has always been keen to distance SEM from any stereotypes fans may have of his profession. Speaking about the reputation of football agents, Jerome Anderson told *The Observer*'s Jamie Jackson in 2006,

> "It is what it is. Partly media, partly the image. I can only speak for myself. I had a university place to study law. I've been chief executive of a plc for two years before we bought the company back. We're not one man in a car park, this is a global management brand for the modern world of sport."

A quick look at information held by Companies House tells you that this is indeed more than just one man in a car park. Jerome Anderson has over 30 appointments as a director or secretary with UK registered companies. Active companies with which he holds, or has held, appointments include Banaram Limited, Sports Holding Limited, The Casedirector Technolgy Partnership LLP, Ingenious Film Partners LLP and Ingenious Film Partners 2 LLP. As well as obvious links with sport - technology and films appear to feature heavily. In 2012 HM Revenue & Customs won a court victory over the proposed use of tax relief for the film investment scheme *Eclipse 35* and other schemes are being looked into.

Whether Jerome Anderson was "one man in a car park" or "a global management brand for the modern world of sport" it was always going to be a difficult task trying to convince your regular football fan that he was one of us. Considering their corporate background the same applied to Philipp Grothe and Philippe Huber. When asked about Kentaro's success Phillipp Grothe once said,

> "Every project is different, but you can measure success pretty easily. Basically, is the client happy with what's coming out at the bottom line?"

How much this has shaped the events that unfolded at Blackburn Rovers remains considerable cause for concern. I don't go to Rovers to support the bottom line. I can't actually find too many examples of representatives of Kentaro coming forward to speak out about their role at Blackburn Rovers. If there are examples out there please feel free to point me in the right direction. Like all Rovers fans, all I want from this is to try and understand why things have gone so badly wrong at the club. When you piece together the facts, as I have done, it doesn't look great. The wall of silence that exists around many of those who have been involved only makes it look worse. Kentaro are one of several companies and key figures that have failed to respond to my numerous attempts to engage in conversation. In each case I have posed the following generic questions in an effort to open up some form of meaningful dialogue:-

1. When and how did your association with Blackburn Rovers start?
2. What were your hopes for Blackburn Rovers when Venky's first took over in 2010?
3. What areas do you feel Venky's have improved the club?
4. With the benefit of hindsight, what do you feel should have been done differently?
5. Things have been going wrong at the club – what changes would you like to see?
6. You have received criticism in some quarters for your handling of affairs at Blackburn Rovers - what is your response to that?
7. What do you think the next twelve months hold for you personally and Blackburn Rovers Football Club?
8. Please feel free to add anything else...

The list of key figures that have failed to respond to these fairly unobtrusive and open questions is extensive. This has been a source of great disappointment. If any of the people involved would now like to respond with honest answers that promote a better understanding of what has gone on my email address is michael.blackburn@live.co.uk. I would still like to hear from those who have anything worthwhile to say. If I do hear back from anyone I will post full details on the rovertaken.co.uk website. Many things in this story don't add up. If I can't provide the answers I feel that it is important the pressure remains on those that can. The exact nature of Kentaro's role in identifying potential suitors, overseeing the sale and then advising Venky's on football matters is a grey area. SEM's Jerome Anderson has been a little more forthcoming about his involvement and from what he has said publicly it appears that he played a significant role in the process.

When Jerome Anderson took on the task of finding a buyer for Blackburn Rovers it wasn't the first time that he had been involved in attempts to source finance for a Premier League football club. He had played an instrumental role in the Fortress Sports Fund fiasco at Everton in 2004/05. Speaking to the club's shareholders at the 2004 EGM, Everton Chairman Bill Kenwright described Jerome Anderson as,

> "The chap who first of all came to me and said 'I know some people who might be able to help you', which I've got to tell you a lot of people do, and Jerome Anderson introduced me to some people that I hope will help you and help this football club."

It all sounded promising enough to Everton fans at the time and they were desperate for new investment following the collapse of the King's Dock project. Jerome Anderson had introduced Swiss-based English fund manager Christopher Samuelson to Everton and had also made a call to a 23-year old Russian Anton Zingarevich about the project. The Brunei-based Fortress Sports Fund was established and the proposal was that the fund would purchase a 29.9% stake in Everton by December 2004. There would then be an option to acquire further shares to give the Fortress Sports Fund a controlling stake – a deal reported to be worth around

£12.8 million. Zingarevich quickly withdrew from the project but Samuelson, who soon started describing himself as a lifelong follower of Everton, was keen to make the deal happen. Unfortunately the money was not forthcoming. Six months passed and various reasons were given for the money not arriving. Samuelson said the money had failed to arrive because he decided to use a cell fund and the delays were procedural. In January 2005, Samuelson was quoted by Mihir Bose of *The Daily Telegraph* saying,

> "Money has been raised for some time but it cannot go into the fund until the fund has a legal existence. You can only have a cell fund in places like Guernsey, Gibraltar, Mauritius and Brunei, which are tax havens. We have an office in Brunei. The funds we have are made of private individuals. They don't want publicity for themselves."

It all sounded very complicated and already there were Everton fans who were wishing that Jerome Anderson hadn't offered to help in the first place. By the following month the money still hadn't materialised and Everton started looking for new investors. The money never did find its way to Everton's account and seven years later Anton Zingarevich has completed his takeover at Reading FC. Everton Director Paul Gregg stated that he had been "led down the garden path and that the whole exercise has embarrassed the club."

Jerome Anderson was back in the spotlight in 2007 when he teamed up with Kentaro to advise former Prime Minister of Thailand Thaksin Shinawatra during Shinawatra's takeover of Manchester City. Shinawatra was a highly controversial figure and by 2011 The Supreme Court had stripped his family of $1.4bn (£910m) in contested assets, over allegations of corruption and conflict of interest. Shortly after Shinawatra arrived at Manchester City Sven Goran Eriksson replaced Stuart Pearce as manager. SEM oversaw at least seven of Eriksson's 10 signings during Shinawatra's season at the helm. Although Manchester City got off to a great start that season the long-term value of many of these signings is seriously debatable. In just over three weeks in the summer of 2007, SEM oversaw the transfer of Geovanni, Valeri Bojinov, Gelson Fernandes, Javier Garrido, Rolando Bianchi, Vedran Corluka and Elano. These guys didn't come cheap. According to *transfermarkt.com* Manchester City paid over £40 million in transfer fees to secure their services. Having now had the benefit of watching these players play on quite a few occasions, from what I can see, bar maybe Corluka and Elano, none of them have gone on to make any great waves in the Premier League. When Manchester City went top of the Premier League after three games the compliments came flooding in for Jerome Anderson. At the time, Wigan Athletic were actually fourth and in truth, a lot of the players that SEM were involved in signing at Manchester City sign soon fell down the pecking order. After Eriksson was released from his duties less than a year after arriving at the club he said of Shinawatra "he didn't understand football – he hadn't a clue." Whether Shinawatra was dependent on advisors or his manager the fact was that after that first season only three of the seven players listed above featured more than a dozen times for Manchester City's first team. None of the players listed were still at the club just three years later. I know that a large amount of new money came in to Manchester City not long after these players were signed but the fact that not one of them made an impact at the club beyond 2009, considering the amounts of money that were involved, didn't fill me with confidence. Despite being top of the league after three games at the start of 2007/08 and hovering around the UEFA Cup places going in to the new year, in the end Manchester City finished ninth that season, two places behind a Blackburn Rovers squad that cost little more than Manchester City had paid for Rolando Bianchi. Jerome Anderson has said of his time at Manchester City, "I will never forget the excitement of the Manchester City fans who really appreciated the work that was done." If Shinawatra hadn't been replaced by Sheikh Mansour bin Zayed Al Nahyan in the summer of 2008 I am not so sure that Jerome Anderson's time at the club would have been quite so fondly remembered. On 30 November 2007, Nick Harris of the *Mail on Sunday* reported that Shinawatra was reducing his involvement with Jerome Anderson. Harris wrote,

> "Anderson was well rewarded for his pivotal role in transforming the City squad and is understood to have earned in the region of £5 million in agreed commissions."
>
> Jerome Anderson said,

> "There is no one else in the world who could have delivered what I did in three weeks. It was my idea to open it up to other agents, and whatever I was paid, and it wasn't as much as City say, they've had it back in spades."

As well as his ongoing work as a football agent and his various business interests, Jerome Anderson and a number of his SEM clients (including Ian Wright, Stephen Warnock and Alex Song) also became a part of the Africa Soccer Developments project. According to the website,

> "Africa Soccer Developments is dedicated to helping young footballers to achieve their potential. It aims to develop the next generation of young professional footballers. We aim to source, develop and place new talent from all over the world, with a particular emphasis on placing African scholars into the European game"

In 2009, African Soccer Developments opened its first Soccer School of Excellence in Cape Town, South Africa. *The Daily Mail* did a feature on the soccer school and highlighted that a number of leading figures in South Africa had been quite vocal about their opposition to such soccer schools. Speaking from a Cairo conference looking at ways of tackling the problem of European clubs poaching young African talent, Chief Executive of the South Africa Football Association Raymond Hack said,

> "You cannot have people coming into your country, investing in your talent, even if the intentions are 100 per cent good. There is a procedure and a protocol which needs to be followed. Because you've got money does not mean that you can come in and invest in the country and decide what you're going to take and what you're not going to take."

In response to the suggestion that this was simply a money-making venture, sponsor of Africa Soccer Developments and SEM client Ian Wright said,

> "If money is made somewhere down the line, that's fine. But that is definitely not the aim of the academy. It will take 10 to 15 years for this academy to make any kind of profit. And any money we do make will be invested back into the school to train more South African coaches, to improve facilities and to give more boys an education and an opportunity. And even if, somewhere very far down the line, someone does make a bit of money from this academy, where's the negative in that?"

When questioned about the African Soccer Developments project, Jerome Anderson said,

> "I invested some money. I believe in the project and at some stage in the future, when the lad is 18, maybe we'll be allowed to sell that player on for the club."

Shortly after the launch of the soccer school in Cape Town, Jerome Anderson was searching global markets for potential buyers for Blackburn Rovers. Even if they had not been aware of his role in the Fortress Sports Fund fiasco at Everton in 2004/05, or were not put off by it, I would have at least thought that somebody at the club would have known of Jerome Anderson's work in the summer transfer window at Manchester City in 2007. Whatever the process behind the decision to involve him, somebody obviously thought he was the right man for the job and it wasn't long before he was leading potential suitors to Rovers' door.

In 2011, Laurence Bassini, a former bankrupt who had changed his name from Lawrence Bazini, said that he had been one of those approached about buying Blackburn Rovers.

> "I was offered Blackburn Rovers, as Jerome Anderson is a good friend of mine, and I went to see some games there. There was talk of it but I decided that I wanted to be near London."

Bassini ended up buying Watford, where his controversial reign lasted just over a year. Shortly after having a member of staff escorted off club premises by the police for refusing to hand over the keys to the safe, Bassini sold the club. Was this the calibre of buyer that was now considered right for Blackburn Rovers? By the time Jerome Anderson had introduced the club to Venky's in 2010, Saurin Shah and Ali Ahsan Syed had also been made aware of the club's sale. To say that Venky's appeared to represent the best option of all of them probably tells you a lot about Laurence Bassini, Saurin Shah and Ali Ahsan Syed.

It didn't take long for Jerome Anderson's association with Venky's to come to the attention of Rovers fans and in November 2010 he was spotted at a number of games with Balaji Rao and Venkatesh Rao. It was now understood that SEM was going to be playing a significant part in future transfer activity at Rovers and Jerome Anderson quickly became a regular face at Ewood Park. Rovers fans were worried that there would be a shift in power from the existing board and management team to a group of businessmen whose long-term use for Blackburn Rovers was not entirely clear. Concern amongst the fans was only exacerbated by what the manager was saying. At a time when Sam Allardyce was still claiming he had barely spoken to the new owners it was reported that representatives of Kentaro were flying out to India to discuss transfers with Venky's. On 13 December 2010, Allardyce was sacked and it was difficult to accept that the management and board still called the shots. Mrs Desai told reporters,

> "Kentaro are our main consultants but Sam had the final call but we didn't even get as far as discussing any names with him. As for Kentaro, they introduced us to the club in August and continue to advise us, but we are talking to a lot of people and we certainly don't have an exclusive deal with them. All our transfers don't have to go through them."

Although there was still three weeks until the start of the transfer window, from what Allardyce was saying, there had been very little effort at all by Venky's to discuss transfers with him prior to his departure. The changes behind the scenes were causing considerable concern to both the fans and the playing staff. Blackburn Rovers belonged to Venky's now and they were free to take advice from whomever they wanted but the fans wanted to see the club going forward on the field. Soon after Allardyce's sacking Alex Ferguson got involved by saying,

> "You've got that issue at Blackburn of an agent involved and deciding the future of the club, Jerome

Anderson, he couldn't pick his nose. It's baffling and it's a serious threat to how clubs get run and how they conduct themselves."

By this stage SEM client Rio Ferdinand had been at Manchester United for eight seasons so Fergie will have been familiar with the work of SEM. In 2005, Manchester United and SEM had been involved in the high profile chase for 18-year-old Nigerian "wonderkid" John Obi Mikel. At the time Obi Mikel was regarded as one of the best young footballers in the world and was even likened to Zinedine Zidane. In April 2005 Obi Mikel and his club in Norway, Lyn Oslo, announced that the player would be signing for Manchester United. That appeared to be deal done but two months later Obi Mikel was making it quite clear that he wanted to join Chelsea. Obi Mikel left Norway and fled to London where he told BBC's *Newsnight* that he had never wanted to play for Manchester United but signed because "some people forced me". Obi Mikel only actually played six league games for Lyn Oslo and although he got as far as putting a shirt on in a press conference, he never actually played for Manchester United at all. The transfer saga rumbled on throughout the 2005/06 season but in June 2006 Obi Mikel signed for Chelsea. It was agreed that Chelsea would pay Lyn Oslo £4 million and Manchester United £12 million. Rovers' fans didn't want to be involved in this sort of story and many expressed their concerns with Venky's and their advisors. There was a big worry that we were going to end up with a load of players managed by SEM – and not Rio Ferdinand and Cesc Fabregas. When Steve Kean was appointed full-time manager he said of his relationship with his agent,

> "I've been with SEM long before I was at Blackburn. They're a worldwide organisation who have got lots of top sportsmen and top managers, including Owen Coyle and Tony Pulis. It's something I'm proud of and glad that SEM are happy to look after me. I don't see that as anything other than positive and good for the rest of my career. I would like to take the Blackburn job. If the new owners brought somebody else in and asked me to be assistant or coach, I'd be open to that too. I'd like to stay in some capacity. It has always been in my mind one day to be a manager of a Premier League team."

Whilst Kean may have been happy with the turn of events, it wasn't just Rovers fans who were questioning why a man with virtually no managerial experience, was now the manager of our football club. David Hytner of *The Guardian* commented,

> "The questions about Kean started with Steve who? But the ones that cut to the quick concerned his representation by Jerome Anderson, the founder of the sports management agency SEM. Some onlookers have wondered why a first-team coach should need such a high-calibre agent but that is slightly disingenuous. It is not usual for assistant managers in the Premier League to have such representation to ensure they get the best possible remuneration on contracts. But Kean's association with Anderson does reveal his ambition. From his days at Fulham, where he began as the academy director and progressed to the post of assistant manager to Chris Coleman, Kean has never hidden

his desire to become a manager. He may have reasoned that having a string-puller such as Anderson in his corner would not hurt him."

Jerome Anderson was undoubtedly a man of influence. The fact is Allardyce was a proven manager and Kean had never been the permanent full-time manager of a professional football club in his life. Kean replacing Allardyce made little sense. This was one of many baffling developments over the next 18 months involving Blackburn Rovers and SEM. I still don't feel that many of them have been adequately explained. Members of Blackburn Rovers board were soon writing to Mrs Desai asking why they were being by-passed on important decisions and asking for clarification on SEM's role on transfers. At one point even Steve Kean accepted that it all looked a bit contrived. When it was put to Jerome Anderson in 2012 that a common accusation directed at him was that he engineered Venky's to take over Blackburn Rovers, then engineered bringing his client Steve Kean into the manager's job and therefore behind the scenes he was controlling events at Ewood Park, Jerome Anderson described these claims as utter rubbish and pointed out that it had been the Trustees that had first contacted him and Allardyce who had first appointed Kean. Throughout this story Jerome Anderson's name would not go away and over the next 18 months the link between SEM and Blackburn Rovers remained.

Chapter 6

On The Pitch (November 2010 – January 2011)

With all the profit making, politics and pantomime that comes with being a part of the Premier League corporation it is often easy to forget that football is essentially a very simple game. It's not about money; it's not about advertising; it's not about television. Sorry Leeds fans but it's not even about how big your attendances are. When you strip away all the baggage, football is about no more than two teams trying to put the ball in the back of the net more times than the opposition. Although in the case of Rovers, the drama essentially came to be played out off the pitch, it would be wrong to ignore what was happening on it. Events on the pitch may not have been the root of fans frustrations but they certainly provided an excellent barometer of the debacle that began to unfold off it.

Saturday 6 November 2010 and one week on from Venky's first public visit to Ewood Park, Rovers played host to Wigan. Whatever football has lost over the years, any fan who doesn't get a buzz from Saturday afternoon derbies at the start of the five-month winter probably needs to hang up their rattle and call it a day. Still Rovers' manager at this point, Sam Allardyce urged players and fans to put any talk of a takeover to one side and to focus all of the club's energies in to seeing off our Premier League neighbours. There will have been grumbles about Allardyce "hoof-ball" on the way to the ground but once inside it was business as usual for Rovers fans – backing the manager and the team and enjoying the day. After tough defeats to Liverpool and Chelsea, Rovers had slipped to 18th in the Premier League. Although the sudden drop down the table owed as much to the fixture list as it did to any obvious deficiencies in the team, even at this early stage it was difficult to bill the game with Wigan as anything other than a must-win. For all his faults, Allardyce could never be accused of downplaying the importance of home games against teams outside the top four. Only Arsenal, Spurs, Manchester City, Chelsea, Everton and Aston Villa managed Premier League wins against Rovers at Ewood Park during his two years at the club. When we came up against the teams around us Allardyce turned these games in to cup finals and there was absolutely no chance of Rovers turning up unprepared. The Rovers line-up that day was Robinson, Salgado, Samba, Nelsen, Givet, Phil Jones, Mame Biram Diouf, Emerton, Pedersen, El-Hadji Diouf and Benjani. Between them they averaged over 100 Premier League games each, not to mention the vast experience most had gained from playing for their country. With Bunn, Dunn, Kalinic, Hoilett, Goulon, Roberts and Chimbonda making up the substitutes, barring the obvious absence of a 15-goals-a-season striker this was a solid Premier League unit.

As I have said, the games were often pretty grim. The first real incident of note in this one came on 32 minutes when Benjani was withdrawn due to injury. This was Benjani's seventh appearance for Rovers and having opened his goal scoring account a week earlier against Chelsea, his next challenge was to play in two different halves of the same game. With the game still goalless Allardyce was left with a straight choice between £6 million Kalinic and Jason Roberts. Despite being publicly panned by Allardyce for a glaring miss at 1-1 against Chelsea, it was Roberts who got the nod and a chance to redeem himself for his costly miss. Both sides had chances at the start of the second half but it was Rovers who took the lead thanks to a Morten Gamst Pedersen free-kick just before the hour mark. Pedersen hasn't always hit the heights that thrust him in to the spotlight between 2005 and 2007 but with a combined total of over a hundred goals and assists since he arrived from Tromso in 2004 he will always hold a place in the hearts of Rovers fans. Anyone who claimed that Pedersen's wickedly bending 30-yard free-kick was an attempted cross obviously hadn't been watching him take corners for the previous six seasons. Wigan spurned the chance to equalise shortly afterwards and it was Rovers who got the crucial second on 67 minutes. Emerton broke quickly down the right and played a perfect ball in to the path of the on-rushing Roberts; the Blackburn End held its collective breath and Roberts guided the ball neatly in to the bottom corner for his first of the season. That should have been game over but N'Zogbia's 30-yard free kick ensured a nervy final 15 minutes. Rovers held on for the three points and by five o'clock it was Wigan who had replaced us in the relegation zone.

15.	ROVERS	P11	W3	D3	L5	Pts 12
16.	Liverpool	P10	W3	D3	L4	Pts 12
17.	Stoke	P11	W3	D1	L7	Pts 10
18.	Wigan	P11	W2	D4	L5	Pts 10

Wigan at home would be the first of three Premier League games in a week for Rovers. There was little time to reflect on the win before it was off to Newcastle and a ground that held no fear for Rovers. We had won our last four league games against Newcastle United at St. James' Park. Even Paul Ince managed one of his three managerial Premier League wins here. As bad as we often were away from home under Allardyce, he tended to fare quite well against the newly promoted sides. There was also the added motivation of going back to the club that had unceremoniously sacked him three years earlier. Rovers' fans were quietly confident we could get something from this one. With Benjani out injured and Allardyce going for five in midfield again, it was Kalinic who got the nod ahead of Roberts and Mame Biram Diouf. Manchester United loanee Mame Biram Diouf had shown flashes of being an OK player but the fact that he struggled to get in the team ahead of Roberts and Benjani told its own story. Rovers' lack of a proven goal scorer was a constant problem. Although the four strikers we did have were handy enough on their day none of them stood out as being better than the other three, nor did any of them really look capable of bagging 10 league goals a season. Rovers were one of only two clubs in the Premier League not to have spent any money in the summer and had Allardyce not spent the best part of £10 million on Kalinic and full-backs the summer before it would have been hard not to feel for him. As it was, we just had to make do with what we had and Allardyce's policy of swapping the four strikers around based on the demands of each individual game appeared to be the best way of muddling through the situation.

Rovers got off to the perfect start thanks to Pedersen's second of the season just three minutes in to the game. Rovers' Norwegian winger tossed a hopeful free kick in to the box and Newcastle's defenders made such a hash of clearing it that Pedersen himself was able to catch up with the play and blast the ball home. Rovers held on to the lead for the remainder of the half but Newcastle equalised early in the second when Andy Carroll out jumped Samba to head home a Joey Barton cross. Barton followed up his assist by inexplicably punching Pedersen in the stomach. It was an unsavoury off-the-ball attack that went unpunished on the night but eventually landed Barton a three-game ban. I accept that some people are susceptible to the red mist but Barton's feeble attempts at an apology after the game were worse than the punch. Pedersen and Rovers had the last laugh. After replacing the ineffective Kalinic shortly after Newcastle's equaliser, it was left to Roberts to fire home the winner for Rovers eight minutes from time. A hopeful ball was launched deep in to the Newcastle half and Newcastle centre-half Mike Williamson bounced off Roberts like an inflatable doll bouncing off a deep-rooted oak tree. Roberts steamed in to the Newcastle box and stroked the ball past the on-rushing Tim Krul. That made it five wins in five for Rovers at St. James' Park and Roberts' second winner in five days. Roberts' angry "remember the name" goal celebration seemed to be directed at Allardyce. It was hard to forget Roberts' name – it had been on the transfer list long enough. It's just a shame it wasn't on the score sheet more often. At that point I didn't actually mind Roberts but I still failed to see how someone who averaged one goal every five games for Rovers could get too angry about being left out of the team. There were times when Roberts would beat three mean and you would think you were watching George Weah but then he would get one on one with the 'keeper and turn in to Iain Dowie. He is one of the few players who you feel has a better chance of scoring with his back to goal than when he is actually facing it. Roberts has proven himself to be an excellent impact player or a bit of muscle when needed it but the fact is his finishing is just not consistent enough to command a regular place up front for a team in the Premier League. The goal at Newcastle would be his last Rovers goal for the best part of three months.

Three wins in a week was always asking a bit much and Spurs away proved one game too many for Rovers. I have had my fair share of good days out at White Hart Lane but the inevitability of this defeat meant that on this occasion I made the shamelessly grown up decision to spend the money on a fortnightly £150 food shop at the supermarket instead. In an open affair that saw chances at both ends, 4-0 to Spurs with 15 minutes to go was a little harsh on Rovers. Late consolation goals from Dunn and Givet restored some pride and on balance 4-2 was a fair reflection of an end-to-end game in which Spurs were the better side. Venky's watched on from the crowd and the uncharacteristically cavalier defeat didn't appear to put them off as six days later they became the new owners of Blackburn Rovers Football Club.

Balaji and Venkatesh made it two games in two when they arrived at Ewood Park for the visit of Aston Villa. Their pre-match walk-on and wave to the crowd has become an unforgettable image. At the time, the mood around Ewood Park was a mixture of intrigue, curiosity, hope and anticipation. Staying in the Premier League season after season with little or no financial investment had been some achievement but the truth was it had become pretty grim as a spectacle for the paying supporter. Almost overnight, fans became more likely to accept that this is what had been needed to get us to this point and now we could strive for the next level – the no-man's land between a relegation scrap and the European places. Maybe we would see the arrival of the big-name striker Allardyce had been searching for and while we didn't expect Venky's to turn us into the *Invincibles*, there was a greater acceptance that hoof-ball had simply been a case of our manager cutting his cloth accordingly. Fittingly the victory over Aston Villa was an exhibition of all that was good about Allardyce's time at Rovers. Villa's team on the day included Ashley Young, Stephen

Ireland, Stewart Downing (all considered top players at the time) but Rovers overpowered and out-fought a team of much greater individual talent to claim another three points at home. Villa manager Gerard Houllier claimed that missed chances told the story of this game but from where I was sitting it was the goals of Pedersen that gave you a better idea of what went on. The game ended 2-0 and once again it was Rovers' Norwegian winger that proved to be the difference. His first came in first-half injury time, thanks in no small part to two Rovers old boys Stephen Warnock and Brad Friedel. When Warnock hacked down El-Hadji Diouf 30-yards from the corner flag it was no surprise to see Pedersen standing over the resulting free-kick. What was a surprise was the total hash Friedel made of Pedersen's cheeky shot at goal. Friedel anticipated a cross and charged out to the penalty spot. By the time he got there Pedersen had fired the ball straight in to the gaping hole left at the near post. Friedel had played 287 games for Rovers and, while I am happy to blame a great many of the goals scored against us between 2002 and 2005 on Lucas Neill, I can't think of more than about half a dozen goals that came from Friedel errors. Legendary status isn't handed out lightly by Rovers fans, particularly when it comes to the new breed of modern day mercenaries that come and go like man flu, but no Rovers fan would ever question Friedel's place in the Rovers Hall of Fame. Not only did Friedel mistakes come along about as often as 90 minutes of Vince Grella, but some of the saves I have seen him make for Rovers have literally defied belief. I swear he made a save against Fulham around the turn of the millennium where he grew wings and flew. Paul

Robinson proved to be an excellent replacement but I am still to come across many keepers who can top Friedel. Ironic then really that, having said all this, he should save this relative howler for his return to Ewood Park. Cheers, Brad! Villa started the second half brightly but when Pedersen diverted Ryan Nelsen's cross-cum-shot in to the net on 66 minutes for his fourth Premier League goal of the month it was game over. Allardyce said that tying Pedersen to a new contract in the summer had been like signing a £10 million player and at this point I had to agree. If Venky's were planning on making wins against teams like Villa a regular event they could come again.

The mood amongst Rovers fans may have been picking up but one member of the Venky household clearly wanted more. Mrs Desai's mid-week calls for games to be more entertaining weren't ideal preparation for the trip to Old Trafford. Perhaps there weren't enough fours and sixes but three wins in four is title-winning form and you would have struggled to find a Rovers fan who wouldn't be entertained by winning the title. The timing of Desai's comments was poor and this became a recurring theme. Good times don't come around every week when you are a struggling side in the Premier League. Why not just enjoy them when they do? Allardyce's retort that six losses in 37 home games is entertainment enough was a fair reply but maybe there are some arguments you can't win.

Despite our impressive home form, it started to look inevitable that at some stage, and sooner rather than later, a team in the top four or five was going to absolutely demolish us away from home. This was not just because most of these teams had players on the substitutes bench that cost more than our entire club but it appeared to me that Allardyce just didn't take these games that seriously. The selection of Goulon may have been entertaining but unfortunately it was for all the wrong reasons. Chelsea, Liverpool and Arsenal had all threatened to do it but eventually it was left to Manchester United to dole out our biggest ever defeat in the Premier League. It was no shock to see players like Goulon, Linganzi, Hoilett and Morris get a run out ahead of our form players – hence why I had given up going to away games about a season ago. When Goulon came off the bench late in the Villa game I thought it was a pitch invasion. He didn't fare any better at Old Trafford and by the time he was substituted after 28 minutes Rovers were already 3-0 down. Goulon is one of the worst players I have ever seen play in the Premier League. Having signed him just weeks earlier, he would continue to be employed by the club for the next two years. The demolition job continued and with 20 minutes still to go Berbatov had five and Manchester United had seven. A late Samba consolation added absolutely no respectability to the 7-1 score line and Allardyce's apology to the fans might as well have been read out with the team sheets. Chimbonda never kicked a ball again for Rovers and was sold in the January transfer window. The media had a field day with this one. Debutant Josh Morris telling the world that he had managed to swap shirts with Berbatov wasn't really what the fans wanted to hear.

Sven Goran Eriksson once said that it is better to lose one game by seven goals than to lose seven games by one goal and I have to agree. If Rovers could recover quickly from the embarrassment of Old Trafford with a win over Wolves then I didn't see that that the 7-1 score line was as big a deal as the national press were making it out to be. Rovers welcomed back key players for the visit of Wolves and in the end we ran out comfortable 3-0 winners thanks to goals from Dunn, Emerton and Nelsen. The football was very similar to what it always had been but the wins were becoming more frequent and everybody could see the bright light of the January transfer window not too far ahead. Allardyce told reporters after the game,

> "We never get credit for things, but that's the way it is. We are just a small town club enjoying ourselves by winning football matches. The fortress of Ewood Park is back and the walls are getting higher."

6. Bolton	P16	W5	D8	L3	Pts 23
7. Stoke	P16	W6	D3	L7	Pts 21
8. ROVERS	P16	W6	D3	L7	Pts 21
9. Sunderland	P16	W4	D8	L3	Pts 20

Bad weather during the week had meant the Rovers had been unable to train for a couple of days so Allardyce had given the players time off. Allardyce now wanted to see under-soil heating installed at the training ground at a cost of around £100,000. Was this the sort of investment the new owners were likely to support? Although Rovers continued to pick up wins it was becoming difficult not to notice the increasing off-field speculation about the future of the manager. When questioned about his future, leading up to the game with Bolton Wanderers, Allardyce told Sky,

> "Irrespective of the length of contract, we're employed to get results and that's the first major thing to achieve. If you get results you stay there, if you don't get results as I say it can be a little quick, the decisions are made and you know the industry that you're in. It's a results game that you've got to keep the right end of, and you will keep your job for as long as you want it if you get that right."

Little did Allardyce know but the next time he lost a game, he would be gone within 24 hours. He didn't have to wait long. Rovers hadn't lost at the Reebok Stadium in the league for 10 seasons but that record was about to end. Two weeks before Christmas and with the live Sunday game still goal-less just short of the hour mark I am sure I wasn't the only Rovers fan in the world wondering whether to stick £10 on 0-0 to help cover the impending cost of Christmas. I did just that and around a minute later one of the most bizarre 24 hour periods in the history of Blackburn Rovers Football Club quickly began to unravel. Mark Davies was sent off for Bolton forcing them to bring on Fabrice Muamba to shore up the midfield. Having come on to protect the back four, it was Muamba who put Bolton 1-0 up on 65 minutes.

With chances coming at both ends, the next goal was going to be all important and it was Rovers who got it with just three minutes to go. This time it was Rovers substitute Mame Biram Diouf who latched on to a

Roberts through ball and dinked home a cool finish. Allardyce's celebration was up there with Marco Tardelli in the 1982 World Cup Final but unfortunately, there would be no trophies at the end of this one – in fact we didn't even get a point. Seconds after the re-start Bolton were back in front through Stuart Holden. Depending on which team you supported it was either a wonder strike or bad defending. Bolton saw out the final few minutes and nobody looked more gutted about it than Allardyce. I often wonder how much Kean knew about what was going to happen next. I have studied the footage of Allardyce, his assistant Neil McDonald and Kean after Holden's winner for Bolton but mind reading is just not my forte. The following day, as the manager was publicly slamming his own players for defending like old women news came through of a message from India. Allardyce was sacked, along with his number two Neil McDonald. Their exit was as quick as it was unexpected. Nobody in football could understand it, not least the players and the fans, and over the next few days silly season reigned at Ewood Park.

Club captain Ryan Nelsen described the decision to sack Allardyce as a "huge shock" after telling the BBC that he had found out by text from a reporter in New Zealand; Mrs Desai talked about links with Maradona and former England manager Graham Taylor claimed that he was going to eat roast beef for Christmas dinner instead of turkey in protest. Do you want any turnips with that? Meanwhile, Allardyce's number three Steve Kean was promoted to the post of caretaker manager. Few Rovers fans saw this as anything other than a short-term stop gap. Many didn't even know who Kean was. Bolton manager Owen Coyle offered a little insight when he told the *Daily Mirror,* "I am sure Steve won't be happy with being called the 'new Owen Coyle.' He is quite a good-looking lad. I am sure Steve will do well."

If Coyle felt that Kean was a good-looking lad I was careful not to read too much in to the rest of what he had to say. Not for the last time I found myself avoiding newspapers and *Sky Sports News.* After a difficult few days it was just a case of sucking it all in and turning up to games. The problem with the West Ham game was, with heavy overnight snow across the country even just turning up to games had suddenly become a problem. With a foot and a half of snow outside my door, I was secretly hoping not to have to get off the settee, put eight layers of clothing on and make the Arctic hike to Ewood Park. As I watched pretty much every other game in the country fall foul of the weather, the nearer it got to three o'clock the more I began to realise that for some unfathomable reason Rovers was not going to be postponed. I have no problem with snow but when there is an 18-inch layer of it across Britain I could not see why Rovers were so keen to press on with this fixture. The official attendance for the game was 21,934 and while Rovers may have sold 21,934 tickets a lot of them must have been hiding somewhere warm because there were empty seats everywhere. The game was an absolute stinker. England's brightest young footballer Phil Jones was dropped to the bench and although David Dunn had a goal harshly disallowed in the 84th minute a point was all either team deserved. Nelsen gave Rovers the lead with a scrappy scrambled effort five minutes in to the second half but West Ham equalised through

Junior Stanislas 12 minutes from time. More worrying than the two dropped points were injuries to Roberts, Samba and Phil Jones. Roberts and Samba would be fit again in no time but Phil Jones had managed to pick up a particularly nasty knee injury and early reports were that he wouldn't be seen again until next season. This was a massive blow for Rovers and it capped off a thoroughly forgettable week. With only two Premier League games beating the weather Rovers were guaranteed an extended slot on *Match of the Day* but there was no way I was watching this one again. Rovers had pulled out all the stops to make sure the game against bottom of the league West Ham went ahead but I failed to see why. Following the most unimpressive home draw I can remember it was announced shortly after the game that caretaker manager Steve Kean would now become our permanent manager until the end of the season. When the *Lancashire Telegraph* asked the question "Is extending Kean's contract until end of season right decision" a massive 82% of the 8,000 polled voted No. Kean may have had the public backing of his SEM counterpart Owen Coyle but he still had a long way to go to convince Rovers fans he was the right man for the job.

Kean's pre-Christmas dash to India to speak with the owners seemed to have put members of the playing staff at ease but as I made the Boxing Day stroll to Ewood Park for the game against Stoke City, few Rovers fans were happy about developments at the club. Stoke City and Blackburn have played out few classics that I can remember and this particular encounter was up there with the worst. Chris Brereton of *The Independent* described Rovers performance as "perhaps the most dreadful Premier League performance by a side all season". The loud boos at full-time would suggest there were others who agreed but it wasn't just our performances on the pitch that had become a concern. Boxing Day games are often the highlight of Christmas for me but with all that was going on off the field, two lousy home performances and the sub-zero temperatures I just wanted to get home to eat turkey butties and watch repeats of *Morecambe and Wise*. Rovers' rookie manager needed a win and he needed it fast.

The games were coming around quick and the big win that Kean desperately needed came away at West Brom two days after the Boxing Day defeat to Stoke City. The fans had started to get pretty angry and the win came just in the nick of time. John Williams was quick to praise Rovers 1500 strong away following and in stark contrast to the game against Stoke City the travelling fans were entertained from the outset. Kalinic struck after just three minutes to give Rovers the lead. His quick burst inside from the wing and cool finish showed that Kalinic was a player of talent – Rovers fans just wanted to see it a little bit more often. West Brom equalised after 17 minutes through Jerome Thomas and at this point I feared we had peaked too early. Rovers continued to play their part in a free-flowing game and as the teams went in level at half-time, more goals were predicted for the second half. Paul Robinson appeared to have suffered an injury in the pre-match warm up and, after struggling on through the first half he was replaced by Mark Bunn at half-time. The injury kept Robinson out of action for the next three games.

It would have been an optimistic Rovers fan that expected Rovers to come out in the second half and play free flowing attacking football away from home but that is exactly what we did. Kalinic was rewarded with a second (a little header from close range) to put Rovers 2-1 up and Mame Biram Diouf made it 3-1 just after the hour. For the first time since we beat Derby County 2-1 at Pride Park in December 2007 Rovers fans were clearing their throats for a rousing rendition of, "Jingle Bells, jingle bells, jingle all the way, oh what fun it is to see Rovers win away." Just as Kalinic should have been going hat-trick hunting, he was red-carded for a needless high challenge on Paul Scharner. Kalinic's brace should have launched his career as a 12-goals-a-season Premier League striker but it was his red card that seemed to have more impact on his future. By the time he had served his three-match ban, he had slipped well down the pecking order and he rarely featured again for Rovers. Kalinic's sending off didn't affect the result and Rovers held on for a deserved 3-1 victory and Kean's first win in charge.

A New Year's Day defeat at Sunderland threatened to derail Rovers mini-revival before it had even started. With the January transfer window now open for business, if Venky's wanted to impress the fans they could have done a lot worse than signing any of Sunderland's goal scorers that day. Bent, Welbeck and Gyan all ended up leaving Sunderland in 2011 and you had to feel that they all represented better value than Ronaldinho. Sunderland manager Steve Bruce dedicated the win to Allardyce. Bruce wasn't around for Rovers next trip to The Stadium of Light when

Sunderland fans dedicated their 2-1 victory over Rovers to their new manager Martin O'Neill.

If Mrs Desai had wanted the games to be entertaining, at this point I was struggling to see exactly how entertaining Kean's four games in charge had been. The West Brom game had been entertaining but from my personal point of view the West Ham game wasn't entertaining; nor was the Stoke City game and if you find getting beat 3-0 at Sunderland entertaining then I would be interested to know more. Then came the Liverpool game. This one really was entertaining and for all the right reasons. When Roy Hodgson's Liverpool arrived at Ewood Park for Rovers first home game of 2011 all the talk was that this was a weak Liverpool side. A quick look at a team sheet containing names like Pepe Reina, Glen Johnson, Martin Skrtel, Joe Cole, Steven Gerrard and Fernando Torres told a different story. I don't know if Liverpool's big names just didn't fancy it on this particular night but Rovers absolutely blew them away – particularly in the first hour. Rovers were full of energy and enthusiasm and the visitors just didn't seem to have an answer. Martin Olsson got Rovers first on 32 minutes. Mame Biram Diouf played him in with a perfectly weighted ball and Olsson drilled it under the hapless Reina. Two minutes later Rovers had a second. Pedersen dinked a neat ball to Benjani; Benjani chested it down, spun sharply and smashed the ball high in to the roof of the net. What a finish! I didn't know Benjani was capable of this kind of football and if he was why did he only unleash it once a season? Rovers continued to press after half-time and deservedly got a third just before the hour. Man of the match Hoilett skipped past two defenders, ran along the by-line and rolled the perfect ball across the goal to give Benjani the easiest of tap-ins for the third. Rovers had been red hot up to that point. Liverpool did come in to the game in the last half hour and had Steven Gerrard not missed a penalty to make it 3-2 late in the game it could have been a nervy ending. As it was Rovers held on for a deserved three points and Kean had another first to his name – his first home win as a manager. Liverpool manager Roy Hodgson was sacked three days later after just six months in the job.

Rovers followed up the impressive mid-week victory over Liverpool with an FA Cup win over QPR on the Saturday. QPR were flying in The Championship and they were undoubtedly the outstanding English team outside of the Premier League. There was a debut for Jason Lowe but there were no wholesale changes for this one. Kean was eager to build on the momentum gained from his first home win in charge. Despite Rovers having the better of the chances the game remained goalless deep in to the second half. Just as an unwanted mid-week replay at Loftus Road started to look the likeliest outcome, Hoilett fired home his first goal at Ewood Park and we were in the hat for the Fourth Round. As usual, QPR manager Neil Warnock had plenty to say after the game. Jamie Mackie had gone in for a 50:50 with Givet in the first half and ended up suffering a double leg break. Whilst absolutely no blame was apportioned to Givet, Warnock was apparently incensed by El-Hadji Diouf's reaction, prompting him to call Diouf "the gutter type". Warnock added, "I was going to call him a sewer rat but that might be insulting to sewer rats." Warnock's childish ramblings couldn't take the shine off another good win for Rovers and after a difficult Christmas period, we were heading in the right direction again.

Even the 2-0 defeat away at Chelsea represented some form of progress. At least Kean put out a full strength team and at least we didn't just roll over and hand them three points. Chelsea were the better side for large parts of the game but it took them 57 minutes to score the first and another 20 minutes to make the game safe. Ryan Nelsen seemed a lot happier now and he even revealed a fresh approach to games that made losing sound fun.

> "We're trying to win games by using our abilities and we are trying to use our strengths when we have the ball. When you do that, in a way, you don't mind losing games because it means you go down fighting. It's very enjoyable. You can express yourself and show off your talents when you have the ball. We have got some players that can do that."

By the time the Sky cameras turned up for the Super Sunday clash between Rovers and West Brom I think it was a bit much to suggest that the club was "rocking" as Jerome Anderson later put it but I did start to sense the very early signs of a feel-good factor winging its way to Ewood Park. A win against West Brom and Rovers would be amongst the teams competing for a Europa League place. Roque Santa Cruz made his Rovers return and there was also a debut for loanee Jermaine Jones. The first half was relatively even and the two sides were separated only by a comedy own goal by West Brom's Gabriel Tamas. Dunn sent in a great cross and Tamas out-jumped Kalinic to fire a bullet header right in to the top corner of his own net. Tamas didn't have a great record against Rovers – he had only just come back from suspension after getting sent off at the end of our game at The Hawthorns in December. Hoilett added a second just after half time with a stunning 25-yard strike. Hoilett had been no more than a fringe player under Allardyce but he had been given a real opportunity under Kean and we were now starting to see what an exciting player he was. West Brom pressed to get back in the game and should have had a penalty when Jermaine Jones inexplicably hacked down Peter Odemwingie just inside the box. The referee deemed the foul to have taken place outside the box, West Brom missed the resulting free kick and at this point it was clear it just wasn't going to be their day. Steven Nzonzi got 30 minutes under his belt after coming back from a long injury lay off and it was also good to see Rovers loanees Santa Cruz and Jermaine Jones both settle in well and get a full game. It was a good day all round for Rovers. Although many were still a little angry about the way Kean appeared to have overhauled Allardyce from his post, a few impressive wins later and Kean was now starting to win over the fans. Alan Nixon of the *Daily Mirror* wrote,

> "Kean celebrated signing a new long-term contract by masterminding a performance of class, skill and imagination that was never part of Big Sam's sterile if successful survival plan."

As hard as it is to imagine now, Kean's name was actually sung a number of times by significant sections of the crowd towards the back end of the game. As Sam Allardyce sat watching it all in the Sky studio already it seemed a case of "Sam who?" In truth it had been Allardyce who had baked the cake and Kean who had put the candle on it.

6. Sunderland	P24	W9	D10	L5	Pts 37
7. ROVERS	P24	W9	D4	L11	Pts 31
8. Newcastle	P23	W8	D6	L9	Pts 30
9. Bolton	P23	W7	D9	L7	Pts 30

January ended with an FA Cup defeat at the hands of Aston Villa. This was the fourth time in two seasons we had been dumped out of a domestic cup by Aston Villa at Villa Park. A decent run in the cup is always nice but with all that was going on at the club maybe this year it was no bad thing that we exited the FA Cup at the Fourth Round stage. 16 points out of a possible 30 since the start of November was a healthy return and the team's performances on the pitch had gone some way towards easing fans worries about the changes off it. With Rovers sitting seventh in the Premier League with two-thirds of the season gone, a period of off-field stability and a top 12 finish had to be the aim for the rest of the season. Unfortunately the honeymoon period was about to end.

Chapter 7

January Transfer Window 2011

There had been so much talk about what may or may not happen at Blackburn Rovers during Venky's first transfer window in charge that it was a relief when January 1st finally came round. Rovers fans still knew very little about our new owners and all the time judgements were being formed. The sacking of Allardyce had done little to endear Venky's to the football world but on the whole Rovers fans were still willing to accept that this was all part of a wider plan. The January transfer window represented Venky's big chance to step away from the media circus that had plagued their first few weeks in English football and really show Rovers fans that they had a serious long-term vision for Blackburn Rovers Football Club.

Very early on in the takeover process there had been crazy talk from certain sections of the media about Manchester City style spending but in fairness to

Venky's none of this had come from them. They had indicated all along that a figure of around £5 million would be released this time, with the promise of "much, much more" in the future. It was nice to have a bit of money for a change but anyone who thought it was going to be straightforward was about to learn otherwise. Whilst there was a degree of clarity on how much we had to spend, those who claimed to know what sort of players we were going to be in for were definitely one step ahead of me. There had been talk of a new approach to transfers that involved targeting new and exciting young players but there had been little public expansion on the plan. Like most Rovers fans, I was still trying to work out who was responsible for driving incoming and out-going transfer activity at Venky-run Blackburn Rovers. It certainly wasn't Allardyce and there was a great deal of speculation about whether or not it was his replacement Steve Kean. Mrs Desai responded to questions about Kean's role in transfers by saying, "It will be discussed with him. He will be involved and will be the final decision-maker." I am not sure whether this was one answer or three. As for the board's role in transfer activity, John Williams had proved more than capable in the transfer market but we now know that his input was minimal once Venky's took over. At the time of the take over Venky's had declared themselves hardcore cricket fans but now news was emerging that there was a football expert in the family. Maybe the family football expert had a say. Far more likely, and since confirmed by the man himself, was that Chairman and Chief Executive of the sports management corporation SEM, Jerome Anderson had been brought in to assist Rovers with the

January transfer window. From the outset, Rovers' fans were anxious to know whether Jerome Anderson was at Rovers in his capacity as an agent or to serve the needs of our football club. If Jerome Anderson was going to be involved in contract re-negotiations what steps would be taken to ensure that sensitive information about the club's players remained protected by the club? At the time the new owners were quick to play down Jerome Anderson's role but assured fans that he was a well-connected man and any involvement he did have would only help strengthen the club's position. No Rovers fan was going to turn their nose up at £5 million pounds worth of new players every January. If somebody at the club had a few names up their sleeve that could better Allardyce signings like Givet, Nzonzi, Salgado and El-Hadji Diouf while one half of your brain was screaming "No!" the other half was telling you to embrace the change and to just enjoy the unseasonal spending-spree for what it was.

It was a new feeling for Rovers fans. Since the introduction of the January transfer window in 2002/03, it wasn't something that we had ever felt the need to get too excited about. Allardyce once described January as "the most horrible month in the football calendar" and he wasn't alone in feeling this way. For fans of clubs outside the financially fortunate few January is a time of fear and trepidation rather than any overwhelming feeling of excitement. Paranoia that you are going to sell all your best players takes over and the thought of signing anyone decent seldom enters your head. In Rovers case it is pretty irrational, as we had actually fared well from our January transfer dealings up to this point. Prior to the arrival of Venky's, the club's approach to the window had been quite straightforward. Unless we were struggling in the league, we rarely looked to bring players in and instead of spending money in an over-inflated market, the focus was very much on keeping hold of the players we already had. This may not be *Sky Sports News* favoured way of dealing with the transfer window but it served Rovers well and, of the players we have signed in January, several have turned out to be big players in our recent history. Nelsen, Samba and Givet all arrived quietly in the month of January. Emergency buys Robbie Savage and El-Hadji Diouf also did a job at Rovers after arriving mid-season. Prior to Venky's arrival, the only high profile departure I can recall is Barry Ferguson and he was never missed at Rovers anyway. Another January arrival Aaron Mokoena wasn't every Rovers fans cup of tea but I liked him and I would argue all day that opposition players would much rather line up against Barry Ferguson than Aaron "The Axe" Mokoena. If we could pull bargains like this out of the bag with no money just think what we could do with a few quid behind us.

Back in December 2010 and with £5 million available for transfers, Allardyce could have been forgiven for thinking that Venky's were just going to hand him the money and sign off the cheques. After all, this way had worked well enough for the previous owners. Between the Walker Trust, the manager and the board, Rovers transfer profits had helped us continually keep pace with clubs who were streets ahead of us in terms of finance. I am not saying every transfer they touched turned to gold but any funds the Walker Trust did release were always spent with consummate care and forward planning. John Williams had said in the years prior to the sale, "we can't go out and spend £5 million on a player who is not good enough. That would kill us because our finances are so finely balanced." Over the years when it came to transfers John Williams and the staff at Rovers were hard to beat. Of the clubs that who started the 2011/12 season in the Premier League, according to *transfermarkt.com* figures collated by Nick Harris from the *Mail on Sunday*, only Blackburn Rovers had made a combined net transfer profit over the previous 10 seasons. Remarkably, whilst no other club had made a penny profit from total net transfer activity, as of 12 August 2011, Rovers had made a whopping £42.5 million. This was over too long a period to be all luck. Basically, somebody at Blackburn Rovers knew what they were doing in the transfer market. More than anything, I thought it would be this ability to turn footballers into money that any new owners would be keen to tap in to.

Once it became clear new money was making its way to the club who could blame those at the top for drawing up their wish list? Allardyce started drawing up his list of potential transfer targets as early as October. Names like Robbie Keane, Roque Santa Cruz, John Carew and David Bentley all got a mention and all represented good affordable options that would undoubtedly strengthen the team. Allardyce may as well have been writing his list to Father Christmas as he was gone within four weeks of Venkys arriving. It emerged later that Allardyce had never really figured in Venky's plans at all. I remained baffled by Venky's comments that things had been going wrong with transfers prior to their arrival. I wanted to know what exactly had been going wrong with transfers because from a fans point of view everything appeared to have been going right. In the main we bought cheap and sold high - allowing us to keep pace with financially stronger clubs. I was also rather curious as to why the board were now being by-passed on transfer decisions at a time Jerome Anderson has said he was sleeping at the training ground to help out. Kean appeared happy enough with the new way of doing things but why wouldn't he be? Rovers had flourished doing it the old way but while we were flying high in the Premier League, Kean was no more than understudy to Chris Coleman. He may or may not have had total control over transfers but either way, the blow had been softened by his baffling promotion, a bumper new contract and the chance to manage a Premier League football club. When quizzed about his role in transfers Kean advised that the owners gave him a list of players and then he had final say. Kean didn't to go in to too much detail about who helped the owners compile this list but Jerome Anderson later clarified the issue. As for Kean having final say on transfers I take my hat off to anybody who can catapult up the employment ladder at a multi-million pound company and then start calling the shots.

Kean opened the transfer window by telling the media that he wasn't sure how much Rovers had to spend but we were looking to strengthen in every area. How helpful. Venky's had told us from the start that the kitty was around £5 million - whether this included wages was anyone's guess. As for the players we needed, we didn't need a goalkeeper, we didn't need a winger and we didn't need any defenders but it looked like Kean was covering all bases. What Rovers were crying out for, and every fan knew it, was a goal scorer, a bit of steel in midfield and someone who could open up a game with a bit of guile. I would have taken any of the strikers Allardyce had suggested - Robbie Keane, John Carew or Roque Santa Cruz. Other names that had been mentioned by the fans, whether on a loan or on a permanent basis, were Charlie Adam, Damien Duff, Scott Parker, Kevin Nolan, Wilson Palacios, Joey Barton and Daniel Sturridge. If those in control at Rovers had the money and connections that allowed them to effectively disregard the vast wealth of experience on the Blackburn Rovers board then at least two or three of these players should have been attainable targets. Rovers had shown over the past 10 years how fruitful the transfer market could be if you knew what you were doing. Most of it isn't rocket science either. A high percentage of our most successful signings have been players who were too good to sit on the bench for a top six team but not good enough to command a regular place in the starting 11 at a top six team (Bentley, Bellamy, Warnock, Salgado, Robinson, Santa Cruz). We could offer these players the combination of money and weekly Premier League football they weren't going to get making up the numbers at a richer club. Rovers also represented an excellent option for any player who felt he had outgrown his current club but perhaps wasn't quite good enough to play for a top six side. Add to this the host of left-field bargains that our scouting network had managed to uncover over the years and it would be fair to say that Rovers real success as a club had come in the transfer market. I could only presume that somebody now had an even better way of doing things. What other reason could there be for ignoring the wealth of transfer know-how that was available to the new owners when they bought in to Blackburn Rovers? Meanwhile Kean remained rather vague on what was going to happen next.

I don't know who was behind Rovers first significant movement of the transfer window but I fear that the Venky family football expert may have been at work here and it looked like somebody had been watching too much *ESPN Classic* over the Christmas holidays. When it was first announced (once again by Alan Nixon!) that Rovers had made an unsuccessful bid for former World Player of the Year Ronaldinho it was so embarrassing that even the very people that had just made the bid felt compelled to deny it. News of the failed bid was met with widespread derision and Venkatesh Rao told reporters, "There is no interest at all. They are just rumours." At pretty much the same time that one member of the Venky family was denying the bid, another, Mrs Desai, was happily telling reporters that a bid had indeed been placed with AC Milan for the services of "Mr Row-now-dean-o", and we were looking to offer him a wage package of around £20 million over three years. This was a long way off the £5 million pound budget that had previously been spoken of and I was praying that we weren't about to blow our entire next four year's January transfer budget on an ageing Brazilian who had little reason to come to Blackburn other than for a pay-day. Kean claimed that the bid for Ronaldinho put Blackburn Rovers on the football map. Had Kean been living up a tree?

Blackburn Rovers had been on the football map for over a century and failed transfer bids for players past their peak wasn't how we had got there. Just in case the Ronaldinho bid wasn't embarrassing enough, it soon emerged that Rovers were also now trying to sign David Beckham on loan. It was like taking over a basketball team and trying to sign Michael Jordan and Magic Johnson. The transfer window was only four days old and already you couldn't get Venky's and Rovers out of the papers. All this media exposure was great for the Venky brand but it wasn't doing the reputation of Blackburn Rovers any good and nor was our squad actually increasing in numbers. Neither Ronaldinho or Beckham ended up making the move to Blackburn and if these were indeed serious attempts to bring global superstars to Blackburn I have to ask what happened to this money in future transfer windows? Even Kean had to concede that the failed bids for Ronaldinho and Beckham had cost the club credibility. Bizarrely though, it didn't stop him going on to say that we were still in the hunt for a marquee signing and if it didn't happen this time it would happen in the summer. Kean denied that the bids had only been made for a bit of cheap publicity and even claimed that it was he who had initiated the move for Ronaldinho. Kean advised that the only reason he hadn't discussed Ronaldinho with the existing board members at the previous Friday's board meeting was because when it came to transfer targets he had a domestic list, a development list and a foreign list and he only discussed his domestic list at that particular meeting. Whichever one of his shopping lists Kean was talking about it was hard to disagree with the wise words of

Michel Salgado when he came out the following week and said we should be looking to sign three or four club players rather than global superstars. Unfortunately, by the time the rest of the football world had stopped laughing, it was no longer incoming transfers that were the main concern.

Unrest had been brewing amongst the Rovers squad since the dismissal of Allardyce three weeks earlier. Club captain Chris Samba went public with his feelings towards the new regime just before Christmas.

> "If this is the way the club's going to be run from now on, I don't want to be part of it and I want to leave. As captain it's very difficult to say this but I've thought long and hard about it. Nobody in football understands the decision to sack Sam. The players and fans need answers about the club's future. Unless we commit to who the manager is, how can we attract big players in January?"

Samba's comments didn't go down well with the majority of fans but I sympathised with him. Here was a guy who had sweated blood for Blackburn Rovers and although he had benefited from the relationship as much as we had it was hard to argue with a lot of the comments he was making. Kean didn't help the situation by stripping Samba of the captaincy and coming out and saying Samba had wanted to move for 12 months. Was this really the action of a manager that was doing everything he could to stop one of the club's best players from leaving? Lack of diplomacy can cost football clubs millions. Samba was reinstated as captain on New Year's Day but he remained open to offers for the remainder of the window. There were reports of interest from Aston Villa and Spurs and it was telling that Samba was reluctant to sign a new deal at Rovers until the transfer window had closed. When he did sign a new four and a half year deal at Rovers two days after the close of the transfer window he looked like he was signing for an unwanted parcel.

Despite interest in Samba, in the end, the only high profile departures from Ewood Park in January were Chimbonda and El-Hadji Diouf. Alan Judge and Alex Marrow both moved on after failing to make the grade and fringe players Blackman, Linganzi and Doran were all sent out on loan. Even though he had done quite well on loan at Motherwell during the first half of 2010/11 there were some eyebrows raised when SEM client Blackman signed a two and half year deal at Rovers before being shipped out on loan again. Chimbonda went to QPR on loan and El-Hadji Diouf was loaned out to Glasgow Rangers. It seemed a sudden fall from favour for pantomime villain El-Hadji Diouf. He had been one of our best players in 2010 and had publicly pledged himself a happy Rover only a month earlier. He may not have been everyone's cup of tea but he did a good job for Rovers. If you look at a lot of the goals we scored that season, El-Hadji Diouf was involved. In stark contrast to his off-field persona, I found El-Hadji Diouf to be a very reliable performer. There was an unsavoury incident with an invisible banana at Everton but other than this he caused Rovers few problems out on the pitch. If he wanted to wear Dalmatian print tracksuits and drive round in chrome plated cars then so be it. Managing off-the-wall characters is part of modern day football management and if Kean felt he couldn't handle big personalities then surely he had made the wrong career move.

One current Rovers player was more than happy with the new regime. Jason Roberts had been told by Allardyce in the summer of 2010 that his time at Rovers was up. Roberts had done a decent enough job when needed but, at that point, his record of 22 goals in 116 games told you everything you needed to know about his number one shortcoming. Allardyce could see it, the fans could see and most of football could see it. He was a big strong bloke, a good athlete, hard working, even quite skilful at times but the fact was he just couldn't be trusted in front of goal. He was a sort of low budget Emile Heskey. Roberts had two months to find a new club and it was no real surprise when we received no serious bids for him. As we couldn't sell him, we didn't have sufficient funds to replace him, so Allardyce named him in the Rovers squad for the season and told him he could either leave in January or at the end of the season when his contract expired. Roberts added just two more league goals under Allardyce and most people expected that, unless Tranmere or Doncaster were about to table a bid, January would be the end of the road for Roberts as a Rover. Following Allardyce's shock departure in December, with a distinct lack of serious interest from anyone else, suddenly Roberts saw a future at Ewood Park again. Allardyce was barely down the drive before Roberts was out in front of the press declaring that he was comfortable with the new owners' vision. I bet he was. Players coming out to big up the new regime around the same time as they were handed a new contract became a common theme.

Kean and Roberts were a match made in heaven. Whilst the rest of the world was still deciding whether the glass was half-full or half-empty a couple of glasses were full to the top and overflowing. Some of the stuff they came out with was priceless. My personal Kean favourite was this cracker when he was trying to justify a mid-season club trip to Dubai when we would have been playing in the FA Cup Fifth Round had we not been knocked out the previous round.

> "Our break in Dubai went really well. From a medical point of view I have been told vitamin D levels were very high in the lads when they come (sic) back due to the sunshine. The lads have not been in the sunshine this season, and Michel Salgado was the only one who had a high level of Vitamin D before because he has been back and forward a few times. Everyone's levels were very low. I don't know physiologically what it does but there is not a spring in your step and there is a general flatness."

Why not just say you went on a mid-season knees-up? Kean definitely missed his calling as a double-glazing salesman and maybe he knows it - hence why he gets so excited when he meets a football manager. Roberts is slightly different but I do find him equally irritating once a microphone is put in front of his mouth. "I scored five league goals last season and kept a £6 million striker out of the team" beamed Roberts when asked about his contribution in 2009/10 season. I would hardly be boasting about five goals all season or keeping Kalinic out of the team for a few games. Allardyce had managed to keep Roberts' media appearances to a tolerable minimum but when Kean handed Roberts a contract extension at the start of 2011, I soon started to wonder if there was a clause in it that said Roberts must appear on the box more often than he appears in the box. Jason Roberts telling strikers how to finish and Clarke Carlisle telling defenders how to defend? It sounds more like an idea for a sit-com than the basis of a credible television sports programme.

Somebody at Rovers seemed to be cottoning on to the idea that keeping the playing staff happy was half of the battle. Whilst contract offers were not too forthcoming for a lot of the younger players who weren't clients of SEM, the new deals came thick and fast for our senior contingent. Roberts, Dunn, Nelsen and Salgado were all handed lucrative contract extensions in the month of January. I felt really dubious about the long-term benefit of these deals to Blackburn Rovers. A lot of the players who signed new contracts were over 30 and had little sell-on value regardless of whether or not they signed a new contract. The fact that a football agent was so involved in this process was seriously worrying. Most of those that did have any significant sell-on value had generous sell-on clauses inserted into their new deal. At 33, Nelsen was not the player he once was and with Phil Jones, Samba, Givet and Hanley in the squad, there was no shortage of decent centre-backs at Rovers anyway. Dunn had been great in the 2009/10 season but how much he has contributed since is very debatable. To me it just looked like an easy way for the manager and owners to buy favour with the more influential voices in the dressing room while being seen to be taking control of the situation. Salgado likened what was happening at Rovers to Chelsea when Roman Abramovich took over. Somebody must have been giving it a really hard sell behind the scenes because I totally failed to see the link. Chelsea spent millions signing exciting young players; not handing out dubious contract extensions to old guys. When Salgado made these comments in the final week of the January transfer window we had secured the services of a few players who were well past their best and added Roque Santa Cruz and Jermaine Jones on loan but we had still hadn't actually signed anyone on a permanent basis.

When defensive midfielder Jermaine Jones arrived at Ewood Park mid-way through January I knew nothing about him at all. He had never played in the Premier League before and he was only on loan until the end of the season so he would have to settle in quickly. He had played in the UEFA Champions League for Schalke 04 and won a few caps for the USA but it was just a case of waiting and seeing with this guy. Roque Santa Cruz arrived on loan from Manchester City around the same time. Rovers' fans knew a bit more about Santa Cruz, having secured himself as a firm fans' favourite during the 2007/08 season. Santa Cruz was a breath of fresh air that first season at Rovers. He was a hard worker, excellent in the air and a good finisher. He ended the 2007/08 season with 19 league goals and was rewarded with a new four year contract. At that point Santa Cruz could do no wrong as far as Rovers fans were concerned but the following season, with a host of club's interested in him, I feel he let us down quite badly. All the transfer talk had an effect on his performances and it was an unwanted distraction. We were fighting against relegation at the time and we needed him out on the pitch playing football. When he left I was happy enough to see him go. We ended up making a very tidy profit on an injury prone player who has only got 10 or more league goals in a season on two occasions. He had failed to make any kind of an impact at Manchester City and, if you ignored the reported loan fee of £1.5 million for half a season, I felt than the return of Santa Cruz represented an OK bit of work by Rovers. Manchester City and Santa Cruz were keen on a permanent move but with his injury record I think a loan deal made a lot more sense from Rovers point of view. There was every chance he would get us a few goals if he stayed fit and if he didn't we could just give him back in May anyway.

By the final day of the transfer window, there had been talk of interest in Sebastian Larsson, Damien Duff, Charlie Adam and Juan Roman Riquelme but the only permanent addition at Ewood Park was assistant manager John Jensen. Steve Kean had said that no player would walk through the door unless it was on his say so. I am not sure the same applied to assistant managers and when John Jensen was brought to Blackburn Rovers, despite both being managed by Jerome Anderson, Kean admitted that he had never met Jensen before in his life. Jerome Anderson was the driving force behind this one but if he was sleeping at the training ground I wanted to see a bit more than John Jensen.

Venky's finally broke their transfer duck on the last day of the window when attacking midfielders Mauro

Formica and Ruben Rochina were brought in from Newell's Old Boys and Barcelona B respectively. Neither player was directly managed by Jerome Anderson but it was he who played a major role in bringing both players to the club. In August 2011, Nick Harris of the *Mail on Sunday* revealed that as part of the deal to bring Ruben Rochina to Blackburn Rovers, as well as the 450,000 Euro transfer fee Rovers had paid Barcelona, a £1.65 million payment had been made to Rochina's agent Manuel Salamanca Ferrer. Harris wrote,

> "That is way over the going rate, which would typically be around five per cent of a player's wages over the term of his contract. With Rochina's two-year deal starting at £23,000 a week, the agent's cut would normally have been around £170,000."

When Jerome Anderson was asked about the story on *talkSPORT* the following day, he said, "Today there are clubs out there that would already pay £6 or £7 million for this player." It seemed an extraordinarily high valuation for a player who still hadn't played 90 minutes in a senior game.

The signing of Formica was a long and complex affair. According to the papers, Barry McIntosh, the agent that had helped Rovers sign Jermaine Jones and Carlos Villanueva on loan three seasons earlier, had offered Formica to Jerome Anderson earlier in the transfer window. McIntosh, a licensed agent of the Cayman Islands national team, said of Formica,

"He is one of the hottest players on the scene in South America at the moment. Maybe he would not make an immediate impact but Blackburn Rovers would be getting a phenomenal talent. Remember, he would be coming from a club who had had great players like Lionel Messi and Diego Maradona."

It looked like another car salesman had missed his true calling. Formica appeared to be heading to Monaco, where we could then take him on loan. In the end the Monaco deal fell through and we signed him on a permanent basis for a transfer fee of £3.5 million. Kean said that the Formica signing had been delayed by a bit of paper hence why he eventually signed on the final day of the window. Kean described Formica as the new Gabriel Batistuta. I couldn't work out whether the new Gabriel Batistuta would get in Kean's team ahead of the new Pele - aka Jason Roberts. Rochina and Formica went on to make just of one first team start between them between now and the end of the season. The Formica transfer has since come under much scrutiny and in January 2012, Nick Harris had this to say on the *Sportingintelligence* website,

"*Sportingintelligence* can exclusively reveal that one of Blackburn's permanent transfer signings in the January 2011 window - that of the Argentinean attacking midfielder, Mauro Formica - was initially disallowed by the Premier League on 'technical grounds'. Impeccable sources have confirmed that the parties involved in the deal presented it for 'international clearance' but the deal involved a 'third party ownership element' that the Premier

League were not happy with. *Sportingintelligence* has learned that the ultimate owners of the player could not easily be identified when the deal was *initially* presented for clearance, but they were linked to an investment vehicle in the British Virgin Islands. After the initial deal was prevented, it was quickly reconstructed, within days, so that Formica moved into the full ownership of Newell's Old Boys; the transfer was then green-lighted between Newell's and Blackburn."

At the close of the transfer window Kean declared,

"I think the fans are starting to realise now what's happening here. There was the confusion of a few weeks ago when people weren't sure what was going to happen. Maybe fans were worried there was going to be an exodus. But then Ryan, Chris, Michel, Jason have all committed and we've also tied up young Phil Jones. They've backed us this month - they've backed us since day one. It's good that we've been able to attract players of this calibre."

If Rovers fans had been hoping that the January transfer window would finally give us some idea of what life was going to be like at Venky-run Blackburn Rovers, most fans ended up with more questions than answers. A lot of the players now seemed happier but ultimately all the fans had seen was a few debatable contract extensions, two players signed on loan and two unknowns signed permanently. If this was just a warm up for the big summer spend and the two unknowns turned out to be good players then fair enough. If this was as good as it was going to get then already some fans were starting to worry. Helped somewhat by three Premier League wins in a month (two of them against West Brom) Rovers fans were still supportive of Venky's but just 10 weeks in to their reign and already there were enough doubts to suggest that difficult times may lie ahead.

Chapter 8

On the Pitch (February 2011 - May 2011)

Once the January transfer window was over, Rovers were again free to concentrate on matters on the pitch. Talk of Ronaldinho and Beckham had cost the club credibility and major question marks remained over the long-term value of our four signings but the fact was our squad did look stronger than it had done at the end of December.

February opened with the mid-week visit of Harry Redknapp's Spurs. Flying high in the UEFA Champions League, Spurs were a different proposition to the Jekyl and Hyde outfit they once were. The bookies quite rightly made them marginal favourites for this one. The pre-match build up was all about Venky's.

Balaji and Venkatesh were back in town and this time they had brought along their sister Mrs Desai for her first game at Ewood Park. The three of them arrived in a fleet of chauffer-driven cars and they stepped out to a rousing chorus of "Venky's" from the 200 fans waiting outside the ground to greet them. Mrs Desai stopped briefly to sign an autograph for a young fan and when asked whether she was excited about the future she replied "absolutely". It is hard to believe now but when a video message from Mrs Desai was played on the big screen prior to the game there were no boos, jeers or obscenities - just smiles and warm applause. Rovers got off to the worst possible start, falling behind after just three minutes thanks to another Peter Crouch goal against Rovers. Some players just always seem to score against Rovers (Anelka, Keane, Van Persie, Heskey) and Crouch is one of them. Rovers rallied well and created much the better chances from here on in. Unfortunately, Spurs' keeper Heurelho Gomes was in inspired form. Gomes may be a figure of fun in some quarters but on his day he is a good goalkeeper. In the end, Gomes was the difference between the two sides and the early Peter Crouch header turned out to be the only goal of the game. While nobody likes to lose, it was a decent effort from Rovers and the fans went away in reasonably good spirits. Little did we know at the time but Venky's weren't just in town to enjoy the football. Two days after the Spurs game it emerged that Chairman John Williams was leaving Blackburn Rovers and Venky's had used the trip to finalise his severance package. It was difficult to understand why John Williams had been pushed to the sidelines and once again suspicions were high towards Kean and Venky's.

"We are trying to find a good experienced chairman and we do have some options," director of marketing at Venky's India, Vineeth Rao, told the *Lancashire Telegraph*. Leading up to the Spurs game most Rovers fans felt that we already had one.

It was announced the following week that Crown Paints would not be renewing their shirt sponsorship deal with the club. Although the decision had been reached prior to John Williams' exit, only a month earlier Crown had publicly stated that they were undecided on whether they were going to be renewing. Rovers thanked Crown and put on record that they were now searching global markets for a successor. In truth it was another blow. The game at Wigan did little to lighten the mood. Rovers started well enough. Roberts opened the scoring with his first goal in three months and Rovers looked much the better side for large parts of the first half. Wigan equalized on 35 minutes and the 4,500 travelling Rovers fans were disappointed not to be going in at half-time in front. Heavy rain and a poor playing surface played their part and the game was turned on its head shortly after the break when Wigan scored two quick goals to take a 3-1 lead. Chris Samba made it 3-2 but Wigan replied quickly with a fourth. A David Dunn penalty ensured a crazy final 10 minutes but Rovers were unable to do enough to force home an equaliser. Conceding four goals against a Wigan side that had only managed eight in their previous thirteen Premier League games at the DW Stadium was not good enough. In the week leading up to the Newcastle game, Kean gave his own thoughts on what needed putting right.

> "We know the areas of the pitch we need to work on: we have been predominantly working on finishing,

> obviously, and defending in the final third so we have split the group with the limited time we have had this week."

Fresh from the 4-4 thriller against Arsenal at St. James' Park, it was almost inevitable that when Rovers and Newcastle United met at Ewood Park the following week it would be an absolute bore fest. Three things of note happened in this game. Santa Cruz hit the woodwork for Rovers, Lovenkrands hit the woodwork for Newcastle and a fan released a chicken on to the pitch. There was no place in the starting 11 for Pedersen and the three players who had played a significant part in most of our goals during the first part of the season (Pedersen, El-Hadji Diouf and Emerton) were notable by their absence. Rovers didn't have a shot on target in the entire game and, considering we were playing at home against a team on the same number of points as us six months into the season, this was not good enough. Kean was happy to cling to the positives but his words were wasted on anyone who had just watched the game. Kean told the BBC,

> "The good thing is we got a clean sheet, we get a point, we finish our sequence of games where we didn't get anything from and we move on and we respect the point."

The games had been coming thick and fast and if player fatigue had contributed to the lacklustre display against Newcastle then that problem was about to be solved. Now we were out of all the cups, Rovers would play just three games in the next six weeks. Shortly after the Newcastle game, Rovers jetted out to Dubai where players and staff enjoyed trips to the tennis, horse racing and the beach - in between hard training. The common man doesn't begrudge pampered footballers the odd break abroad mid season but they have become so regular that it does begin to grate when you see your entire club jetting off to a different country four times a year - especially at a time when the good teams are playing in the Fifth Round of the FA Cup. I don't know how these things are funded and I would hope that a large proportion of the costs are covered by the players themselves. For me, if your whole squad comes back with a sun tan when they should have been playing in the FA Cup, you have got to put in a performance in your next game and Rovers just didn't do that. Prior to the trip to Dubai, Kean told reporters,

> "We have done it the last couple of years and there has been a big response - a spark, a number of points added to the board. I am hoping that they can energise themselves and we can all come back for the game at Villa in a couple of weeks bright and breezy."

Upon their return, Rovers were beaten 4-1 at Villa Park and the poor run of results continued. Rovers' record at Villa Park has been awful over the last few years. Villa usually beat us and they usually end up scoring three goals or more in the process. With Villa hovering just above the relegation places, the fans were right to expect more from this one. After a goalless first half the second half went very much according to the script. Having been out through injury for months, Keith Andrews walked back in to the side and duly gave away the crucial penalty by attempting to Cruyff turn Ashley Young in his own box. Once Villa had scored the first, the customary Villa Park implosion followed. Rovers conceded four and Ryan Nelsen was sent off deep in to injury time. Kalinic managed to get a consolation goal but it was too little too late for Rovers. Of Kalinic's 13 goals for Rovers up to that point, five had come at Villa Park. Having also netted twice for his country earlier in the month, Kean was still likening Kalinic to Croatian legend Davor Suker. Despite conceding four goals and Nelsen being sent off, Kean also felt the need to single out our central defensive partnership of Hanley and Nelsen for special praise for their performance in keeping two-goal Ashley Young quiet. The disturbing thing is I don't think he was being ironic. Even at this stage it was difficult not to notice Kean's strange approach to reality. I felt that he needed to be very careful. Although glossing over poor performances by highlighting less significant positives has become an infuriating feature of the modern game, ultimately few proper fans are ever fooled by it. After the game, Nelsen was sent home to New Zealand to be with his family following the tragic earthquake in Christchurch.

The players may have been putting pen to paper on lucrative new contracts and publicly backing the manager but what the fans now wanted to see was Premier League points. Kean had the seemingly unconditional backing of the new owners but he was still on probation as far as the fans were concerned. Two league wins in January had helped his case but one point from a possible 12 in February was not good enough. March started no better. Kean was targeting 10 points from 10 games for Premier League survival but a defeat at Fulham left Rovers still 10 points short of Kean's target. After the poor showing at Villa Park, the manager made six changes for the trip to Craven Cottage. Rovers fell behind twice to Rovers old boy Damien Duff but showed plenty of character to level things up on both occasions. Rovers' first goal came courtesy of a heavily deflected Hanley shot; the second a quality strike from the ever-impressive Hoilett. With just 90 seconds left Rovers looked to have done enough to have secured a well deserved point but referee Mark Clattenburg was about to spoil the journey home. A Fulham corner was floated in to the box and Clattenberg pointed to the spot for an innocuous tug by Hanley. It was the sort of tug you see from John Terry and Nemanja Vidic almost every week. Bobby Zamora slotted home the resulting penalty and that was game over. It was a devastating blow and the defeat left Rovers just two points above the relegation zone. To compound the misery Givet was sent off after the final whistle for verbally abusing Clattenburg. Over the next 12 months Kean would be critical of the local newspaper, the fans and even MP's but for whatever reason he was reluctant to blame Clattenburg for this costly penalty decision. This would be the first of a series of dreadful refereeing decisions against Rovers during Kean's time in charge.

13. Aston Villa	P29	W8	D9	L12	Pts 33
14. ROVERS	P29	W9	D5	L15	Pts 32
15. Blackpool	P28	W9	D5	L14	Pts 32
16. West Brom	P29	W8	D8	L13	Pts 32

Having looked comfortable leading into February, everybody was now very much aware that Rovers were back in a relegation scrap. Speculation was growing about Kean's long term future and the rumours had travelled far enough for Venky's to feel the need to put out an official statement on the Rovers website.

> "I do not know the source of these rumours but I would like to clarify that there is absolutely no truth in these reports. I would like to put on record that we have a contract with Steve Kean and he will continue in his present position with the club. There is no question of the manager being changed."

Only wins would really stop these rumours and Kean needed to start with the visit of Blackpool. Newly promoted Blackpool came to Ewood Park with a growing fan club and I looked forward to seeing what all the fuss was about. Every year the media like to champion the cause of an unfashionable club and this season it looked like it was Blackpool's turn. The first major talking point of the game was Luke Varney's disallowed goal on 20 minutes. Blackpool weren't happy about it but for all the fuss the fact remains that Varney was offside. Five minutes later and Blackpool were handed an absolute gift courtesy of referee

Howard Webb. I couldn't begin to explain why Webb felt the need to give a penalty for a coming together between Nelsen and Taylor-Fletcher that was even more innocuous than the Hanley incident two weeks earlier. If Webb has ever watched the incident back I am sure he will agree that it is well up there with the two dreadful decisions he made at Ewood Park back in 2006 when he gave West Ham a goal that didn't cross the line and a penalty that effectively kept them in the Premier League.

I really don't like blaming referees but have a look at the decisions in question and try and explain them in any other way. Blackpool's Charlie Adam slammed home the penalty to make it 1-0 to the visitors. I don't know why Adam felt the need to stand in front of the Blackburn End goading Rovers fans but it showed all the class of a player who would be playing in the Premier League the following season whatever happened to Blackpool. Adam arrived at Ewood Park with a big reputation but, bar a great free kick on 30 minutes to make it 2-0, I wasn't that impressed with what I saw of him. Rovers were there for the taking but Adam seemed too busy blowing kisses to the crowd and patting himself on the back for his two goals to play much of part in the remaining hour of the game. Half-time couldn't come soon enough for Rovers and the fans made their frustrations clear as the players trudged off the field at the end of the first half. When Blackpool fans started singing "you're getting sacked in the morning" in Kean's direction there were pockets of angry Rovers fans that joined in. I'm not too sure if Kean still has a hair-dryer but whatever went on at half-time, Rovers came out a totally different side. We played at a much higher tempo and the chances came thick and fast. Samba made it 2-1 five minutes in to the second half and Blackpool were hanging on for dear life. The team received a massive lift when Phil Jones returned from injury just before the hour mark but it was his namesake Jermaine Jones that continued to catch the eye. In stark contrast to his opposite number Charlie Adam, loanee Jermaine Jones didn't appear too concerned with the pretty stuff, this guy was a monster and the longer he was at Rovers the more his pedigree shone through. When a friend asked me what sort of player he was, the best way I could describe him was the engine of Steven Reid, the no-nonsense attitude of Nigel De Jong and the finesse of Patrick Vieira. I'd had a few beers at the time but, basically, he was just what we needed. I was disappointed Rovers didn't have the option to make the deal permanent but as with most things at new Rovers if it was good it was short term; if it was bad it was long term. Rovers continued to press and Martin Olsson, Samba and Hoilett all had chances to equalize. When the fourth official held up the board to show three minutes injury time it looked like Rovers had missed the chance to get something from the game. Robinson launched the ball in to the Blackpool box in the 93rd minute, the ball fell kindly to Hoilett and the smallest man on the pitch nodded in to the net to spark wild celebrations. Rovers were unquestionably poor in the first-half but the team showed enough quality in the second to let people know that we were more than capable of doing enough to stay in the Premier League. I wasn't so sure about Blackpool and now at even money to go down that looked a good value bet to me. There would now be a lengthy international break in which the rapidly unfolding shambles at Rovers was high on the media agenda. There was talk of press officer Paul Agnew being promoted to the still vacant Chairman's role, Venkatesh Rao said Venky's would continue to back the team and there were even reports of Rovers signing Jerome Anderson's son. Many Rovers fans were still prepared to put a lot of the stories involving Rovers down to media mischief making and instead of joining in with the hysteria chose to focus on backing the team to Premier League safety.

Nobody expected much from Rovers first game back after the break. I have been to The Emirates three times to watch Rovers and we have been beaten 6-2 twice and 4-0 the other time. So you will understand when I say there was nothing boring about this 0-0. It was a real team performance and we fully deserved our point. It was difficult to pick out individuals but once again Jermaine Jones was superb, as were Nelsen, Nzonzi, Martin Olsson and many fans' player of the season Michel Salgado. Nzonzi was harshly sent off with 15 minutes to go and whilst we still held on for the point we really could have done without his resulting three match ban. I would have liked to have seen an appeal go in against the Nzonzi red card but appeals against red cards have become a rarity at Rovers since the arrival of Venky's. The point against Arsenal was undoubtedly a bonus but with seven games to go it was now crunch time for Rovers. Only eight teams had made it to the magic 40-point mark and every other team had to consider themselves in a relegation battle.

Just eight points separated last place Wigan on 31 points from ninth placed Newcastle on 39 points. With 34 points, Rovers were right in the thick of it. Problems were mounting for Kean. As well as Nzonzi's three match ban, Santa Cruz still hadn't got a goal since his return, top scorer Kalinic wanted to know why he wasn't even getting in the squad, there was still no sign of January signings Rochina and Formica and now news was emerging of a contractual issue with Givet that threatened to put him out for the rest of the season. At this point, the most cutting criticism of Kean wasn't actually coming from the fans; it was coming from the media. Allardyce chipped in by saying that Rovers wouldn't have been in this mess if he was in charge and it was hard to disagree with him. The fans were not happy about what was happening but were in full agreement that this was not the time for protests. On the face of it we had just had a bad February and a bad March but when you looked deeper and considered the vast wealth of experience that had left the club it was difficult not to fear that this was now the start of a fatal slide. Nelsen said we had seven cup finals to play, starting with Birmingham, and the fans remained behind the team.

Givet pulled out of the Birmingham game at the last minute claiming he was not in the right frame of mind to play. Kean would not be drawn into detail about the contractual issue that was causing the problem with Givet and said he would prefer to keep it in-house. When details of the problem were made public it was abundantly clear why the club were keen to keep this one out of the public eye. Most other players would have suffered a reaction from the fans for pulling out of games but Givet had become a real fans-favourite since arriving from Marseille two years earlier. This was a player who you feel would dive head first through a post to save a corner. Whatever the problem was, it was clearly serious. Martin Olsson stepped in for Givet and whatever we were about to lose defensively hopefully we would now gain going forward. Birmingham went 1-0 up just after the half hour and again Rovers fell victim to the now customary piece of poor refereeing as Lee Bowyer nodded home Cameron Jerome's cross from an offside position. Bowyer waited for the flag but the goal was allowed to stand. Birmingham could have made it two moments later when a 20-yard Sebastian Larsson free kick came back off the post. Rovers got an equaliser with the only other goal of the game just before half time. Liam Ridgewell dwelled on the ball and Hoilett dispossessed him. Still 30 yards out, all that stood between Hoilett and the goal was Birmingham keeper Ben Foster. Hoilett raced in to the box, coolly rounded Foster and slotted the ball in to the empty net. A close to capacity Ewood Park breathed a sigh of relief. Rovers had much the better chances in the second half but the game ended a draw. The absence of Kalinic from a team that scored two goals in five games in April was bizarre. Exactly what Santa Cruz, Benjani and Mame Biram Diouf were doing to keep him on the sidelines I really don't know? Santa Cruz looked good in training according to Kean but with the massive loan fee and Rovers perilous league position we hadn't signed him to score goals down at Brockhall. The result suited neither team and this was Rovers third consecutive home draw against beatable opposition. We were somewhat lucky that the teams around us had stopped picking up points or the situation could have been a whole lot worse.

On the eve of the Everton game at Goodison Park, Kean announced that Nelsen would be out for the rest of the season as a result of the knee injury he picked up against Birmingham. It was a cruel blow for Nelsen and nobody wanted to lose his experience and big-match composure but with Givet back and Phil Jones in his best position of centre back, Salgado, Jones, Samba and Givet was probably our best back four anyway. Ruben Rochina was handed a first start in place of the injured Hoilett but bar this enforced change it was a Rovers team full of Premier League experience. Rovers were poor. We offered little going forward and lost out to second half goals from Osman and Baines. Losing to a better team is no crime but losing to an Everton team who didn't really have to get out of second gear was wholly unacceptable. Kean said that Rovers were excellent in the first half prompting Chris Brereton of *The Independent* to write,

> "If this was Blackburn in "excellent" mode then heaven knows what they must look like on a bad day, although Everton were no better in a poor first half. That Rovers never showed a hint of desire to get back into the contest is what should worry their fans the most. Kean, it would appear, has serious work ahead."

Brereton didn't have much luck when he was sent to watch Rovers games but in fairness his summary of the afternoon at Goodison Park was a lot closer to my own personal take on the game than Kean's post-match analysis. Five more performances like this and we were going down.

By the time Rovers played Manchester City the following Monday in the live Sky game we were just one point off the relegation places and the fight against the drop appeared a straight race between West Ham, Wolves, Wigan, Blackpool, Rovers and Birmingham. There was no chance of any selection favours from Manchester City - Roberto Mancini's expensively assembled squad was still looking to secure a place in next season's UEFA Champions League. City could have taken the lead as early as the third minute when David Silva's shot came back off the woodwork but Rovers weathered the early pressure and ended the first half looking as likely to score as Manchester City. Martin Olsson, Samba and Benjani all had good chances in the second half but it was Manchester City's Edin Dzeko who got the game's only goal 15 minutes from time. Once again, Rovers felt they were hard done to as Mario Balotelli was in an offside position as he blocked Robinson's sight of the ball. This one was a lot less clear cut than some of the previous bad decisions but it was hard not to feel we were well overdue a break. Overall, the performance was much better than the sub-standard showing at Everton but at this stage it was points we needed. Rovers' 11 game winless streak was now the club's longest run without a win for 25 years. With 34 games gone we now had chance to compare the points return from Allardyce's 17 games and Kean's 17 games. Of the 35 points we had picked up during the 2010/11 season Allardyce had won 21 of them and Kean just 14. Pundits including Mark Lawrenson, Lee Dixon and even ex-Rover Robbie

Savage were tripping over themselves to tip Rovers to go down. When somebody like Mark Lawrenson tips your club to go down it gives you fresh hope that your team will avoid relegation and this was just the boost I needed.

15. Birmingham	P34	W8	D14	L12	Pts 38
16. ROVERS	P34	W9	D8	L17	Pts 35
17. Blackpool	P34	W9	D7	L18	Pts 34
18. Wigan	P34	W7	D13	L14	Pts 34

It had reached the point where little, except maybe a win, would surprise Rovers fans and in the build up to the Bolton game Kean found himself having to answer questions about whether or not Venky's knew you could get relegated from the Premier League. Kean was quick to dismiss these rumours but just the fact that the question had been asked in the first place was embarrassment enough. Bolton came to Ewood Park off the back of a 5-0 humiliation at the hands of Stoke in the FA Cup semi final. Riding high in the Barclay's Premier League, Bolton manager Owen Coyle pledged that there would be no FA Cup hangover and was challenging his team to aim for Europa League qualification. Coyle was left disappointed as a fine Martin Olsson solo effort proved the only goal of the game and at last Rovers got the win we had been so desperate for. Rovers could have added to Martin Olsson's first half goal against a Bolton side that looked way off the pace for long periods of the game. For all the talk of this being a Bolton side with the potential to go far (SEM client Owen Coyle was being tipped for the

Arsenal job at one point!) they actually ended the 2010/11 season just one place above Rovers in the Premier League. Rovers were by no means out of the woods yet but with all the teams around us either losing or drawing Rovers' first Premier League win in over three months meant we were back in the driving seat.

For months Kean had been giving his predictions on how many points Rovers needed to ensure Premier League safety and with three games left to play there was no chance of him hanging up his crystal ball yet. "If you've got 40 points and a good goal difference, which we have, that's going to see you safe," said Kean after the Bolton game. With Rovers now on 38 points, I felt that we needed more than two draws from our final three fixtures and Kean ended up revising his prediction before the end of the season. I felt Kean would have been better off just saying we were trying to get as many points as possible rather than guessing how many points it would take us to creep over the line. The fixture list had not been kind to Rovers and there was no chance of any easy points from our final three games.

Every one of our fixtures was against a team with just as much to play for as us. West Ham, were now in danger of becoming cast adrift at the bottom of the table and manager Avram Grant insisted they had to beat Rovers to stay in the Premier League. The last time Rovers had won at Upton Park Ian Pearce scored the winner and 22 of the 26 players who featured that day were English! Leading up to the game Kean was now targeting one more win for survival but, having not won at Upton Park since 1994 and with Manchester United at home coming up next nobody wanted to leave it the final day of the season against fellow strugglers Wolves at Molineux. We need to get something from the game at West Ham and just hope that the teams around us didn't win. Rovers had injuries to Salgado and Phil Jones but Givet and Emerton were ample cover and the news that Scott Parker was out for West Ham softened the blow. Rovers had much the better of the opening exchanges and deservedly took the lead on 13 minutes through Jason Roberts. Roberts was about to hit form just at the right time. I have never been a fan of Roberts as a media personality and there are times when he is frustrating as a player but when he hits a purple patch the guy can be unplayable. Urged on by another excellent away following Rovers continued to create chances and for large parts of the game looked the most likely to score next. West Ham were bottom of the league for a reason and without Parker to drive them on there didn't appear to be the urgency that the situation demanded. Just as it looked like West Ham were about to surrender without so much as a whimper Thomas Hitzlsperger found the net with a low drilled shot on 78 minutes - suddenly it was game on. Roared on by the home support and desperate for the win that would put them back in the race they threw absolutely everything at Rovers. All the momentum was with West Ham and having looked second best all afternoon now it looked like a West Ham winner was inevitable. Only a Samba super show saved Rovers. He was Superman, Spiderman, The Incredible Hulk, the lot. Even then, Robbie Keane still missed a glorious late chance to make it 2-1 but with the game finishing all square West Ham were as good as down. Rovers had fluffed chances to make it 2-0 but when the final onslaught was taken into account, it was probably a point gained on reflection. Unfortunately for us, bar Birmingham, all the teams around us also picked up points. Had Blackpool not conceded a late equaliser at White Hart Lane, things could have been a lot worse. We were edging nearer to safety but we still weren't there.

In the week after the game Kean's comments that Rovers had now picked up five positive results from seven games were wholly inappropriate. This wasn't the time to be quoting misleading statistics and the manager was in danger of a backlash if he didn't stop insulting the intelligence of the fans. The sequence of results Kean was referring to amounted to seven points from seven games - and three of those points were draws against teams that went down. Relegation form in other words. We wanted a win; not spin.

Manchester United arrived at Ewood Park needing just one point to secure the Premier League title. Rovers welcomed back Phil Jones and Salgado and the Rovers line-up of Robinson, Salgado, Givet, Samba, Phil Jones, Jermaine Jones, Nzonzi, Emerton, Martin Olsson, Hoilett and Roberts looked like our strongest 11. Manchester United still had the UEFA Champions League final to come in two weeks so they rested Van der Saar but other than that it looked a pretty much full strength team. Manchester United dominated the early stages but it was Rovers who took the lead on 20 minutes through Emerton. Manchester United stand-in goalkeeper Tomas Kuszczak made a hash of an Emerton cross-come-lob and pushed the ball towards the left corner flag. Martin Olsson collected the ball and after a neat exchange with Hoilett delivered a perfect ball for the on-rushing Emerton to slam in at the far post. Ewood Park went wild. There was the expected rally from the visitors but they were unable to get on the score sheet before half-time. Rovers looked much more settled in the second half and Manchester United started to get edgy as their chances became less and less frequent. As if, 1-0 wasn't enough, Martin Olsson had a great chance to double the lead on 65 minutes but his header came back off the woodwork. I could see Fergie's face getting redder and redder and even though you knew Manchester United would get an equaliser from somewhere, with 20 minutes to go, it was difficult to see where from. Then on 73 minutes Javier Hernandez took down a long ball and raced in on the Rovers' goal. Hernandez appeared to have taken too strong a touch but before the ball could go out of play, Robinson dived down at his feet and the Mexican striker needed no second invitation to take a tumble. It was a rare error from Robinson who had just received Rovers' Player of the Year award prior to the game. Rovers' fans were furious that it took so long to give the penalty but the referee did eventually make the right decision so, in hindsight, it is difficult to argue that it shouldn't have been given. Rooney made no mistake with the penalty and I don't know how he celebrated because I looked the other way. I would have put my fingers in my ears as well if I wasn't 30 years old. With just 15 minutes to go and both teams satisfied with a point, the champions in waiting then set about passing the ball along the back four for the remainder of the game. Both teams were criticised for what was seen as unsporting behaviour but no rules appear to have been broken and up until this very late stage of the game both teams had gone for the win.

Like most Rovers fans, I didn't hang around for the Manchester United post match celebrations. Allardyce and Kean never seemed to have got their head around this one but the average Rovers fan doesn't like Manchester United. Constant references to the achievements of "Sir Alex" (Fergie to anyone who remembers his first few years in England) might as well be dished out to a room full of Liverpool fans. Once again, results from elsewhere took the gloss off an otherwise excellent result. Although West Ham were now down, no matter what, wins for Blackpool and Wolves meant the fight for survival was going to the last day and it was any two from five. Billed as "Survival Sunday" by Sky, just one point separated Wigan, Blackpool, Birmingham, Wolves and Rovers. The cost of relegation had been reported at £80 million in one newspaper. A number of the clubs involved didn't have pay-cut clauses in the contracts of big-earning stars - meaning that many of the players would still be entitled to Premier League wages even if their club dropped down in to The Championship. Rovers held the upper hand in the fight for survival with a point more than three of our relegation rivals and a superior goal difference but anyone who thought that we were out of it had probably been spiked by Fergie. Despite Kean's predictions, it had been clear to me for some time that this was going to the final day. I had bought my ticket to Molineux well before the Manchester United game. I have been to hundreds of away games but I had got out of the habit of going during Allardyce's first full season. When money is tight something has to give and it was either the house or 10 away games a season. I love going down to Ewood Park but nothing beats the buzz of leaving your house at the crack of dawn with a plastic bag full of cans to make the make the epic journey to... Luton or Sunderland or Watford or West Brom or wherever. When I woke up at 4 am to the sound of a heavily inebriated old man singing Rovers songs in the street, I was more excited than nervous. It had been a terrible week for Rovers, a terrible six months in fact, but it all came down to one thing - beating Wolves - and I was confident we could do it. The seven days leading up to the game had been a mini-disaster. Kean was charged with drink driving on the Sunday; he then disappeared off to India for two days; an alleged irregular payment made by Gael Givet to a contact of Sam Allardyce was front page tabloid news; other clubs continued to be linked with our players and Rovers had suddenly become everyone's least favourite club. In 11 hours time none of that would matter. All that would matter was beating Wolves - something we had done on numerous occasions over the last few years. Wolves' manager Mick McCarthy had been giving it large all week but I didn't fear any team lead by this guy. With Wolves also needing a win to be certain of staying up the atmosphere inside a full to capacity Molineux was electric. The free burgers did little settle the nerves or the stomach but it was a nice touch from Rovers all the same. Kean picked the same team that drew with Manchester United and it was hard to argue that this wasn't Rovers strongest team. Talk about saving your best performance for when it matters, Rovers absolutely blitzed Wolves in the first half. Roberts opened the scoring on 22 minutes, steering in a wayward Salgado power driver past Hennessey in the Wolves net. It was no more than Rovers deserved. The pressure continued and Emerton made it 2-0 on 38 minutes with a dream of a volley from the edge of the box. The 3,000 travelling Rovers fans were in heaven. A massive weight lifted off my shoulders and anxiety I didn't even know I was carrying around just evaporated instantly. We still weren't mathematically safe but it would take an absolute horror show to cock this one up. Just as we thought life couldn't get any better, Hoilett arrived on the scene with a solo goal of the highest quality. Forget maths - we were safe. Let the party begin. Wolves were in total shock. They had started the day a point above three of the other teams but their first half non-show meant they were now in the relegation places with just 45 minutes of the season remaining. Wolves' manager Mick McCarthy was bearing the brunt of the fans frustrations and it was comforting to know that it wasn't just Rovers fans who didn't particularly like their manager. Wolves created more in the second half but it was Rovers who had the best chance to get another. When the ball fell to Roberts just eight yards out, he took a touch and tried to bend one round Hennessey. It was a great chance and Roberts really should have made it 4-0. It was hard to fault Roberts other than this. On the day he was excellent. With just 17 minutes to go, O'Hara made it 3-1. It still wasn't enough and news was coming through that Wolves were down if they didn't get another. With five minutes to go Stephen Hunt became a Wolves legend when he bent an exquisite curling shot into the net to make it 3-2. This was no consolation goal, Hunt's goal took Wolves out of the relegation places and condemned Birmingham to the drop - Blackpool went with them. Wigan, Wolves and Rovers were safe.

15. ROVERS	P38	W11	D10	L17	Pts 43
16. Wigan	P38	W9	D15	L14	Pts 42
17. Wolves	P38	W11	D7	L20	Pts 40
18. Birmingham	P38	W8	D15	L15	Pts 39
19. Blackpool	P38	W10	D9	L19	Pts 39
20. West Ham	P38	W7	D12	L19	Pts 33

When the full-time whistle went the ground erupted. Rovers had been safe for the best part of an hour but after goading Wolves fans for the entire second half, it was great to be enjoying a joint party. It was a fantastic day to be a Rovers fan and it will always be right up there with my most memorable games following Rovers. In stark contrast to how the year would end, Kean was quick to praise the supporters. "I am overjoyed for the supporters who have been first class" beamed Kean. Rovers were in the Premier League for another season and all the problems of the previous six months already seemed a distant memory. I made a promise to myself to start going to more away games next season - even if it did mean falling behind with a couple of the less important bills. Kean and Venky's came out and hailed this as the start of better things. With bumper funds promised for the summer the only mistake Rovers fans made was believing them.

Chapter 9

Summer Transfer Window 2011

To understand fully the problems that took hold at Blackburn Rovers Football Club it is important to understand the backdrop against which the events took place. In 2010/11 the 20 teams that made up the Premier League recorded losses of £361 million. Taken in isolation, the substantial losses didn't look great. When you consider that that the 20 teams involved in this £361 million loss generated income of £2.3 billion the figures become absolutely astounding. Despite the huge amounts of money the Premier League had been generating for years many of the clubs involved in the corporation continued to operate at a loss. Where had all this money gone? When I looked around Blackburn, the 17th most deprived area in the country according to one study, it was clear where it hadn't gone. In 1992/93 the average Premier League players wage was £1,482 a week. By 2011, not accounting for generous bonuses, the average Premier League players wage was up to an eye-watering weekly figure of £22,353. To put it simply, the vast amounts of money being generated by Premier League football had been used to make a small group of individuals (some talented, some lucky and some just basically taking advantage) obscenely rich. This had undoubtedly been to the detriment of the game and I would argue society.

From a personal point of view I was very much aware what the Premier League was all about but I still loved football and I still loved Rovers. The Premier League was the league Rovers were in so once you are in it you have got to make sure everything is in place to stay competitive. The summer transfer window is a vitally important part of the process and I went into the summer transfer window of 2011 feeling good. The final six months of the 2010/11 season had proved a real baptism of fire for Venky's and Steve Kean. There had been changes, mistakes, new faces and poor decisions but the fact was, when the curtain closed on another season we were still in the Premier League. Rovers had finished the 2010/11 season strongly and with the promise of "substantial" transfer funds it was time to move onwards and upwards.

The fans had grown frustrated with the avoidable teething problems that had dogged Venky's time at the club but in the main football fans are fairly easy to pacify and splashing the cash has always been a good starting point when it comes to buying a bit of popularity. The owners and management had confidently declared that we wouldn't be selling any of our best players and to quote Kean our summer transfer kitty was "miles bigger than Rovers have had in the past". For now at least, most Rovers fans I knew were happy to put any growing doubts about the new regime to one side while we drew up our shopping list of big summer transfer targets. Fans had grown used to seeing large outgoing transfers at Ewood Park (as the table below illustrates) but not since 2003 when the board released funds from the sale of home grown talent Damien Duff and David Dunn had we seen anything like the substantial transfer kitty's that were commonplace at other Premier League clubs.

BLACKBURN ROVERS TRANSFER REVENUES AND EXPENDITURES
(figures taken from transfermarkt.co.uk)

Season	Departures	Revenue	Arrivals	Expenditure	Total gain/ (loss)
10/11	26	£242,000	28	£4,444,000	(£4,202,000)
09/10	34	£32,252,000	34	£11,616,000	£20,636,000
08/09	31	£23,320,000	29	£10,278,400	£13,041,600
07/08	18	£3,498,000	24	£5,456,000	(£1,958,000)
06/07	26	£14,880,800	26	£14,542,000	£338,800
05/06	27	£2,376,000	26	£872,000	(£5896, 000)
04/05	22	£6,776,000	22	£6,930,000	(£154,000)
03/04	32	£31,988,000	28	£19,685,600	£12,302,400

The talk of a "substantial" summer transfer kitty was an exciting development considering the players we already had at the club anyway. By the end of 2010/11, whether by accident or design, Kean seemed to have stumbled across Rovers strongest looking team. Robinson had proved himself to be a top goalkeeper and in Bunn we had a decent deputy. At the back, Samba and Phil Jones would get in most Premier League teams and Givet was a solid performer who was at home anywhere along the back four. Hanley had shown that he was more than capable as a fourth choice centre-back. Nzonzi and Jermaine Jones had looked strong through the middle and Hoilett had been a revelation since breaking in to the team. In Martin Olsson and Emerton we had two experienced Premier League performers who were as comfortable on the wing as they were at full-back. We also had good options on the bench in Pedersen, Dunn, Santa Cruz and Mame Biram Diouf. Up front we were a little short but, bearing in mind Rovers had almost got in the UEFA Champions League in 2006 with Craig Bellamy partnering a mixture of Paul Dickov, Sinama Pongolle and Shefki Kuqi I felt that Roberts and Kalinic could both play a part in 2011/12. I had always liked Roberts as an option and we had done the hard bit with Kalinic, it just seemed mad not to use him now he had served his costly apprenticeship. Bearing in mind we still had January signings Rochina and Formica to enter the equation, I felt we had the core of a mid-table Premier League squad provided we had £10 million to spend and it was spent wisely. Wholesale changes weren't needed but the squad did definitely need freshening up. One area of concern was the number of over-30s in the squad. Emerton still had a good engine on him, as did Roberts, but I couldn't really see Nelsen, Salgado or

Dunn standing up to the rigours of a 38 game season in the Premier League. Each one of these players had contributed greatly to the Rovers cause and I am not questioning their place in the club's history but securing cover for them had to be high on the agenda for me. We also had three loan players in the first team squad and Kean had to work quickly to either sign them or replace them. Kean had already told reporters,

> "Obviously Mame goes back to Manchester United, Roque goes back to City and Jermaine goes back to Schalke, so if we can get the three of them in then that is fantastic if not then that is (sic) three positions we will definitely fill."

For me, Santa Cruz hadn't done enough to suggest he was worth signing on a permanent basis; Jermaine Jones was definitely a player I would have liked to see Rovers sign and although Mame Biram Diouf divided opinion, provided the price was right, personally I think he was worth a punt. Kean's job over the summer had to be to keep our best players, generate extra cash by getting rid of players like Vince Grella and Keith Andrews and then try and sign Jermaine Jones, Mame Biram Diouf, a full-back and a proven goal scorer to work alongside Kalinic, Roberts and Hoilett. Kean would end the year on the sort of money the normal man in the street could only dream of so now he had to show the fans why the owners felt he was worth it.

The Rovers hierarchy were careful not to be drawn in to revealing how big our transfer kitty actually was. Venky's and Kean wanted to show that they had learnt lessons from the embarrassment of January. Someone had finally worked out that telling the seller how much you have in your pocket doesn't always work in your favour when you are trying to negotiate the lowest price on something. Kean was still more than happy to play human thesaurus however and whilst he would not be drawn on exact numbers he was happy to tell everyone that would listen that we had a "sizable budget", "very healthy budget", "competitive budget" or depending on his mood a "substantial budget". The way I looked at it, if Spurs could expect to command a transfer fee of £10 million for a half decent player like Peter Crouch, I would expect a transfer kitty described as "substantial" to be at least £10 million.

The first signing of the summer was truly bizarre and certainly a log in the fire for the anti-Venky's camp. With all the bad feeling surrounding agent Jerome Anderson's reported involvement at Blackburn Rovers the last player in the world we needed to sign was Myles Anderson – his son. Myles Anderson had reportedly signed a pre-contract agreement with Rovers in March 2011. I am not one of the 7,371 fans who was at Pittodrie to see his one and only appearance for Aberdeen (he came off the bench after 88 minutes when Aberdeen were already beating Kilmarnock 5-0) nor do I have an encyclopaedic knowledge of inter-school football so I couldn't really tell you much about Rovers' controversial signing. Kean likened him to Manchester United's Chris Smalling so I presumed he was a defender. This was confirmed by a quick scan of the SEM website. Kean defended the signing by saying,

> "We think he has a lot of potential but there was the opportunity for him to go Scotland in January and we and he felt that would be a good experience for him. There was interest in him from a couple of Spanish clubs but he is our player and will be at our club full time in July."

On Kean's first point, I am not sure how good an experience it had been for Myles Anderson going to Aberdeen and being kept out of the team by Zander Diamond. Around the same time that Myles Anderson signed for Rovers, Diamond signed for Oldham Athletic and has since moved on to Burton Albion. On Kean's second point about Myles Anderson attracting interest from Spain, this was exactly the sort of comment that saw Kean become so unpopular with the fans. Were we talking Real Madrid here or were we talking the Spanish equivalent of Leyton Orient – another club that Myles Anderson couldn't get a game for? Jerome Anderson moved quickly to dispel talk that there had been anything sinister about a Premier League football club signing a 22-year-old who had played just five minutes for Aberdeen in his entire professional career. Anderson senior claimed that Rovers had wanted to sign his son after he impressed on trial the previous year. He has said that his son did a tackle in a trial game that was so good that people still talk about now. My son did a painting in nursery that was so good it is still on the fridge now but it doesn't make him an artist. I knew Rovers were struggling financially towards the end of the Walker Trust days but surely we could have found some money from somewhere if Myles Anderson had impressed enough.

If we couldn't afford to offer contracts to non-league players, why offer them a trial in the first place?

Myles Anderson was soon making his way up the Rovers pecking order, jumping from eighth choice centre-back to seventh choice centre-back as news began to emerge that Rovers star defender Phil Jones would be leaving the club. Given football's loyalty issues there were few Rovers fans who expected Phil Jones to stick around at Rovers forever, however his sudden departure left a bitter taste. Soon after making his debut at the age of 17, Jones had quickly been identified as a player with immense potential. Ironically it was Kean himself who was taking much of the credit for his discovery. In video footage that emerged 12 months later Kean shared with Rovers fans the moment he told then-manager Sam Allardyce about his new discovery,

> "I said to Sam, I've got a player for you – he is better than John Terry at his and he said... FUCK OFF."

Arsenal, Chelsea, Liverpool and Manchester United had been circling ever since. It was hoped that Phil Jones' declaration that he was a lifelong Rovers fan would help keep him at the club longer than the lengthy list of departing mercenaries. Having signed a new and improved five-year contract only four months earlier most Rovers fans expected at least another season out of him. At the time Kean said of his capture,

> "This is great news, especially on the back of so many other key players committing themselves to the club. Phil has made incredible progress over the

> past year or so and his form, prior to his unfortunate injury setback, attracted a lot of attention. It speaks volumes that he is happy to stay here for the long term and we are all absolutely delighted."

Phil Jones had been aware of interest from other clubs for some time and whilst he publicly played it down it was something that was difficult to get away from. In response to interest in Phil Jones earlier in the year, Kean had told reporters that Rovers were no longer a selling club.

> "In the past, because of the financial state the club was in, we had to sell players. The owners now have installed a financial stability where we don't have to sell players. It is really important we try and hold on to the likes of Phil Jones and Chris Samba. I hope Phil stays here and he's just signed a five-year contract."

It became a common theme for Kean to declare that a player was here for the long term and then for that player to be sold. Phil Jones was the first high profile example. When Phil Jones had signed his one-year contract extension in February 2011, keeping him at the club until 2016, it was the length of the contract that offered most comfort to Rovers fans. Little did we know then that there was a release clause in the contract allowing Phil Jones to open talks with any club that agreed to meet his asking price of £16.5 million. Within two weeks of the 2010/11 season ending the vultures were circling again. Kean was yet to excel in hands off warnings and instead told reporters,

> "You always brace yourself for bids – we have had offers before for him and I am sure there will be solid ones in again. He will move on some time, but I can see him being captain here first."

Just a week later, Phil Jones appeared to have signed for Manchester United for just £16.5 million. Rovers' fans were in uproar. Another season would have been nice and the transfer fee was pathetic. Kean had said earlier in the year that it would take "the biggest bid we have ever had, for Phil to move to anyone". I was surprised that the release clause was less than the £17 million we had received for Roque Santa Cruz in 2009. Barring injuries, Manchester United have every reason to expect 12 years of service out of Phil Jones. At a time when Andy Carroll and Jordan Henderson had signed for Liverpool for the best part of £55 million how had we just given away a 19-year-old, widely tipped to be the next England captain, for £10 million below what most Rovers fans had generally come to presume he was worth? The key to the entire deal appeared to be the £16.5 million release clause. Why had it been put in to his contract and had Manchester United been alerted to it? Liverpool were now reported to have put in an offer of over £22 million. There was also interest from Spurs, Arsenal and Chelsea but Phil Jones' representatives claimed that he had already agreed terms with Manchester United. At this point Mrs Desai stepped in and demanded to know how Manchester United had been made aware of the £16.5 million release clause. There was even talk of legal action against Manchester United and claims that the clause did not necessarily mean we had to sell to them if there were other offers on the table. For all the big talk, Rovers predictably stepped down. We had become so weak in transfer market negotiations that it appeared that we were now struggling to sell our players to the highest bidder. If Rovers didn't need to sell players anymore and Phil Jones had only just signed a five-year contract fans wanted to know why he had been sold? Saying that he was following a dream wasn't good enough for me. This is football; not *Jim'll Fix It*. It turned out to be another embarrassing episode for Kean and Venky's – one that would have been hard to imagine under the guidance of departed Chairman John Williams.

The transfer of Phil Jones to Manchester United was completed on 13 June 2011 and although Rovers eventually managed to negotiate a fee that could rise to £20 million with add-ons (£100,000 for each of his first 20 England caps plus £2 million the first time Manchester United won the Premier League or UEFA Champions League with Phil Jones at the club) it was hard for Rovers to claim any kind of triumph. Fergie got his man and over the next six months the football world heaped nauseating praise on "Sir Alex" for turning a £25 million player in to a £25 million player. Fergie later admitted that the signing of Phil Jones had been an absolute bargain. Anyone with a Rovers season ticket could have told you that in June. I am still not entirely sure how Fergie has picked up this reputation as being some sort unique spotter of talent. Maybe he is but the majority of players he has signed since the turn of the millennium have been pretty obvious signings. Players like Rooney, Berbatov, Ferdinand, Hargreaves, Carrick, Valencia, Ashley Young and now Phil Jones, were hardly leftfield bargains – they were proven performers who were all signed for a fair amount of money. Phil Jones was just the latest in a long line.

After the sale of Phil Jones, it became harder to accept Kean's transfer declarations.

> "This season will differ because for the first time I am able to bring the players that I want to the club. It is the first time I have experienced this and I think it is very important to bring in the right players for our philosophy and the way we want to play. We want to be dynamic, we want pace in the wide areas and we want to play as much as we can with two strikers. We want to play fast flowing football and if we can do that and keep the back door shut then I think we will have the fans on their feet."

Just like he had done in the January transfer window, Kean seemed to be covering every eventuality. This only added to the speculation about how big a role he had in transfers. The words weren't matching what was actually happening and fans were struggling to see where selling the club's best young player featured in this new philosophy that was going to get us on our feet. It was another case of one step forward, two steps back for Venky's and Kean and any kudos they had gained from the final few games of the 2010/11 season was fading fast. Fans had remained patient but the mood was quickly starting to turn. We had stood by the owners following the puzzling removal of Allardyce, John Williams and other key figures. Even the baffling promotion of Kean had attracted more criticism from the media than it had from the fans. Rovers' fans had recognised that Venky's had stumped up a significant amount of cash to buy our club and as a result the fans had given the new owners a real chance to bed in at a time when most of the football world were still more concerned with chicken jokes. The fans now wanted to see the club going forward. Despite the bold early transfer promises, two months on from our final day escape at Molineux and the only transfer activity Rovers fans had seen was the potential future captain of England replaced by a guy three years his senior who had never started a professional first team game in his life.

Kean had been flown out to India at the special invitation of Venky's to work on a transfer strategy with the owners. The only thing Rovers fans wanted to know was where was the money; how much did we have to spend and who were we going to buy? By this stage Rovers had made no attempt to re-sign Santa Cruz and had started to concede that the re-signings of Jermaine Jones and Mame Biram Diouf were both looking unlikely. When questioned about a permanent move to Rovers Jermaine Jones had told reporters, "My team in Germany have told me to come back but my agent knows what I want. I've been talking with Steve Kean and he needs to talk with the owner." If this wasn't a come-and-get-me plea I don't know what was. According to newspaper reports, his parent club Schalke 04 wanted £10 million for him. This is where the highly paid non-playing staff at Rovers needed to be justifying their big salaries. 29-year-old Jermaine Jones was worth £5 million and somebody at Rovers should have been trying to make it happen. Rovers ended up missing out on Jermaine Jones – something

Kean would publicly regret by the end of the year. Mame Biram Diouf also ended up staying at his parent club for the remainder of 2011. Reports were that Manchester United wanted £6 million for him. Again, I don't think it would have taken international hostage negotiator of the year to have chopped £4 million off that asking price and wrestled Mame Biram Diouf away from the bright lights of a League Cup run with Manchester United reserves. Mame Biram Diouf eventually signed for Hannover 96 in January 2012 for a transfer fee reported to be less than £2 million. He scored six goals in his first 10 games for the club.

Rovers were linked with Robbie Keane and Emanuel Adebeyor but both were quick to distance themselves from talk of joining Rovers. Keane eventually signed for MLS side LA Galaxy. Around this time an unnamed Premier League target was reported to have told his agent he would rather retire than sign for Rovers. Talk of landing Ruud Van Nistelrooy appeared to be just talk. There were reports of interest in £12 million rated Roma striker Mirko Vucinic and £10 million rated Freiburg striker Papiss Cisse but neither player ended up at Ewood Park. Vucinic signed for Juventus and Cisse went on to establish himself as one of the hottest strikers in the Premier League shortly after signing for Newcastle United in January 2012.

By mid-July, there was sufficient speculation about the lack of incoming transfer activity at Rovers for the club to release an official statement on the Blackburn Rovers website. As well as calling for fans to remain patient key excerpts from the statement included a reference to "optimising the current playing squad in a manner which is sustainable and beneficial to the long term interests of the club" and clarifying that the club "will only enter into negotiations with other clubs and agents on terms which are commercially viable and are within the market norms accepted by every other club".

Whatever had motivated the release of the statement it was now evidently clear that we were chasing a much lower calibre of player than those we had been linked with at the start of the summer. It was one thing asking fans to remain patient but why on earth were we trying to sign Benjani? It was debatable how good Benjani had been in his prime and after three goals in 18 games for Rovers and just seven goals in the previous three seasons he was maturing more like milk than wine. From a fan's point of view, things were not looking good and there was more uninspiring transfer talk to follow. News was that Rovers were now looking to add free-agent Mariano Pavone and Monaco's Cedric Mongongou to the ranks. I had never heard of Pavone and although Mongongou's name rang a bell I would be lying if I said I knew why. As was becoming the case with most of Rovers latest batch of transfer targets, the Internet was my first port of call for clues on these two. Pavone was a 29-year old Argentine journeyman striker who had been a flop at his one and only European club Real Betis. Mongongou was a 22-year-old 6'2" defender that had played 79 games for Monaco between 2007 and 2011. It was hard to make too much of a judgement on Mongongou's stats but there was nothing too impressive about Pavone's résumé. Pavone's agent Barry McIntosh was talking as though the deal was done at one point,

> "Mariano (Pavone) is delighted to get his chance in English football. He has spoken to several clubs but he was particularly impressed by Steve Kean. Steve made him feel very welcome and explained his plans, and Mariano was delighted with what he heard. He is now looking forward to the next chapter with an ambitious club like Blackburn."

Both Pavone and Mongongou appeared eager to sign for Rovers but despite newspaper reports saying that they were on the verge of signing neither ended up joining. Mongongou signed for French side Evian and in 2012, Pavone signed for his forth club in just over two years. Around the same time that Rovers were looking at signing him, Pavone's agent Barry McIntosh became embroiled in a very public spat with Newcastle United over another of his players – Tranquillo Barnetta. Newcastle were looking to sign the Swiss international from Bayer Leverkusen and had proposed wages of £40,000 a week. McIntosh claimed that the offer was "derisory" and the deal didn't happen. Barnetta is a solid player but no world beater and if £2 million a year was considered "derisory" it was further evidence of the madness that was eating away at our national game. Back at Rovers and Kean's travels around the world in pursuit of obscure names the average football fan had never heard of continued. The *Airmiles* were quickly stacking up but unfortunately the quality acquisitions were not and neither was Rovers transfer strategy. If we had "the biggest transfer kitty of recent times" and Kean was believed to be stronger than Allardyce in the transfer market why were we chasing players like Vierinha,

Simon Vukcevic, Bruno Ribeiro and Mariano Pavone? Was this a genuine strategy to improve the team or just an easy way to make money? As fans became increasingly frustrated, the press began to crank up the pressure and Kean told reporters,

> "It is not just simple bids, you have things like passports to check, things like who actually owns the player fully. These type of things have to be checked to make sure things are fit and proper."

I don't want to over-simplify things but Birmingham's Roger Johnson had just signed for Wolves for £7 million. Did Wolves need to check who Johnson was owned by and check his passport to make sure things were fit and proper? Johnson may not have had the greatest time of it at Wolves but I felt that a half decent manager could have got a tune out of him. At the time we were still out chasing a load of players few Rovers fans had heard of. I am not saying that just because a player is unknown to the average football fan he is no good but the plain fact is that for every Ryan Nelsen or Chris Samba there are easily 10 players who go on to have all the impact of Herold Goulon. Sticking together a load of unknown foreign players with absolutely no proven top league pedigree was a clear recipe for disaster and I could not believe that anyone with an ounce of football knowledge did not already know this. Rovers most successful signings over the last five years had been cast-offs from bigger or richer clubs – Bentley, Warnock, Bellamy, McCarthy, Santa Cruz, Robinson, Givet, Salgado and Jermaine Jones. If we had the contacts and the money it made no sense whatsoever to abandon this strategy. Questions were asked about Rovers financial position and frustrations were growing amongst Rovers fans. Kean did little to ease concerns when he responded to the growing speculation by saying,

> "Finance is not the stumbling block, there is certain paperwork that has to be done. I can totally understand the fans' frustrations and I hope they bear with us because it is not a case where we are twiddling our thumbs and not doing any work. I have a good relationship with the owners and we have a management panel in place. There is activity. I am possibly frustrated we have not managed to finalise one. It is a lot harder to get them done than I first thought."

This was a remarkable admission and one that only served to make the shoddy disposal of decades of boardroom experience even more difficult to fathom.

Kean eventually broke his summer transfer duck on 3 August 2011 when it was announced that Rovers had completed the £3 million signing of Dundee United striker David Goodwille. Reports have suggested that Kean himself was not overly excited by the prospect of signing Goodwillie and would have preferred Pavone. Personally, neither would have been on my wish list if the club had the kind of kitty Kean had hinted at back at the start of the summer. I could pretend I was familiar with the work of Goodwillie but I am going to be honest and own up to the fact that prior to being linked with Rovers I had never heard of him. The fact is

I don't play *Championship Manager* and my knowledge of the less high-profile leagues of Europe pretty much nose-dived soon after getting a girlfriend. I knew one thing, not many strikers have come down from Scotland in the last few years and set the Premier League on fire. Kris Boyd, Jan Vennegoor of Hesselink, Chris Porter and Peter Lovenkrands had all got goals for fun in Scotland but most of them had struggled to make an impact in The Championship let alone the Premier League. Even our own Nick Blackman had managed 10 goals in 18 games at Motherwell but still struggled to get a game at Rovers. Goodwillie's record of 25 goals in 129 games at Dundee United was nothing to write home about – especially considering 40-year-old defender David Weir was named the league's best player in 2010. Kean said of his 22-year-old new addition, "David has always been put on a parallel with a young Wayne Rooney and you can see that when you see him play." If you say so, Steve.

At least now players were starting to come through the door. Less than a week later and Rovers were at it again. Having been priced out of a move for midfield general Jermaine Jones, Kean had turned his attention to Serbian international Radosav Petrovic. 22-year-old central midfielder Petrovic had scored 17 goals in 70 games for his native FC Partizan and also had UEFA Champions League experience. He already had over 20 caps for Serbia and had been part of the 23-man Serbia squad that went to the 2010 World Cup in South Africa. Rovers completed the deal on 9 August 2011. At just over £2 million, on paper, Petrovic appeared to be a decent buy. Upon his capture, Kean told reporters,

> "He is a dynamic midfield player, with a great box-to-box mentality and a good passer of the ball, who I believe will go on to make a big impact with Rovers. It is a fact that many European clubs were in the race for his signature and we consider getting him to Ewood Park as a major coup."

I must admit, I did find it slightly worrying that Kean didn't liken Petrovic to Zinedine Zidane.

Just as things threatened to move forwards it was outgoing transfers that came to the fore once again. Kean was developing reputation for freezing out players that were no longer part of his plans. Keith Andrews, El-Hadji Diouf and Nikola Kalinic were all critical of Kean after leaving the club and unsurprisingly all three of them now saw their future away from Ewood Park. Andrews ended up going to Ipswich on loan, El-Hadji Diouf went to Doncaster and Kalinic signed for Ukranian side FC Dnipro. As I have said previously, Kalinic was by no means the finished article but I couldn't understand why Kean had treated him so shoddily. When Kalinic arrived in 2009 he was too lightweight and the £6 million price tag appeared to weigh heavily on his young shoulders. He did have a bit of ability however and Rovers had done a great job turning him in to a Premier League player. He improved month on month and just as we were starting to see the hard work pay off Kean decided that 33-year-old goal machine Benjani was more worthy of a place in the team. No wonder Kalinic and his agent wanted answers. Here we had a talented 23-year-old striker approaching the prime of his career and just as he starts to get a few goals the manager tells him he is not even good enough to get on the bench. Kalinic had made it clear that he was happy at Rovers provided he featured in the manager's plans. Rovers claimed that they wanted to keep Kalinic but how long did they really think he was going to wait last in line behind Roberts, Santa Cruz, Mame Biram Diouf and Benjani? By the time Rovers pre-season tour to Hong Kong came round Kalinic had gone public about his desire to leave the club and his relationship with Kean appeared to have hit rock bottom. Kalinic arrived at the airport with the rest of the squad but as soon as the management team got on the plane, he collected his bags and hit the road. Kalinic's representative Tomislay Erceg told the *Daily Mirror*,

> "Nikola has been disrespected by the club. He tried all day to speak to them about his transfer request. We even called India to speak to the owners and to the manager Steve Kean, but no-one would talk to us. There is an offer in, and it is worth more than £6 million with bonuses. Nikola does not want to play for Blackburn again. I spoke to him (Kean) three months ago and he said he (Kalinic) was his best player. Then he never plays him after that. Nikola cannot play for Croatia if he does not get in the Blackburn team. He has to go. He is finished there."

Within a week of the airport incident Kalinic had signed for Ukrainian side FC Dnipro. Embarrassingly, Mrs Desai had slapped a £12 million price tag on him but in the end he went for less than half that. Kalinic's 10 goals in 19 games for FC Dnipro in 2011/12 helped secure him a place in the Croatia squad that went to Euro 2012.

28-year-old full back Bruno Ribeiro was signed on a 3-year deal the same week and even though Kean said players in the squad had likened him to Denis Irwin an unknown 28-year old Brazilian was not really what Rovers fans were looking for. Not to be confused with the Bruno Ribeiro who had played for Leeds and Sheffield United at the turn of the millennium, Bruno de Paula Ribeiro Ingracia (to give him his full name!) turned out to be as bizarre a signing as Myles Anderson. Having spent the majority of his career at Sao Paulo based state clubs and now managed by London based sports agency Velop4 Sports Ltd, the Premier League was an unlikely jump in class for Ribeiro and this is exactly the sort of signing that infuriates football fans.

The summer transfer window was turning in to a total wash out for Rovers. On the eve of the 2011/12 season, Paul Wilson of *The Guardian* summed up the feeling of Rovers fans best when he said,

> "Steve Kean's Blackburn recruitment drive needs action, not words. Unless the Blackburn Rovers manager backs up his transfer claims with new faces, the club will struggle next season. Most clubs and most managers prefer to do the business first and the talk later."

Rovers had agreed fees in excess of £22 million for departed players and by the time the new season kicked off, we had spent just £5 million on replacements. By the time the Wolves game came at the start of the 2011/12 season the club was in absolute disarray. Three of Rovers recognised back four were absent for reasons that weren't entirely clear and the central defensive partnership of Nzonzi and Hanley was not acceptable. Pretty much the same Wolves team that Rovers had pulverised less than three months earlier were full value for their 2-1 win and still Kean was telling anyone that would listen that Rovers were stronger than last season and on course for a top 10 finish.

All that was really missing was another laughable bid for a global superstar involving bits of paper and a fax machine. Right on cue, Rovers made a bid for Raul that was akin to the school nerd asking the best-looking girl in school out on a date. As a Rovers fan, at a time when we couldn't get Hoilett to agree to a new contract, I found the bids for global superstars beyond embarrassing. I am not going to dwell on this one but Raul said thanks but no thanks and more importantly time was running out for Rovers. With just 10 days to go before the close of the window even Kean himself was starting to show signs of concern.

> "We are making realistic bids and they are not coming off. Maybe we will have to pay over the odds to ensure that we get people here. We have to speed up the process because I don't think we can go another couple of games having to play central midfielders at centre-half. We certainly need bodies."

Rovers were linked with over 70 players during the summer. Many of these links were no more than paper talk and idle speculation. Rovers spent a large proportion of the final few weeks of the transfer window chasing 1899 Hoffenheim striker Vedad Ibisevic. This guy appeared to have no problem scoring goals in the German Bundesliga and at £6 million he looked like just the sort of player we needed. At various points it looked like he had signed for us but worryingly the deal was taking far longer than transfers used to take under the previous administration. In the end Rovers pulled out of the deal at the last minute – citing Ibisevic's injury problems as the reason. Rovers said they might take another look at Ibisevic in January but I couldn't see him being in any rush to re-open talks with Rovers. This was a high quality striker who had proved himself in the German Bundesliga. In January 2012, Ibisevic signed for VfB Stuttgart and scored eight goals in his first 13 league games for the club.

Rovers also went to considerable lengths to set up the signing of 24-year-old FC Dallas defender George John but this was another deal that wasn't closed. John was meant to fill the gap left by Phil Jones but the fact that dual national John still hadn't broken into either the Greece or USA team hardly filled me with great optimism. At this point the power of positivity had been unleashed from the armoury again and Kean was back playing the "do you want the good news or the really good news" game. The really good news was that Rovers had signed Simon Vukcevic – only really known outside of Britain to his friends, relatives, work colleagues and people who play too much *Championship Manager*. Vukcevic had signed from Sporting CP of Lisbon for around £3 million. It is difficult to judge a player that you have never seen play before and with so many unfamiliar faces Rovers fans again had to wait to see if different was better. The good news (also known as bad news to people of a less positive outlook) was that it had now emerged that Brett Emerton would be leaving Rovers with immediate effect. This was a tragic loss for Rovers and considering the problems we went on to have filling the right-back role with a fit, experienced defender of Premier League quality it had to go down as one of the worst decisions of Kean's entire reign. Rovers had allowed Emerton to sign for Sydney FC on a free transfer as a gesture of goodwill for his services to Rovers. Yes, Emerton had been a great servant to Rovers but three games in to the season, why were we so keen to make dreams come true when those dreams involved losing one of our most valuable players?

By the final day of the transfer window Rovers fans were bracing themselves for absolutely anything. Forget who was coming in – Hoilett still hadn't signed a new contract, Samba had indicated he was ready to leave and there had been reported interest in Nzonzi, Pedersen, Givet and Martin Olsson. The big talk at the end of May had amounted to absolutely nothing and it was now just a case of damage limitation. It was a massive day for the football club. If it went wrong, make no mistake, we were about to challenge Derby's record of 11points in a Premier League season; if it went right, we still had an outside chance of ending the season 17th. It was a horrible, tense, uncomfortable day but ultimately it turned out to be one that got Rovers back in the fight for survival. Despite all the talk, none of our first team players left and money was spent on three new players. In came Scott Dann from

Birmingham and Yakubu from Everton. *Sky Sports News* had reported 24 hours earlier that Yakubu had snubbed the advances of Rovers to stay with Everton. Whatever had happened in the meantime at least we had now spent a bit of cash and signed a couple of players with Premier League experience. Dann came with a good reputation and although the signing of Yakubu raised some eyebrows it was hard to fault his goal scoring record. Yakubu had been around for years. Pini Zahavi, one of the football agents involved in the Carlos Tevez third party ownership controversy, famously negotiated a £3.64 million agent's fee when Yakubu transferred from Portsmouth to Middlesbrough in 2005. It would be interesting to know what the financial rewards were for the people involved in bringing Yakubu to Rovers but there was no denying that the Premier League journeyman was a decent player. I actually thought Yakubu was in his early-30's but once I found out that he was only 28 his impressive scoring record of 119 goals in 313 games in England made him look a good buy.

The signing of Jordan Slew from Sheffield United was an odd one - £1.1 million for a League One striker with 11 league appearances and three goals to his name? Shortly after Slew's move to Rovers, Danny Wilson, his manager at Sheffield United, told the *Daily Star*,

> "I think it's the wrong move for Jordan and I told him so. He needs to learn his trade and won't do that in the reserves at Blackburn. He could have stayed with us and maybe gone in January, by which time he'd have had 20 first-team games with us under his belt.

But this is what happens, I'm afraid. If the Premier League is dangled in front of people, it is very difficult to turn it down. In my opinion, his progression would have been best here, but it is down to the player and agent."

Kean had said throughout the summer "judge us at the end of the transfer window". By the end of the transfer window Rovers were bottom of the Premier League having picked up no points from three games. Kean claimed that he was delighted with the business Rovers had done in the transfer window and publicly declared that we were on track for a top 10 finish. It wasn't just Kean who was coming out with this sort of stuff – David Dunn and several other members of the Rovers staff all went on record with the "finishing top 10" line. For me there is a point where spin and the power of positive thought becomes claptrap. Rovers had been 90 minutes from relegation in 2010/11 and by the close of the 2011 summer transfer window I was happy to argue all day long that we now had a much weaker squad. This is not hindsight – most Rovers fans were saying exactly the same thing in September 2011. If you compared the squad we had at the end of 2010/11 to the squad we had now – Phil Jones had been replaced by Scott Dann; Brett Emerton by Myles Anderson; Jermaine Jones by Radosav Petrovic; El-Hadji Diouf by Simon Vukcevic; Nikola Kalinic by David Goodwillie; Mame Biram Diouf by Jordan Slew; Keith Andrews by Bruno Ribeiro and Roque Santa Cruz by Yakubu. Kean could sugar coat it all he liked but it was glaringly obvious to anyone who had been a football fan for longer than nine months that the players that were departing Ewood Park were of a much higher calibre than those that were coming in.

We had signed a few players but at least half of them didn't appear to be Premier League quality. If we weren't signing players that were good enough to play in the Premier League, why were we signing them? According to *transfermarkt.co.uk* figures Rovers had made a net transfer profit of £6,952,000 over the summer. We will have to wait for the 2012 accounts to come out to get a better idea whether this money went on wages, running costs, bonuses or covering the £4,679,349.22 spent on licensed agents between 1 October 2010 and 30 September 2011. Wherever it went it was not really what Rovers fans had in mind back in May when Kean was telling *Sky Sports News*, "It's a very exciting time for Blackburn Rovers." It may have been an exciting time for certain people at the club but it wasn't an exciting time for the fans. The ridiculous amount of money that had been spent on agents (well over 25% of the share value of the entire club!) was hard to justify considering the quality of the players that had come in. Manchester United had spent a similar amount on agents during the same period but had actually spent three times as much as Rovers on transfer fees. The summer transfer window had been Kean and Venky's big chance to put right the wrongs of the previous season and I wasn't the only Rovers fan who felt that they had failed miserably. Fans will only take so much before eventually they say enough is enough. Rovers fans had walked away from Molineux in May full of hope. Those feelings of hope had been encouraged by Kean's transfer declarations. 10 weeks of the transfer window and the feelings of hope had been replaced by feelings of anger, frustration and disappointment. Rovers' fans didn't expect to see the world's best 11 players running out of the Ewood Park tunnel kissing the club crest. What we did expect to see was actions that backed up the bold statements. Once again *The Guardian* was right on the money. This time it was Amy Lawrence and Paul Doyle. Not only did they predict that Rovers would finish the season 19th but they summed up the mood amongst Rovers fans perfectly when they wrote,

> "If you could bottle and sell the mood around Ewood Park, you'd be banged up for peddling toxic moonshine. Blame the Indian chicken barons who, since buying the club last November, have failed to produce the readies to genuinely pursue their grandiose ambitions. Ronaldinho? Champions League in four years? Dreaming is good, but to keep declaring your dreams while doing little to realise them is lame. And annoying. Most Blackburn fans are annoyed."

Chapter 10

Out With The Old

It would have been easier to handle our transfer market failings if things didn't appear just as chaotic behind the scenes. The club that was once considered the best-run club in football now looked like it was being run with all the professionalism of a kindergarten tuck shop. When the takeover was completed in November 2010 Venky's made a written pledge; "to continue to support the existing management team and staff". Understandably, most people took this to mean that there would be no wholesale changes to the non-playing staff in the immediate to short-term future. David Brown (the director who provided the link between Blackburn Rovers and the Walker Trust) resigned at the time of the takeover but other than this predictable development few other changes were anticipated. Provided Blackburn Rovers continued to perform as a business and a football club as well as it had done for the past 10 years there was no obvious need to change things at all. Yes, the club's success owed a lot to hefty outgoing transfers but if the board knew how to buy low and sell high then it could hardly be considered cheating. Senior boardroom figures acknowledged that under the previous ownership they had received enormous freedom in terms of managing the affairs of the club. They also recognised that this level of freedom would change now that Venky's had taken over. The understanding amongst fans was that Venky's had bought Blackburn Rovers to increase awareness of the Venky brand, make money and help the club grow on the field. With this came the presumption that the core of the existing board were the ones best placed to help Venky's achieve this goal. Prior to the takeover, publicly at least, Venky's did little to discourage this view.

Within four weeks of Venky's taking over, the outlook had changed somewhat. Rovers' Chairman John Williams was told via a long-distance phone call that Sam Allardyce and his assistant Neil McDonald no longer featured in the owner's long term plans. It was Williams who took on the task of breaking the shock news to his two close colleagues.

Whatever those on the board had chosen to believe at the time of the Venky takeover it now appeared that the Venky way was quite different to the way things had been done under the Walker Trust.

Williams spent the day after Allardyce's removal locked in talks with Venky representatives and reports in the press were that he would now resign. Two days after Allardyce's removal, with rumours rife that Williams would be the next to go, he told the *Lancashire Telegraph*,

"It has been a very difficult few days for everyone involved with the club. The departure of Sam and Neil was unexpected and I would like to add my thanks to them both for their efforts over two years. It is widely accepted that they did a very good job for us. However, the decision has been taken and we must move on. I would like to appeal to all Rovers stakeholders to fully get behind Steve, an out-and-out football man and a true professional, on Saturday. We are not in crisis - in fact, we are well placed in the table."

Rovers' fans begrudgingly accepted Williams words but looking back, who would want to tell their close work colleague he had been sacked after being given the instruction over the phone by a group of people you had publicly endorsed just six weeks earlier? Williams continued in his role at Rovers and the new order continued to declare that he had a part to play. You can drip feed the public all the information you like but if something doesn't look right invariably questions will continue to be asked. Watching Williams at the time he had the look of an international hostage reading out a statement on state television. As a result the questions continued to be asked. The new order pressed on with their plans and although the January transfer window had failed to see Rovers land Ronaldinho and Beckham, Venky's still received a warm Ewood Park welcome when they arrived in Blackburn for their first game of the New Year. It would be the last time Rovers fans would welcome Venky's with anything but contempt and suspicion.

On 4 February 2011, it was announced that John Williams would be leaving his position at the club with immediate effect. A compensation package had already been agreed and Venky's thanked Williams for his work. In a statement released by Rovers, Williams said,

> "There is a new order, a new way of doing things and I believe the time is right for me now to move on. I would like to take this opportunity to wish the club, its owners, management, players, employees and supporters all the very best for the future."

Not for the first time, Venky's disposed of a key member of staff and then advised that they didn't have a replacement lined up.

If the departure of Allardyce, had sent shock waves through football, it was the departure of Williams that was undoubtedly felt hardest by Rovers fans. Allardyce had his critics so whilst his removal was ill timed and his replacement puzzling the general sentiment of his sacking was not something that was lost on the average fan. Williams on the other hand was widely regarded as a modern day Rovers great and few could see how his departure would be for the overall good of the club. I accept that as a Rovers fan my club was protected from the worst side of the Premier League's descent into lunacy by the Rovers board led by John Williams. As Rovers attendances dropped from 26,255 in 2002/03 to 23,479 in 2008/09, John Williams had the foresight to recognise that fans paying £200 a season was better than the prospect of 10,000 empty seats. It is rare for boardroom figures to be so well thought of but the fans recognised the part that Williams had played our club's success. Williams had the priceless ability to communicate with players, fans, managers and business leaders to create a club that was bigger than the sum of its parts. He was more than just a football chairman. In 2007, when he was made aware of the existence of John Lewis' overgrown grave in Blackburn Municipal Cemetery (John Lewis is the founder of Blackburn Rovers Football Club), he quickly took steps to locate John Lewis' family. Along with the various family members that John Williams managed to track down, members of staff at Rovers then played a pivotal role in restoring the grave to its former glory – testament to how much the history of Blackburn Rovers meant to those running the club. In his 13 years at Blackburn Rovers, Williams had pulled Rovers through difficult times to help ensure our longest run of top-flight football since the war. Players past and present, former managers, local MPs, members of the local press and thousands of Rovers fans paid tribute to Williams' outstanding contribution to Blackburn Rovers.

Feeling towards Williams has changed somewhat in the time since he has left Rovers. While the majority of fans still recognise all the good things he did for the club there is a greater tendency to focus on the mistakes he made - notably, being part of the process that left Rovers in the hands of Venky's. Personally, I am happy to accept that anyone can get a judgment call wrong but the deafening silence that has followed his departure has been the real source of my disappointment. Non-disclosure agreement or not, he was at Rovers in the crucial period between the summer of 2010 and January 2011 and I still feel there are many dots in this story that he could help the fans join up. It is a shame that this has to sour memories of the good times he oversaw but the fact is that it does. Part of me hopes that John Williams will put this right and offer a little bit more insight in to the process that brought Venky's to the club and then the chain of events that followed. I know that John Williams is one of the good guys. I have spoken to dozens of people connected with Rovers and without exception they have all spoke highly of the man.

Following the departure of Williams, Mrs Desai told the *Lancashire Telegraph,*

> "I think that after Sam left, John lost a lot of interest in the club. After that happened I think he knew that he wanted to move on. I know that he did not get along with Steve (Kean) and he had struggled to accept Jerome (Anderson)'s role at the club."

I wasn't really buying that John Williams had lost a lot of interest in the club but why wasn't he coming out to defend himself against these slurs on his professionalism? Allardyce revealed in 2012 that departing staff all agreed to not say anything bad about each other in public. Did the agreement only work one way? This agreement has been little help to the Rovers cause and the wall of silence that exists around Venky's is an area of grave concern. Despite fears amongst fans that the club is not being run in a way that makes results on the pitch the number one priority we have just had to feed of the scraps of information that have leaked out whilst our club continues to go backwards.

On 15 January 2012, Nick Harris of the *Mail on Sunday* revealed a letter sent to Mrs Desai on 4 January 2011 that quite clearly showed that there was far more to John Williams' departure than the claim that he had lost interest. The fascinating two page letter sent by three Executive Directors (Chairman John Williams, Managing Director Tom Finn and Finance Director Martin Goodman) was made available in full on the *Sportingintelligence* website. In the letter the three directors questioned what their role now was at Blackburn Rovers and wanted to know why they were not being consulted on fundamental decisions like the appointment of the new manager. They expressed their concern that the manager had been given the instruction to no longer report to the board on transfer matters. Bear in mind that we weren't talking about Arsene Wenger here - we were talking about a guy whose most senior role previous to this was as Chris Coleman's assistant at Fulham. Williams, Finn and Goodman wanted Kean to report directly to the board through the Chairman who would then seek approval from the owners - a model that had worked successfully for Rovers in the past and been best practice for clubs at our level. They advised that it would become difficult to present a united front to shareholders if they continued to be marginalised and voiced concern about an upcoming catch-up meeting with Barclays as they didn't actually know what the strategy was for the current transfer window. It wasn't just Rovers fans that were confused as to the role SEM were playing in transfers. The letter closed with this paragraph,

> "Finally our football secretary has this morning been instructed by SEM to issue a mandate to a third party without any reference or approval from the board. We are not familiar with the player concerned nor is he one that has been mentioned to us by the manager. Could you please therefore clarify the role of SEM in our transfer policy?"

I don't know if Williams, Finn and Goodman got their answers but they were all out of a job within six months. More changes followed. We had already seen Gandhi Babu and Mahesh Gupta appointed to the board of directors but anybody who knows their whereabouts please get in touch. Vineeth Rao, no relation to the Venky family, was also added to the board in August 2011. Vineeth was meant to be the link between England and India and Rovers fans were told that this was the man that gave the staff in England hour by hour access to the owners. When questioned on whether he was based in England or India, one member of the Rovers board interestingly declared, "both". Vineeth was a family friend of Venky's and at times I wondered if this was the famous football expert that had been mentioned during their first few months at the club. He might have known more about football than Mrs Desai but the recently graduated student of Osmania University, Hyderbad, was still some way short of Williams, Finn and Goodman - about 100 years short. In truth, Vineeth came to be looked upon as a figure of fun by many Rovers fans. Not only did he regularly post cringeworthy photos of himself on Facebook (including the day the day he met Hitler at the waxworks) but he was also known to have conversations with fans that exposed his chronic lack of knowledge of football at the highest level. Kean said that as manager he had final say on transfers but all the signs were that Vineeth and new Sporting Director Simon Hunt were the main driving force behind transfers. I didn't hold out much hope with Vineeth so I just hoped that Simon Hunt had the ability and authority to take control of transfers and at the same time bring in a few decent players. The actual announcement about Simon Hunt's arrival was pretty low key, something that Kean himself mentioned a few months later when the Director of Football rumours started. Like Kean, there was nothing earth shattering about Simon Hunt's achievements in the game. He had worked underneath George Burley at Southampton between 2005 and 2007 and then took the role of Sporting Director at West Brom in 2007. He was only in the West Brom job for six months before leaving for family reasons. In his short time at West Brom the club was involved in close to £50 million worth of incoming and outgoing transfers. A remarkable amount of money to be going in and out of any club - let alone one that was in The Championship. After leaving West Brom, Simon Hunt worked at as a international scout at Ipswich for 12 months. Between leaving Ipswich in 2009 and joining Rovers in the summer of 2011 Simon Hunt was a Director of Hunt Consultancy (Southampton) Ltd but the company was dissolved shortly before he took the Rovers job.

The changes behind the scenes at Rovers continued throughout the summer. The club severed links with their accountants of over 100 years - Blackburn-based PM&M, a new club doctor arrived, 27 year-old Anthony Bloch became the youngest club secretary in the Premier League and David Lowe came in from Tranmere to become the club's head of youth coaching. Finance Director Karen Silk from Stoke City wasn't actually appointed until the end of of the year. Rovers did retain a handful of senior staff from the Walker Trust days. Robert Coar needed to remain on the Blackburn Rovers board in order to retain his position at the Football Association. Ken Beamish stayed on in his role as Commercial Manager and John Newsham kept hold of his job as Stadium Manager. The profile of press officer Paul Agnew seemed to rise significantly after the arrival of Venky's. I found it odd that Agnew's prominence at the club seemed to coincide with the quite apparent breakdown in public relations with the fans. Agnew established a close working relationship with Kean and having gone out to visit Venky's in February 2011, shortly afterwards he was even answering questions about becoming the next Chief Executive. In April 2011, Agnew told *Sky Sports News*,

> "I don't know if they are looking for someone in that position or whether they want to restructure it. They want to see me and ask me if I want to talk about anything. I don't know what they have in mind but I am interested to hear what they want to say. I believe there is a job to be done in communication because that is going to be key."

Press officer to Chief Executive appeared an even bigger leap than first team coach to manager. It was a leap Agnew was familiar with having enjoyed a similar rise at Preston North End earlier in his career. I am always quite wary of people who play such a significant role in handling the public relations of figures who are as unpopular as Steve Kean. Agnew said he was a Blackburn fan of 45 years but he wasn't being paid for being a fan. In the years that I first started going to Rovers, he was actually writing books about Tom Finney and Preston North End. Having started out at the now defunct Blackburn Times in the 1970s, as well as running his PR company Paul Agnew Public Relations (PAPR) Agnew had been a regular sports writer for the Sunday Mirror.

People have found it very difficult to get inside the inner circle at Rovers to find out exactly what has motivated all these changes and to find out why the owners have continued to show faith in a group of staff that has ultimately failed to deliver on the pitch. Some have said it is cost cutting. Looking at the club accounts for 2011, I am not so sure. According to the figures on the Financial Report, in 2010 Rovers had 3 executive directors who between them were paid a total of £700,000 in salaries, rising to £796,903 with Pension and Benefits with the highest paid of the three receiving a total of £358,387. In 2011, there were four executive directors who between them were paid a total of £599,933 in salaries rising to £699,053 with Pension and Benefits with the highest paid of the three receiving a total of £290,566. This is indeed an annual saving until you take into account the £671,451 compensation for loss of office – payments made to directors who have left. The number of staff employed at Blackburn Rovers in 2011 is also very similar to what it was in 2010.

Number of Staff at Blackburn Rovers

	2011	2010
Senior Football Players and Management	76	76
Academy Football Players and Management	60	52
Commercial, Sponsorship, Media and Merchandising	54	53
Adminstration	24	23
Building, Ground and Pitch Maintenance	49	49
TOTAL	263	253

This only makes the departure of former board members even more baffling. As John Williams said, is there simply a new way of doing things?

The feeling is that a lot of the big decisions are made in the monthly meetings Kean travels to India for. Not only do we have little idea what is discussed in these meetings we don't even actually know who attends them. I have approached many of the key figures in the story and asked them for their take on the last two years. In the main, my requests have been ignored, declined or countered with a solicitor's letter. Unfortunately, what snippets of information have come out of Ewood Park do not reflect well at all on the people that are now there. When Keith Andrews left Rovers for West Brom in January 2012 Neil Moxley of the *Daily Mail* gave the most comprehensive account of Andrews' feelings on Venky-run Rovers:

> "I went to Ipswich and loved it. But when I went back to Ewood Park there was no communication. They were of the impression I'd be out playing against

Fulham when I came back from Ipswich. But I told them I had no inclination to play for that club again after the way they had treated me. I told them that I wanted to leave the club and he (Steve Kean) was fine with that, which might indicate that it wasn't his decision. Certain people at the club wanted me in the team. They had seen me scoring goals in The Championship and they wanted me back in the team. Whether they thought the Championship was a higher division than the Premier League, I'm not too sure."

Asked whether he would be surprised at the rumours that Venky's did not know whether or not the club could be relegated, Andrews answered,

"Not in the slightest. I've never really had any dealings with the owners. There's so many financial directors, sporting directors and god-knows-what directors at that club. It's a shame the way it has gone. I'm glad I'm out of there."

This was a completely different picture to the one Kean was painting and a lot of credit has to go to Andrews for being one of the few people who has actually been prepared to stand up and speak out. Andrews turned his back on close to a million pounds when he walked away from his contract at Rovers and with this he appeared to retain his basic right to speak his own mind.

Back at Ewood Park and while all these new faces were arriving during 2011, the experienced heads that had brought so much success to the club were being thrown away like flat batteries. Managing Director

Tom Finn resigned from his post shortly after the end of the 2010/11 season. By this stage Rovers' Premier League status had been secured and the club had announced one of the cheapest season tickets in the Football League for the forthcoming season. Sadly his departure had looked somewhat inevitable since Williams left earlier in the year. Finn had been at the club for 15 years and was instrumental in helping set up the club's Academy. It was reported that Finn had also played a significant part in the subsidised match tickets for our final game of the season against Wolves and it was a personal touch that had all the hallmarks of a man that was very much in touch with the fans. Finn was a popular figure amongst players, fans and colleagues and Venky's apparent disdain for his vast experience made little sense. Finn has been another, however, who has shed little light on what was going on behind the scenes at Venky-run Rovers. When asked by a Rovers fan on Twitter, "are you allowed to share some information about what went on under the ownership of Venky's" Finn's reply of, "Not really and future that matters (sic)" was another blow for the fans.

Once Finn resigned from his post Rovers quickly descended into a national joke. Selling the club's best players and replacing them with cut-price alternatives was the root of most Rovers fans anger but our problems weren't just limited to the transfer market. Nobody appeared to be running the club with any sort of real leadership and over the summer there was a whole catalogue of incidents that ranged from the embarrassing to the totally unacceptable. In a clear cost cutting move Venky's made the position of Chief Executive redundant and appointed Paul Hunt to take up the role of Deputy Chief Executive. Paul Hunt had been employed at Bolton, Wigan and Leicester but, much like Kean and all the other new faces, there was little to suggest that this was a man who was ready to be handed ultimate responsibility for the day-to-day running of a Premier League football club. Were we now meant to believe that Venky's had entrusted Paul Hunt with the duties of both John Williams and Tom Finn? Anyone who you felt may have had the gravitas to say no to Venky's and their people had gone and a real vacuum of power had emerged. Venky's were now free to do with Blackburn Rovers whatever they liked and they were soon recruiting members of Rovers playing staff for the fried chicken advert that has come to symbolise the Venky era at the club. There were things I wanted to see happen at Rovers over the summer of 2011 but David Dunn and Jason Roberts racing each other to the changing room to eat chicken drumsticks wasn't one of them. They may have been licking their lips and nodding but Salgado gave an interesting insight in to what chicken lollipops really tasted like when he told *Four Four Two* magazine the following month, "I had to pretend to love it but the truth is, one bite and my stomach was in knots!" Was this the same football club I used to watch from a wall or just a cheap marketing tool for second generation millionaires? Never mind what the Burnley fans had to say, even the Accrington Stanley fans were getting involved. One suggested that the embarrassing advert, shot in the changing rooms of Ewood Park, was a punishment for pulling out of a planned pre-season visit to India. The Rovers squad were due to fly out to India prior to taking part in the Asia Trophy in Hong Kong. The plan was to fly out to

Mumbai and then travel to Pune to play an exhibition game and do a few public appearances in and around the Venky family base. At one point Kean had even said that Rovers would be playing Brazilian giants Flamengo. Terrorist bombings in Mumbai shortly before the planned trip threw the tour in to doubt and Rovers eventually pulled out the day before they were scheduled to leave. Tabloid speculation was rife that the trip was cancelled because a handful of senior professional just didn't want to go. An announcement that the trip had been re-scheduled for October, when most senior players would be away on international duty, did little to quash these rumours.

Stories like Steve Kean's drink-drive charge and David Dunn being handcuffed to a dwarf were becoming more common in the national newspapers. In isolation, they probably would have slipped under the radar but in these difficult times it was difficult to argue that they did much to enhance the club's rapidly diminishing reputation. In August 2011, the *Daily Mirror's* Alan Nixon even claimed that four of Rovers unwanted players were being touted around other clubs in a brochure that had been produced to try and get them off Rovers' books. Not only this but the brochure concerned gave full details of the four players' wages. I haven't seen the brochure so you would have to ask Nixon how true this one was but we were told El-Hadji Doiuf was on £30,000 a week plus £5,000 a game; Grella £30,000 a week plus £6,000 a game; Keith Andrews £21,000 a week, rising every five games, plus £2,000 a game and a one-off yearly payment of £26,667 and Nikola Kalinic a flat rate of £30,000 a week. I am sure that this did not go down very well with the four players involved, or the rest of the playing staff. Andrews later said that he was under the impression that he was going to feature in the club's long-term plans until his agent found out otherwise. Nixon claimed that Rovers tried to deny the existence of the brochure but it became difficult when he told them that he had seen the brochure with his own eyes. Even more shocking than the brochure itself was the claim by Nixon that Krish Naidoo, the boss of a nightclub in Dublin, was the man who was touting the brochure around. As a Rovers fan, the whole sorry story left me lost for words.

Our three- year sponsorship deal with Crown Paints had been reported to have been worth £5 million. At the start of 2011, when Crown Paints said they would not be renewing, the clear message coming out of Blackburn Rovers was that the search for a commercial sponsor started here. By the time the new home strip was due to come out in August they still didn't have one. Shortly after came the announcement that we had given our shirt sponsorship for the season to The Prince's Trust. Of all the things at Blackburn Rovers I wouldn't have minded giving to charity (one of the players in that brochure would have been a good start) a shirt sponsorship deal worth well over a million pounds wasn't one of them. Rovers may have gained kudos for giving the club's shirt sponsorship to charity but one high profile Rovers fan has publicly stated that Kentaro were meant to be providing the shirt sponsorship deal but the deal didn't materialise. The announcement was made so late that when our new shirt eventually came out, the sponsor had to be ironed on after you had bought it. It was hardly surprising that

Barclays were cranking up the pressure on Rovers when so much money was being lost to bad decisions and mismanagement. The shirt sponsorship fiasco was indicative of the rapid decline in Rovers commercial activities.

The club had started to forget the little touches that had made fans feel they were part of a family club. Jack Walker's legendary status at Blackburn Rovers cannot be overstated. His money, foresight and passion is the reason Rovers fans have enjoyed Premier League football for 17 of the last 19 seasons and the principal reason Venky's had a club worth buying in the first place. Recognising the anniversary of his death with some kind of fitting tribute from the club may not have seemed a big deal to the newcomers but to Rovers fans the one line acknowledgement and old photo of his statue that appeared on the club website half way through the day was a long way from being good enough.

I wanted to know who these intruders were at the club that meant so much so many people. I could not see what connection they had to the town of Blackburn. For me, the club may have belonged to Venky's on paper but the heart and soul of Blackburn Rovers Football Club is the people who were here 10 years ago and the people who will still be here in 10 years time. All the rest are just doing a job. What do normal fans do when they are totally exasperated with their club? I am not a member of any supporters groups or forums; I don't have any connections to anyone in power at the club. Like thousands of other Rovers fans, I am just a normal bloke who enjoys going to Rovers. One day, if my son is interested, I want him to be able to enjoy the same opportunity. With all that was going on at Blackburn Rovers, it now felt like this basic birthright was seriously under threat. During the course of the 2011/12 season certain people in the media tried to paint a picture of Rovers fans that just isn't true. Rovers fans could see as early as the summer of 2011 that things were going badly wrong and all we wanted was a little help putting things right. Rovers fans had always been happy to let senior figures get on with their jobs but why should we just throw our money in to the pot and keep quiet now that we didn't like the direction the club was heading? For whatever reason, people weren't exactly clambering over one another to come to our rescue and the list of media personalities that consistently backed Rovers fans is unsurprisingly short. A lot of people back-tracked once it became clear that the fans were right to be voicing their concerns all along but when Rovers fans needed help in many cases it wasn't forthcoming.

It was the feeling of helplessness around the summer of 2011 that ultimately spawned the beginnings of this book. Around the same time that I was making a start on the book, frustrated Rovers fans were coming together to form the very early beginnings of the BRFC Action Group and the Blackburn Rovers Supporters Investment Trust was also just around the corner. This wasn't the beginning of a campaign of hate as some chose to report it. This was the start of a campaign that really showed the depth of affection Rovers fans have for the club. Around this time, I ended up putting all my frustrations down in an e-mail and sending it to the address on the Rovers website. I challenged the club to give me a reason to renew my season ticket when it just felt like I was throwing money in to a big black hole of uncertainty and suspicion. I knew that I was going to get a season ticket but I just needed to get it down on record that I would be buying one because I was a Rovers fan not because I supported the way Venky's appeared to be running my town's football club like a 3rd 11 pub team. A week later and I still hadn't received a reply so I revised my demands and challenged Rovers to simply respond to e-mails. We hear plenty of guff about the importance of the fans but you find out how important you are when you ask for something.

At least this time I got a reply - in fact I got two. One was an out of office auto-reply from Paul Hunt and the other was an out-of office auto reply from his secretary. It wasn't all bad news, Paul Hunt would be back in a week and one of his other secretaries was still available. Unbelievable. This only served to make me even angrier. The start of the season was just weeks away and the person we were meant to believe was responsible for the day-to-day running of the entire club was off on holiday. I couldn't take this any longer. I sent a reply saying I would rather spend my season ticket money playing golf (I have never played 18 holes of golf in my life!) than continue funding this shambles. I asked what was going on in the transfer market and how long Venky's thought people would take them seriously if they continued to fail to deliver on promises. Rovers were by now on a major drive to boost season ticket sales and over the next week or so I got a few cut and paste responses to my questions. Nothing about the answers I received gave me any confidence that the people that were now running Blackburn Rovers were able to take us in the right direction. I wasn't looking for spin and smart ways of avoiding important questions - I was looking for a bit of straight-talking truth.

I sent Paul Hunt one final e-mail and within 24 hours he was in touch to initiate a chat. We arranged a meeting and he came round to my house just before the start of the season. It might seem incomprehensible to fans of other Premier League clubs for senior figures of a football club to go on house calls but this is how it has always been done at Blackburn Rovers. We are a proper club - or at least we used to be. Tom Finn and John Williams built up trust with the fans by being available to discuss concerns by e-mail, phone or face-to-face when needed. It was one of the key things that set Williams and Finn apart from your average football chiefs and equally helped set Rovers apart from many of our lesser-achieving rivals. Paul Hunt will have been made aware of this practice and was at least making some effort to honour his predecessor's methods. Paul Hunt has since expressed his disappointment that fans have felt the need to go public with details of private conversations. He would have more to worry about when people started leaking his emails. Personally, I don't see what the big secret is all about. We didn't discuss anything he wouldn't have been expecting to be asked in a press conference and, in any case, my concern is with the long-term future of Blackburn Rovers Football Club.

To Paul Hunt's credit, he didn't just pop his head through the door and go. He was prepared to spend time discussing the points I wished to make. Basically, I just wanted to know what was going on and what I could expect from the forthcoming season. At the time of our conversation Rovers had already sold Phil Jones to Manchester United and Kalinic was also on his way out of the club. The combined transfer fees for these two players alone were well in excess of £20 million. Not only were the owners not putting any of their own money in to the club - they didn't even appear to be re-investing funds from outgoing transfers. The only players we had signed at this point were unknowns of debatable pedigree from weaker leagues with absolutely no Premier League experience. The worry was that more players were on their way out. Paul Hunt said he would be amazed if Samba went and he was also confident that Hoilett would soon be putting pen-to-paper on a new deal. I asked why we hadn't tried to sign Jermaine Jones and Mame Biram Diouf. He said that at 29 years old Jermaine Jones was too old and newly signed Petrovic would fill the gap left by him anyway. Of Mame Biram Diouf he said he didn't really earn his money at Rovers last year and he was a strange signing by Fergie in the first place. He tipped Formica, Rochina and Goodwillie to come good this season. I advised him of all the players with better records than Goodwillie who had come down from Scotland and failed to make the grade. Paul Hunt said that Goodwillie was a good player from a poor league. He said that our first team was top 10 comfortably and we only just missed out on a top 10 place in 2010/11. I reminded him that we were 90 minutes from relegation last season with a better team than we had now. When pressed, Paul Hunt admitted that Rovers would be "knackered" if the transfer window closed today. I asked what was happening with dead wood like Goulon and Vince Grella. I was told that Goulon was on his way out and Grella was back fit again. Paul

Hunt claimed that there were a few journalists out to get Rovers. He also said Kean and Fergie "are all right with each other" because they are from the same area. I didn't really care whether Kean was friends with Fergie or not to be honest. I asked why we sold Phil Jones to Manchester United. At this point he was saved by a phone call. It was Kean.

I am not making any of this up by the way - it actually happened. I sat there for the best part of 10 minutes with Paul Hunt sat opposite, talking to Kean about trying to sign players on loan from Manchester City. It was like listening to two students playing a game of *Championship Manager*. Eventually Kean stopped jabbering and Paul Hunt's attention was back in the room. I asked him why we sold Phil Jones to Manchester United for £16.5 million when there were bigger offers on the table. He said that a release clause was put in his contract in January because Rovers feared he was going to go to Chelsea for £8 million. Rovers wanted to hold out for £25 million but Jones wanted to go to Manchester United. Rovers had been held to ransom by Phil Jones and his agent in January. They had seen Venky's takeover as their opportunity to "bust a deal out" while there was division at the club. Paul Hunt then attempted to focus on the players we did still have. He said that David Dunn had just had his best pre-season ever. I said that Dunn was poor last season. Paul Hunt said his heart wasn't in it and Allardyce's long ball game didn't really suit him. I told him that Dunn actually played his best football under Allardyce and his dip in form seemed to coincide with the arrival of Kean. Paul Hunt then admitted that he was just playing Devil's Advocate and I knew more than him. I advised him that Nelsen and Salgado had been great servants at Rovers but they were past it and their legs would probably go half way through the season. He laughed and said they would both be fine. He told me that we were hopeful of re-signing Benjani. I told him not to bother. I said, instead of signing players like Benjani why didn't Kean insist on a players plus cash deal when Phil Jones went to Manchester United. I would have taken any combination of John O'Shea, Wes Brown, Gabriel Obertan, Mame Biram Diouf and even Darron Gibson and Federicho Macheda if they were going cheap. Paul Hunt declared that Rovers had first refusal on all these players but he and Kean felt that none of them were good enough for the Rovers squad. Oh dear. In the end, we chatted about football for the best part of an hour and, all in all, I got a lot of the information I was looking for.

Anybody still buying in to the myth that everybody who is employed in football is worth every penny of their salary could probably benefit from spending an hour in the company of a senior employee at their club. I went down to the ticket office that week to buy my season ticket but I made sure I took a detour past the bookies. Rovers were now 7/2 to be relegated and this was the easiest £100 I have ever spent. If there were people at the club who honestly thought that players like John O'Shea, Jermaine Jones and even Mame Biram Diouf couldn't offer us more than Myles Anderson, Benjani and a handful of untested foreigners then, when you considered all the other stuff that was going on off the pitch and took last year's final day escape into account, I just couldn't see how we hoped to avoid relegation. I sent e-mails to all the other names on the board - people like Gandhi Babu and Mahesh Gupta. These were now key members of the Blackburn Rovers new order but nobody knew anything about them. Bizarrely, it was Paul Hunt who answered every one of my e-mails, no matter who it was addressed to. It didn't add up. Why was such a senior figure at a company with a multi-million pound turnover spending his time responding to other people's e-mails? I feared that our Deputy Chief Executive was just another minor player running around putting out fires.

Chapter 11

On the Pitch (August 2011 - October 2011)

Normally the start of the season brings about feelings of hope, joy and excitement. I can recall many a season and not even that long ago when regardless of how unproductive the summer had been, as far as I was concerned, UEFA Cup qualification was definitely on the cards until at least November. Fans of some clubs get it worse than others. I remember all the Spurs fans that came on *talkSPORT* in 2008 predicting big things because they had just beat Roma 5-0 in a pre-season friendly. Two months later they were bottom of the Premier League with two points from eight games. You've got to laugh but it is this kind of optimism that makes football what it is. As I made my way down to Ewood Park for the first game of 2011/12 - forget feelings of hope, joy and excitement - I would be lying if I said I felt anything other than the feeling you get just before a car crash. Senior members of Rovers' staff were still asking fans to judge the club at the end of the transfer window. Fans tend to judge their club from the first game of the season and strange requests like this did not bode well for the three otherwise winnable Premier League fixtures we had to fulfil in the meantime. I had seen the Rovers line-up before leaving the house and I was left with more questions than answers. Robinson started in goal; Salgado and Martin Olsson were at full-back. Samba, Nelsen and Givet were all unavailable for whatever reason. With the departure of Phil Jones, Rovers had only two centre-backs to choose from. It was no shock to see Myles Anderson left out of the starting 11 and whether his hand had been forced or not, Kean's decision to partner Hanley with Nzonzi had calamity written all over it. Hanley had been the club's fifth choice centre-back earlier in the year and here he was being asked to partner a guy who was a midfielder for a reason. Kean opted for a five-man midfield made up of Dunn, Emerton, Pedersen, Hoilett and debutant Formica; Roberts started up front on his own. The seven substitutes named had a total of three Premier League appearances between them. If anyone was still in any doubt about the extent of the rapidly snowballing crisis at Blackburn Rovers then the opening game of the 2011/12 season would surely provide yet more evidence.

The fixtures had paired us up against the same Wolverhampton Wanderers that we had comfortably brushed aside on the final day of 2010/11. A lot had happened in the intervening 12 weeks and whilst Wolves had undoubtedly strengthened, few observers were ready to argue that Rovers had gone anywhere other than backwards. Rovers actually started the game quite well. Hennessey made a smart save from Hoilett early on and following good work from Roberts, Formica slotted home a well-taken opener on 20 minutes. Unfortunately, Rovers had peaked with 70 minutes still to go. Wolves levelled almost immediately and it was ex-Burnley beanpole Steven Fletcher who rose above Salgado to nod home from close range. Both sides had half chances but it was Wolves who took the lead at the start of the second half. Again it was Salgado who found himself under the cosh. The last thing a 35-year-old full back wants to see is a young winger attacking him at pace. When Salgado forced Matt Jarvis to the ground the referee had no hesitation in pointing to the spot. Robinson saved Kevin Doyle's penalty but Rovers failed to clear and within 10 seconds Stephen Ward had fired home a sweetly struck volley. Wolves were the better team from here on in and although Rovers created the odd chance there was absolutely no cutting edge. When Goodwillie was called from the bench on 70 minutes he ran on to the pitch like a dog that needed a wee. Nothing gets the crowd going like the sight of a new guy charging on to the pitch like he has three seconds to save the world but we saw little else from our £3 million striker. Rovers failed to find an equaliser and in the end Wolves ran out comfortable winners. No disrespect to Wolves but if we weren't ready for the start of the season, part of me wished we had been playing against one of the top four because Wolves at home was a game we needed to pick up points from.

Kean did manage to pick up a few points during the week but unfortunately it was for a drink driving offence. He was banned from the road for 18 months and quickly added "driver" to the list of things he needed to buy before the close of the transfer window. By the time we played Aston Villa that weekend at least Ryan Nelsen was back, allowing Nzonzi to return to his usual midfield role. This turned out to be Nelsen's last ever game for Rovers. As had now become a pattern, Kean dropped a goal scorer to the bench and Formica made way for Goodwille. I couldn't understand the logic behind the decision to play one up front at home to Wolves and then Roberts and Goodwillie together away at Aston Villa. We used to have the SAS; now we had RAG. I couldn't see it working. Rovers' dreadful recent record at Villa Park continued. Villa were 2-0 up after 25 minutes and although Rovers pulled one back just after half-time courtesy of a thumping Pedersen header, a mistake at the back by Hanley on 67 minutes allowed Darren Bent in for Villa's third. You didn't need to be sitting in the stands at Villa Park to know that this was game over. As I have said earlier I go to as many games as I can but it is just not possible for a man on an average Blackburn wage to support a family, a mortgage and 19 away days a season. I am down to home games, five away games a year and following the remaining games any way I can. I listened to this one on *Absolute Radio* and for most of the first-half I couldn't work out who Villa were playing. This is no criticism of Tony Dorigo's commentary skills - by all accounts Rovers weren't really at the races for large parts of the game. Watching the game back on *Sky Sports* later that night only served to confirm this. At this point the fans were still under the impression that results would determine our manager's future and Kean was now favourite with bookmakers to be the first Premier League manager to get the sack. Already Kean was trotting out the age-old rhetoric about injuries and understanding fans' frustrations. If this was the case he would be best advised not to come out with statements like this,

> "Looking at the stats after the game we are in Villa's box 36 times and they are in our box 36 times. They have had 11 shots and we have had nine. I don't think there was anything in the game."

This kind of talk may have impressed some but it impressed few Rovers fans I came in to contact with and the "Kean Out" campaign was just around the corner.

A thick gloom had descended around Ewood Park and Rovers badly needed a win to lift spirits. The transfer window was entering its final week and the fans were yet to see anything like the big spending we had been told to expect. The midweek visit of League One Sheffield Wednesday provided a bit of respite from rigours of the Premier League and gave Rovers fans a chance to get a better look at the few of the players we had actually signed. In the end a mixture of first team players and squad members quickly dispatched the visitors and the game was all over after seven minutes. Rovers raced in to a three-goal lead thanks to two smart finishes from Rochina and a well-taken third from Goodwillie. Sheffield Wednesday managed to pull one back in the second half but Rovers had done enough to show that, at the very least, we had the makings of a decent League One side. Just as the fans got ready to celebrate the first win of the season the night's result became overshadowed by the announcement that Brett Emerton would be leaving Rovers to return to Australia. Only three days earlier Kean had claimed that a lack of experience had cost us at Aston Villa and here we were giving away a bloke who had made almost 300 appearances for the club. We were effectively losing quality, experience and versatility all in one go. *BBC Radio Lancashire* put it to Kean, "Does it make it a nightmare to replace him, bearing in mind you are losing three positions at least?" Kean acknowledged that Emerton had been a model pro - then pointed out that Vukcevic and Ribeiro had now been brought in.

Emerton was made captain for the visit of Everton and, like Nelsen the week before; this would be Emerton's final game for Rovers. The high earners were dropping like flies. Emerton had been a great servant to Blackburn Rovers and he was given a fitting send off by the fans. That is not to say that many fans weren't more than just a little angry that the powers-that-be had given away a player that still had plenty to offer the team. We were told that Emerton had gone for family reasons rather than football reasons but that didn't appear to be his manager Simon Konstantinidis' take on it. Konstantinidis told the *Sydney Herald*,

> "If he was offered an attractive contract, he may well have stayed another year. Those things are speculation at the moment. We knew from the outset Sydney can't pay a transfer fee. It was always on the table and made clear and transparent to everyone

concerned, including us. We can't speak to you and do a deal if we have to pay a transfer fee."

For all the talk of letting Emerton go back home for family reasons I was quite clear that Venky's were just chopping another high earner off the wage bill. Even Emerton's new club couldn't get over how accommodating Rovers were being. Sydney FC chief Dirk Melton said of the transfer negotiations,

> "The spirit which they've undertaken this transfer negotiation has been incredible. I personally look forward to going over there and having a beer with the CEO, Paul Hunt, and saying thank you."

It seemed an expensive beer to me considering Emerton's ability and all round value to the club. Why wasn't more done to keep him at Rovers for just a few more months? Even if we could have kept hold of him until January surely that would have given the new players chance to acclimatise. From the fans' point of view it was another baffling development. Whatever anyone may claim, going to play out the final days of your career in Australia is retiring from football at the highest level and I just wasn't buying it that Emerton was as keen on this move as Rovers were making out.

Unfortunately, Emerton failed to get the final day result his many years of service deserved. Rovers welcomed back the central defensive pairing of Samba and Givet and straight away we looked a more solid unit. Everton were a club with their own off-field frustrations and for large parts of the game it showed. The visitors had plenty of decent players but they seemed to be missing the spark of a "what-would-Steven-do-Pienaar" type player. Rovers overran them for long periods and considering how bad we had been in our previous two Premier League games I was somewhat surprised that our opponents weren't putting up more of a fight. The game ultimately hinged on three penalties. The first was awarded to Rovers for a foul on Formica midway through the game. With regular penalty taker Dunn having been withdrawn with injury shortly after the half-hour mark it wasn't entirely clear who would take the resulting spot-kick. I can think of five different players (Hoilett, Formica, Dunn, Yakubu and Roberts) that ended up taking penalties for Rovers during the 2011/12 season. Roberts later claimed that a stand-in penalty taker hadn't actually been named - a shocking oversight by the management if true. In the end it was Hoilett who did the honours and Tim Howard comfortably saved his lame effort. Rovers continued to press and with less than 10 minutes to go we were awarded a second penalty for another foul on Formica. This time it was Formica himself who stepped up to take it but he too failed to score. Kean has referred back to this game more times than I can remember but the plain facts are that missing penalties cannot be fully blamed on bad luck. The players have to give themselves a chance by first of all knowing who is taking the penalty and in the case of Formica, hitting the target. The rest involves some element of luck but if you get two penalties and miss them both it's hard to blame it entirely on misfortune. Having played pretty poorly up to that point it was almost inevitable that Everton would now sneak a winner. Deep in to injury time, referee Lee

Mason inexplicably pointed to the spot for a third penalty. This time it was Everton who benefitted. Samba was adjudged to have fouled Everton's Marouane Fellaini and although David Moyes claimed that it looked more of a penalty than Formica's two dives there were few who agreed with him. Even the television sofa-monkeys said it wasn't a penalty. Mikel Arteta showed Rovers how it should be done and with pretty much his last kick in an Everton shirt he slotted home to give the Toffees all three points. Whether the result had been harsh or not, defeat left Rovers rooted to the foot of the Premier League with zero points from three games. Kean was untroubled by Rovers start to the season but I thought it was about time he started to get real. We weren't going to get in the UEFA Champions League; we weren't going to get into Europe and we weren't going to finish in the top 10. We were in a relegation scrap and it was time he was troubled by it. Rovers had been bottom of the Premier League before but this was different. When we picked up just two points from our opening four games in 2006/07 there were no calls for manager Mark Hughes to be sacked. Fans recognised that Hughes was the best man for the job. Back in 2006, we could see that the slow start to the season was no more than a short-term blip and we fully trusted Hughes to take us up the table. The same could not be said of Kean. Whereas Hughes had shown that he could win Premier League games, bought and sold wisely, set and achieved realistic targets, made a connection with the fans and worked alongside a board that the fans knew and trusted to get the best out of the players, we were seeing none of these attributes from Kean. With Kean it became clear to anyone who was following Rovers game by game that the slow start to the 2011/12 season was not a short-term blip. The power of positive thought was starting to come across as pure delusion and I personally started to feel that it was of no benefit to the club. Our league position was a consequence of how the club was now being run and Kean's management. Whatever role Kean did or didn't have in the decision-making process the fact remained that he was the very public face and voice of the new order.

Rovers' poor start to the season prompted an open letter from fans asking the owners to relieve the manager of his duties with immediate effect. The letter, put together by members of the *Vital Blackburn* website highlighted the growing frustration amongst Rovers fans. The transfer window had now closed and although we had seen the addition of Scott Dann and Yakubu, for all the big talk the only thing that Kean appeared to have excelled in during his eight months in charge was losing games and talking jive. The open letter was soon receiving national exposure thanks to an article by Henry Winter in the *Daily Telegraph.* With plans under way for a demonstration prior to the home game against Arsenal in two weeks time this would be the start of the ongoing fight for change at Blackburn Rovers.

Rovers' next opponents Fulham had also suffered a difficult start to the season. New manager Martin Jol was still to win a game and there were already grumblings coming out of Craven Cottage. Sky had chosen a bit of a stinker for the 4 o'clock Sunday game and there were few predicting a classic here. There was a Rovers debut for Dann; and Givet replaced Martin Olsson at left-back. Both sides looked nervy from the off and there was little quality on show until Ruben Rochina lit up the game with a stunning goal just after the half-hour. Rovers lead was short-lived and six minutes later Bobby Zamora levelled for Fulham. The home side had much the better of the play from this point but they created few clear-cut chances and Rovers held on for a point. The subject of Rovers' under-fire manager continued to dominate conversations amongst Rovers fans and failure to get a win against Fulham took his Premier League win percentage to 20% after 25 games in charge. Kean said after the game,

> "I'm happy with the squad and I think we will finish in the top half. I'm sure if the fans stay with us they will see plenty more performances away from home like that where we take three points instead of one."

I had watched Rovers finish in the top 10 of the Premier League 10 times in 19 seasons. Like most Rovers fans, I had a fair idea what a top 10 team looked like and it didn't look like this. The fans had kept their frustrations under wraps for nine months of bold statements, baffling decisions and abject failure. There comes a point where enough is enough and it became inevitable that some form of protest would now follow.

17. Norwich	P4	W0	D2	L2	Pts 2
18. Fulham	P4	W0	D2	L2	Pts 2
19. Swansea	P4	W0	D2	L2	Pts 2
20. ROVERS	P4	W0	D1	L3	Pts 1

A call for the removal of Kean on supporters' website *BRFCS* two weeks into the season appeared to have struck a chord with a section of Rovers fans. Venky's were clear that they were here for the long haul. If this was the case then the majority of Rovers fans felt that the removal of Kean was the only way forward. By the week of the Arsenal game the details of the first protest march had been announced and the *Lancashire Telegraph* was reporting that a thousand supporters were expected to take part in a pre-match march against Kean. With the game to kick off at 12.45 pm, season ticket holder and key figure in the organisation of the march Glen Mullan told the *Lancashire Telegraph,*

> "We don't want it to interfere with people coming to the game who don't want to be involved and we want it finished by 12.10pm or 12.15pm so everyone can support the team. It will be a peaceful and professional protest. At a conservative estimate I'd say there will be 1,000-plus on the march. There have been a few people who have said they don't think it's the right thing to do but I've had hundreds of e-mails of support."

Venky's were made aware of the march and issued a statement reminding fans of the importance of getting behind the players as well as reaffirming their own commitment to the club. Balaji and Venkatesh would be in attendance at the Arsenal game and when asked whether Kean's job was safe Venkatesh told the *Lancashire Telegraph,*

> "It's very much safe, there's no problem with Steve. He's a very nice man and I'm sure he'll deliver the

goods. It's been bad luck in the last few matches. In one, two or three matches we will be at number 12."

In the lead up to the game Kean took part in a question and answer session with the chief reporter from the fans website *BRFCS*. Kean answered questions for over half an hour and a recording of the meeting was made available on the *BRFCS* website. Kean expressed his disappointment that the fans planned to demonstrate and confirmed that he had the full backing of the owners. When asked in the pre-match press conference if he had ever contemplated walking away Kean was quite clear, "No, never, not once, not for one minute."

I felt it was a bit like asking a lottery winner if he ever contemplated tearing up his winning ticket.

For all the big build-up, the Arsenal game did not disappoint. The march went ahead as planned and although the turnout was lower than expected the message was clear for all to see. Kean's post-match claims that the low turnout indicated that 99% of fans were happy were way off the mark. There were many reasons for the lower than expected turnout. As well as the horrific weather and early kick-off, many unhappy fans were still buying in to the message that what happens outside the ground an hour before kick-off drastically affects what happens on the pitch once the whistle blows. The protest was well over before the start of the game and Rovers fans did nothing but support the team whole-heartedly from kick-off to full-time. Far from affecting the team's performance, Rovers actually won for the first time all season and the game itself was one of the most entertaining games

I can ever remember. Tactically, Rovers had become like a snooker player that just goes for his shots every time he visits the table. Admittedly, the one frame in 10 that it does come off (like the Liverpool and Wolves games) it does look good - it's just a shame about all the frames you have to lose in between. The Arsenal game was just another case of the carefree approach coming off. The game had everything a great game should have - 34 shots, seven goals, own goals, debut goals, great saves, astonishing misses, managers under fire, David beating Goliath and all live on Sky for the rest of the country to watch and enjoy.

Arsenal were far from the force they used to be but they still had enough quality to expect to beat a Rovers team without a win in the league all season. The first quarter of the game went pretty much as expected and Rovers were lucky to only be one down by the time Salgado limped off on 18 minutes. Despite Arsenal's superior possession, Rovers crept back in to the game and there were excellent chances to score either side of Yakubu's equaliser on 24 minutes. Arsenal stepped it up again and Rovers were chasing shadows for the rest of the first half. Arteta made it 2-1 on 34 minutes and had Gervinho passed to Robin van Persie just before half-time Arsenal surely would have gone in at the break 3-1 up. At half-time the game was still Arsenal's for the taking and there were few sane people who would have predicted the opening 25 minutes of the second half. In a bizarre role-reversal suddenly Rovers went through the gears and ran a shell-shocked Arsenal absolutely ragged. Two Arsenal own goals either side of debutant Yakubu's second meant that, with 20 minutes to go, unbelievably Rovers were 4-2 up and Ewood Park was absolutely rocking. Rovers' fans come in for plenty of stick for the lack of atmosphere at Ewood Park but when everything is going to plan, forget your 70,000-seater stadiums, as any good fan will tell you, there is no better place to be than dancing on your seat in your home ground. The party atmosphere was quickly put on hold as Arsenal got one back through Marouane Chamakh. His well-taken header triggered a 10-minute onslaught only really seen in the closing minutes of a do-or-die cup tie. It was full-on backs-to-the-wall stuff as the Arsenal chances came almost by the minute. In the end Rovers were saved by the full-time whistle and Ewood Park erupted again. The media hailed it a triumph for Kean and suggested that the protests should now stop. Had the fans been protesting about a one-off result then the well-paid ex-pros may have had a point. Rovers' fans were not protesting because they thought we would never win a game ever again - the fans were protesting because since Kean had taken charge we didn't win nearly often enough. Consistently picking up points in the Premier League might change a few opinions but one win every two months wasn't going to take the heat off Kean. Arsene Wenger was quick to offer his support for Rovers' under-fire manager and told Rovers fans to back him. Kean may have drawn consolation from Wenger's words of support but when Mark Hughes was qualifying for Europe every other season I clearly remember a host of visiting manager's, including Wenger, regularly running off to the press room for a public moan. That was the real compliment.

Kean made eight changes for the midweek visit of Leyton Orient in the League Cup. Vukcevic and Nick

Blackman made their Rovers debuts and, although he ultimately hung around until his contract expired, Vince Grella became the third highly paid Antipodean in a month to make his final start for the club. These sort of games can be a real banana skin if you don't approach them in the right way and many a manager has been shown the door following a cup defeat to lower league opposition. If fans thought that Kean was now fearful of getting the sack he didn't look too worried to me and if he was it didn't really show in the team's free flowing attacking display. Rovers had clearly gained confidence from the victory over Arsenal and the final 3-2 score line made the game look closer than it was. There were goals from Roberts, Rochina and debutant Vukcevic on a night when Rovers always looked in control. It may only have been against Leyton Orient but a win is a win and that was two in four days for Rovers.

In the week leading up to the Newcastle game you had to feel for young Robbie Cotton. Kean said he was confident that Hoilett would sign a new contract and Grella would overcome his injury nightmare - he also tipped 17-year-old Cotton to be a big player in Rovers future. I don't know how far into the future Kean was looking but unsurprisingly the new Steven Gerrard didn't make it in to the squad for the weekend's Premier League clash with Newcastle. It looked like the new Steven Gerrard was back in the reserves with the new Denis Irwin, the new Chris Smalling and the new Wayne Rooney while the rest of the squad headed off to St. James' Park. Rovers were now looking for their third win in a week and their sixth in six at the home of the Magpies. Rovers had a strong looking team out and I saw no reason why we couldn't get something from the game. Unfortunately Rovers just didn't turn up on the day. Newcastle's Demba Ba scored a hat-trick and although Rovers had got it back to 2-1 through Hoilett just before half time, Ba's third 10 minutes in to the second half sealed it for the home side. Rovers had been linked with Ba 12 months earlier but for whatever reason the deal didn't happen. Kean blamed bad luck and poor decisions for the 3-1 defeat but I agreed with club captain Chris Samba when he said, "We need to have more will, more heart, we can improve everything, every department."

If you need to improve in every department the last team you want to come up against is the most expensively assembled football team in the world. This is especially the case when your club appears to be lumbering from one crisis to the next almost by the week. The latest crisis was the sudden departure of assistant manager John Jensen. It was unclear why the owners had decided to dispose of the services of Jensen but I hoped that he wasn't being made the fall guy for Kean's failings. As the Manchester City game loomed few Rovers fans were predicting anything other than another defeat. There was a faint glimmer of hope. Earlier in the week City striker Carlos Tevez had caused a stir by appearing to refuse to come off the bench in a UEFA Champions League game and since then all hell had broken loose at the Etihad Stadium. Whilst the departure of Jensen had received few column inches in the national press, the Tevez saga had become a major worldwide news story and the negative attention it was piling on Manchester City was clearly working in Rovers' favour. Over the course of the season, we played so many teams at the right time. I think almost half the clubs we played against were coming off the back of some form of high profile crisis or bad run of form. If we hadn't been in similarly bad shape ourselves we perhaps could have taken more of an advantage.

On the day of the game the weather was unseasonably hot - even in Blackburn. I wasn't really surprised because it always gets hot in Blackburn when I go abroad - which shows how little I go abroad. I watched this one in a bar in Fuerteventura and in fairness it was hotter in the Canaries than it was in East Lancashire. I saw at first-hand how the commercial appeal of certain teams can affect business. There were around 200 people in the bar for the early kick off between Liverpool and Everton. By 3 o'clock the same place had totally emptied and it was just me and a bloke painting the walls for Rovers versus Manchester City. That suited me fine. As I watched the game on Arabic television, shaded from the 90-degree heat in an empty bar, I got the feeling that the stresses of the Tevez affair were playing on the Manchester City players' minds. They just didn't seem to be able to get going. As if the absence of Tevez wasn't enough, on 27 minutes star striker Sergio Aguero limped out of the action. With the game still at 0-0 suddenly everything was falling in to place for Rovers. Dzecko was on the bench but he too was in the bad books for a midweek bust-up with manager Roberto Mancini. Ex-Arsenal man Samir Nasri was brought on to offer support to lone striker Mario Balotelli and whilst Nasri is clearly some player, Manchester City were undoubtedly a much less daunting proposition without Tevez, Aguero and Dzecko up front. As half time approached the visitors slowly began to wake up but in truth they had created few clear-cut chances. Annoyingly, Rovers offered absolutely nothing to counter City's under par first-half display. We seemed to be playing for a 0-0 and if Kean thought we were good enough to defend for 90 minutes against a side of Manchester City's quality you had to wonder why we had only managed four clean sheets all calendar year. Whoever's idea it was to play for a 0-0 had effectively invited City to attack whenever they felt like it. Without even having to play that well, once they got their first goal the second, third and fourth predictably followed. At 3-0 Rovers woke up a little bit and desperately went in search of a meaningless consolation. It didn't come and following another sub-standard display a post-match sit-in followed. I am sure the fans didn't expect us to beat Manchester City but whether Rovers are playing Manchester City or Barcelona are playing Jossy's Giants there is a certain level of performance that any fan demands of their club and Rovers were just so far away from it on so many occasions under Kean. As another protest raged, I went looking for a pub that didn't show English television and the Rovers squad headed home to pack for the re-scheduled club trip to India.

17. Wigan	P7	W1	D2	L4	Pts 5
18. Fulham	P6	W0	D4	L2	Pts 4
19. ROVERS	P7	W1	D1	L5	Pts 4
20. Bolton	P6	W1	D0	L5	Pts 3

One of the main criticisms of the new regime at Rovers was the serious lack of communication with the fans. There had been less inclination to open up direct communication with the Walker Trust because the fans were happy with the people they had in place at ground level and things were going right on the pitch. A great deal was changing at Rovers and if the changes were being made for all the right reasons then all the fans wanted to know was what these reasons were. The fans weren't asking Balaji Rao and Venkatesh Rao to walk in to The Aqueduct pub and start doing a slide show (and they didn't by the way!) but if the owners and the fans wanted the same thing it was difficult to see how effective two-way communication wouldn't benefit the club.

The Blackburn Rovers Fans' Forum had been in place since the end of the 1990s and was re-launched in 2006. Members of the Fans' Forum met regularly with senior club officials (John Williams, Tom Finn, Paul Hunt, etc) and this was seen as an effective way to maintain a link between the club and the fans. The Fans' Forum was open to all fans and there would be around six meetings a year with a pre-meet prior to the main meeting where fans could come along and set the agenda for the forthcoming meeting with the club representative. The meetings weren't used to discuss football matters - it was more things like ticketing issues, up-keep of the ground, feedback and suggestions regarding catering and merchandising and just generally trying to maintain the overall fan experience at games. Following the change in ownership the meetings continued and although members of the Fans' Forum made strenuous efforts to open up communication with the owners it quickly became clear that this was not how Venky's intended to run the club.

In August 2011, nine months in to Venky's ownership, the Fans' Forum received the surprise offer for nine of its members to accompany the club's staff on the trip to Venky's home city of Pune. Earlier in the month Simon Williams (John Williams' son and also Head of Commercial and Marketing) had met with Balaji Rao and discussed ways that the owners could engage with the fans. It was agreed that it would be a good idea for a group of fans to be invited over to Pune and the forthcoming club trip seemed the ideal opportunity. The decision was made to open up the invitation to ten fans but with Greg Coar (Robert Coar's son and also another member of the Rovers marketing team) taking up one of the places. Rovers were now looking for nine fans to accompany the club's staff on the trip. As the club had experience in dealing directly with the Fans' Forum it was decided that they were the obvious choice. The offer came as a somewhat of a surprise to members of the Fans' Forum but they were happy to accept. With 13 members putting their names forward, those that wanted to go put it to a vote and the *Pune Nine* was decided upon.

By the time the trip came round the protests were now in full swing and there were calls from fellow Rovers fans for members of the Fans' Forum not to go to India. Members of the Fans' Forum didn't see what declining the invitation would achieve and felt that the trip still represented the best way to present the concerns of the fans directly to the owners. The main concern amongst the fans continued to be the employment of Kean so personally I wanted to see this topic high on the agenda if members of the Fans' Forum got the chance to talk to anybody from the Venky's set-up.

The trip itself provided a fascinating insight in to how the club had changed since the takeover. It had been hoped that players, management, staff and the fans could travel out to India as one. A large executive plane was reserved but for whatever reason there were delays at Rovers end and the plane eventually ended up being taken by President Obama's team. A smaller plane was reserved for the main Rovers party and the majority of the players, management and staff travelled directly to Pune on this. The fans and a handful of other club staff flew separately on a scheduled flight to Mumbai where they then had to make the journey to Pune by road. Once in Pune, the high profile nature of the trip and terrorist concerns meant that security levels were high throughout and a lot of time was spent in the hotel. The main focus of the trip would be the game between Rovers and local I-League side Pune FC. There was also due to be a gala buffet rooftop dinner where members of the party got the chance to meet the owners. A thunderstorm just at the wrong time meant that the dinner had to be abandoned. Mrs Desai was due to attend but it was a case of rain stopped play for her. The party retreated indoors and most headed for the hotel nightclub. Unfortunately for members of the Fans' Forum, this event seemed a little more exclusive. Rovers' hardcore super fan "Birdy" (he painted his recycling bin blue and white because he doesn't like claret!) did manage to get inside and he quickly sparked up a conversation with Balaji Rao. The two shared a drink and members of the Fans' Forum were soon inside as the unlikely pairing of Birdy and Balaji Rao talked Rovers tattoos. Birdy and three other fans had travelled out to India independently and Balaji Rao did end up settling their hotel bill for them. At this point it wasn't clear how the dynamic of the Venky family worked and many fans still presumed that Balaji, Venkatesh and Mrs Desai all had an equal input in the decision making process. It was thought that relationships that developed with any of them could only help the Rovers cause. There was a second, more formal, meeting with Balaji Rao on the final day. Members of the Fans' Forum put their concerns to him and at the time they felt that he was receptive to what they were saying.

The game against Pune FC was as one sided as you will ever see. A problem with ticketing meant that there were more fans outside the ground than inside and the attendance was some way short of the 22,000 capacity. Kean put out a relatively strong team, arguably stronger than the team we ended the season with, and I-League opposition was no real challenge for an English Premier League side. Pune FC had a man sent off after 20 minutes and the game was hardly a contest from there. Two goals from Roberts and one from Rochina ensured that Rovers ran out comfortable 3-0 winners. Arun George of *The Deccan Chronicle* singled out Pune FC goalkeeper Shahin Lal Meloly for special praise, "Had it not been for Shahin Lal's heroics, the home side would have conceded at least a dozen goals." That just about summed up the game.

Football is still some way behind cricket in India and will probably never get close in my life time but there are signs of growth and the first visit of a Premier

League club did attract a significant amount of media attention. The passion was clearly there but looking at some of the media coverage I am not sure all the locals were quite there yet in terms of knowledge. Salgado was referred to as "Sal-dago", Nzonzi was introduced as Rovers third striker and Ruben Rochina was apparently Japanese! The fans and media in India were aware of the Kean Out campaign and local Rovers supporters in Pune had even made up their own Kean Out banners. Certain people at Rovers were obviously keen to direct attention away from the manager and this was not a part of the trip they wanted to focus on. The media were granted controlled access to Kean and select group of senior players, resulting in some of the most painfully contrived-looking television footage you are ever likely to see.

Overall, the trip to Venky's homeland was hailed a success by those who went out there and predictably the management team remained "positive" in outlook. At the time members of the Fans' Forum also felt that the trip had been worthwhile - they had got a face to face meeting with Balaji Rao and had also met Venkatash Rao. Members of the Fans' Forum came in for no small amount of criticism at the time from Rovers fans who felt they had sold out for a free holiday. I genuinely believe that the Fans' Forum went out to India for all the right reasons. They hoped that the trip would be the start of better things for the club but they now accept that it wasn't and any promises they were made in India have not been delivered.

Two weeks on from the Manchester City spanking and it was back to business in the Premier League. I had returned from Fuerteventura and having missed the

Manchester City game I decided to head off to London for the game against QPR at Loftus Road. The Kean Out campaign was growing game by game and although Kean was still claiming he could turn the situation round questions continued to be asked about his future. On the day of QPR game Venkatesh Rao was shown telling the BBC's *Football Focus*,

> "We don't want to change anything there. We just want to change whatever minor things like for the management purpose otherwise we are going to run the club as it is and as it was (sic). That is our motto."

I preferred "Arte et Labore" but I wasn't going to let Venky's spoil my first pint of the day and anyway I still had to find the ground. Surely the hardest football ground to find in England, Loftus Road also isn't a great place to go if you think you suffer from claustrophobia and if you are overweight it may be worth getting two tickets. There is a good atmosphere around the place though and a real authentic feeling about the football club. The game was a frustrating one. Few managers outside the top handful of clubs get the sack after drawing away from home and for large parts of the game against QPR I strongly suspected that Kean was aware of this. QPR took the lead early on through Heidar Helguson. If Helguson meant to chip Paul Robinson from the corner of the six-yard box then he is a better player than I ever realised. It looked suspiciously like a cross to me. Samba equalised with a monstrous header and at 1-1 with just 24 minutes on the clock the game threatened to rain goals. The downpour of goals didn't come and Samba's header proved to be the final goal of the game. It wasn't just the bad results and drink-driving that made Kean so unpopular amongst Rovers fans. More than anything, most fans, including myself, just felt that he talked absolute garbage a great deal of the time.

The QPR game was a great case in point. Kean said after the game,

> "Of course having the fans behind you like that makes a difference. They were brilliant. Especially in a ground like this, where the fans are on top of you, we could hear the fans from the first minute. They are probably slightly disappointed, like us that we didn't go home with all three points because QPR scored against the run of the play. Everyone wants to see the club climb the table and I think we are in a false position; we could have four more points. But that is a little bit of momentum and we will move forward."

I am sure this all sounded great to any members of the Steve Kean fan club but since when has two losses and a draw ever constituted momentum? Or was Kean including the 3-0 victory over Pune FC in his little revival? Rovers weren't in a false position at all. We were bottom of the league for a reason. We deserved to lose against Wolves; we deserved to be beaten by Villa; we deserved to get no points at Newcastle and we deserved nothing from our performance against Manchester City. As "unlucky" as we were against Everton, we were pretty poor against Fulham and as entertaining as the Arsenal game was, on another day we could have easily lost 7-2. As for the fans being behind the team during the QPR game, yes they were, but during the last half-hour it was difficult to make out too much support for the players due to the hundreds of Rovers fans screaming for Kean to bring on a striker. Before turning up at Loftus Road, unused substitutes Yakubu, Rochina and Formica had scored half of our Premier League goals in 2011/12; Roberts and his replacement Goodwillie hadn't scored a league goal between them since the final day of last season. Managers bore fans with statistics about possession and miles covered when things don't go their way but it is so frustrating when the basic fundamentals of the game (like scoring!) are totally overlooked. Talking to QPR fans after the game, they couldn't believe Rovers hadn't gone for the jugular. QPR had been poor and any one of the strikers we had on the bench could have made all the difference. On the face of it, an away draw was an OK result but most of those crammed in to the away end at Loftus Road walked away feeling this was two points dropped rather than one gained.

The next game at home to Spurs saw a march before the game and a sit-in afterwards. The numbers were now well up on the 200 Kean claimed had marched before the Arsenal game but it still wasn't clear how much notice the owners were taking of the protest. Kean was still in charge so if they could hear they didn't seem to be listening. All of those who had watched Rovers on a regular basis knew exactly why the protests were taking place but significant sections of the media, particularly the ex-pros on television, appeared to be taking exception to paying customers exercising their right to peaceful protest. Even the Rovers players started to get involved. David Dunn came out and said "to be leading protests is poor". It was a strange line and I had to wonder whether Dunn was playing football when all the other pupils were inside learning about history. The protest was being turned into the "us versus them" situation that the protesters were doing everything they could to avoid. Rovers' fans just wanted a manager who was able to communicate effectively with the fans and win enough games to keep us in the Premier League. It was that simple. Anyone who was trying to make out that the protests were anything more was wrong. It didn't help that everyone in football suddenly had an opinion on Rovers and it wasn't always those talking the most sense that people were listening to.

Opposing managers would almost invariably start the pre-match build up with public words of support for Kean while pouring scorn on the protests. On this particular occasion it was Harry Redknapp's turn to tell Rovers fans to back the manager. Who knows whether or not the enquiry about the availability of Ryan Nelsen came around the same time? I could see why opposing managers wanted Kean to remain in employment - three relegation places suddenly became two, no points became three and as well as the increasing likelihood of a decent end-of-season sale, there was every chance that future trips to Blackburn would soon be limited to scouting missions and cup games. For some reason it became the norm for Kean to value the words of people with whom we were in direct competition. The actual game with Spurs didn't stray too far from the script - we lost, Rovers' fans shouldered a large proportion of the blame and Kean claimed we were unlucky not to win. Rovers played

OK in patches but I don't think the result created too false a picture of events out on the pitch. Spurs won the game 2-1 and although Rovers had a few chances, Robinson was the busier of the two keepers and Spurs never really got out of second gear. I didn't expect us to beat better teams than us every week but I think Kean was out of order trying to claim some kind of moral victory for losing to a Spurs team that was playing away from home three days after a Europa League tie.

As the post-match music was cranked up to nightclub level, angry protesters were drowned out by the PA system and Kean told the media," I'm not paying attention to anyone who's staying behind." If this wasn't the new order sticking two fingers up to the fans I don't know what was. Once again it became clear that I was following a different football club than the one I had done for the previous 20-odd years. Rovers released an official statement asking for the fans to continue to support the team as they had done against Spurs. After six weeks of intense protests Kean did not appear to be going anywhere and it wasn't long before even rumours of a director of football coming in were being emphatically quashed.

17. Fulham	P9	W1	D4	L4	Pts 7
18. Bolton	P9	W2	L0	L7	Pts 6
19. Wigan	P9	W1	L2	L6	Pts 5
20. ROVERS	P9	W1	D2	L6	Pts 5

With a massive league game away at Norwich coming up, the midweek League Cup tie against in-form Newcastle United was a bit of an unwanted distraction.

Birmingham fans had shown six months earlier that winning that League Cup does little to soften the blow of dropping out of the Premier League. It was time for Kean to make a decision on exactly how important the League Cup was. Rovers' fans made a statement about how important they felt the game was - of the 10,682 fans who made it to the game almost half were Geordies. Kean didn't agree and, except maybe for Bunn, Petrovic and Goodwillie, there was an argument to say that the team he put out wasn't far off our strongest available 11. When questioned before the game whether Rovers could win the League Cup Kean told the *Lancashire Telegraph*,

> "Why not - and I said that to the players before the game. There's teams that have fancied it in the competition in years gone by and prospered and we fancy it."

Rovers took the lead through an early Rochina goal. Newcastle then had a big shout for a penalty turned down midway through the second half. Rovers went straight up the other end and were awarded a penalty, which Yakubu coolly converted. At 2-0 up with 20 minutes to go Rochina, Yakubu and Hoilett were all replaced and as the game entered injury time it looked like job done by Rovers. Newcastle had other ideas and when Danny Guthrie struck home a long-range effort on 93 minutes, the visitors backed themselves to get an equaliser. This arrived in the sixth minute of injury time when Yohan Cabaye curled home a 30-yard free-kick. It wasn't quite Sheringham at the Nou Camp in 1999 but it was a sickening blow for Rovers all the same.

Newcastle were in the ascendency and as the game went in to extra time they were surely now the favourites to progress to the next round. To Rovers credit the team re-grouped well and Givet's header in the last minute of extra time was enough to dump Newcastle out of the cup. We were through to the next round but was a two-hour Wednesday night workout the best preparation for Norwich City away? I guess we wouldn't find out until we reached the last 20 minutes at Carrow Road.

Rovers made three changes for the trip to East Anglia and for large parts of the game were much the better team. Hoilett gave us the lead on the stroke of half-time and it was hard to think of another player in the Premier League that could leave defenders for dead like Rovers young contract rebel could. Norwich equalised shortly after half-time courtesy of a fine Steve Morison volley but Rovers made sure Norwich weren't on level terms for long. Goals from Yakubu and Samba gave Rovers a 3-1 lead with just 25 minutes plus injury time to play.

Unfortunately Rovers had forgotten how to see out a game and it was almost as if we were too scared to win. On 82 minutes Jason Lowe charged at a Bradley Johnson shot and the ball looped over Paul Robinson's head Paul Parker Italia '90 style. It was another fluky goal but you make your own luck in this game. Rovers panicked and invited Norwich to attack for the rest of the game. When the Norwich equaliser did come it was not totally unexpected but it was a terrible penalty decision all the same. How Nzonzi could have stopped the ball striking the top of his arm when he didn't even know where the ball was or exactly what advantage he gained from doing so, only the referee knows. This was the fourth disgraceful penalty decision against Rovers in the Premier League in 2011 - three of them coming in the last five minutes of a game. Substitute Grant Holt tucked away the resulting penalty and despite Kean continuing to claim we were a mid-table side Rovers remained firmly in the relegation places. Norwich had got lucky but Rovers weren't blameless. Kean was never going to acknowledge his own failings so it was only a matter of time before injuries got a mention - it seems to be the final plea of every desperate manager.

> "We have got Dunny on the pitch, he hasn't got 100 per cent fitness yet, but we need players like Dunny, Ryan Nelsen, Michel Salgado and Scott Dann. These players have played the game and near the end would be able to help us take the sting out of it."

If Kean was waiting for Nelsen, Salgado and Dann to save the day the situation was even worse than I thought. Following Kean's comments, *Life's a Pitch* panellist Adrian Clarke of the *Red, White and Blue* podcast summed up the feelings of many Rovers fans when he said,

> "You do wonder if there is an element of delusion there with Steve Kean. Who's he trying to convince? Is he trying to convince himself?"

Rovers ended October sitting 18th in the Premier League with six points from 10 games. With unrest high amongst the fans and our Premier League status already looking precarious beyond 2011/12 it was now time for change.

CHAPTER 12

Venky's 1st Anniversary

Saturday 19 November 2011 signalled the end of Venky's first full year in charge of Blackburn Rovers Football Club. Anyone who was in any doubt about how their first year had gone would have got all the answers they needed in the week leading up to the official anniversary of the takeover. The week was declared a week of mourning by Rovers fans and wreaths and flowers were left by Jack Walker's statue to represent the death of our club. With 11 games gone in the Premier League, Rovers were 18th with only one win all season. Rovers' long-term residency in the relegation zone was just the tip of the iceberg. By this stage, there was a massive campaign against the on-going employment of manager Steve Kean and feeling towards Venky's was little better. Rovers fans' issues with Kean were well documented. More than anything the fans began to see Kean as the public face of the shambolic reign of Venky's. Anger towards Kean manifested itself in a number of different ways and although the vast majority of Rovers supporters backed the campaign and as a club we have no history of turning on our own in this way, the protests were generally looked upon by outsiders with widespread scorn. People weren't even sure why Rovers fans were waging war on Kean and not the owners. The answer was simple - how could fans wage a war on people that lived over 6,000 miles away and only visited Blackburn once every two months? Wayne Wild, group director of WEC Group, the club's only remaining corporate sponsor was about to go public with his feelings on Venky-run Blackburn Rovers. Wild told the *Lancashire Telegraph*,

> "Being a supporter is hard enough to take but paying for the privilege of sponsorship to be linked to this is both embarrassing and damaging to our company name and brand. One of my key issues is the lack of leadership at the top. I have no one to contact. Steve Kean is reporting direct to the owners. It should be going through a board of directors. There is nobody there. I am having to go to the commercial department who then go to a representative of the owners. In terms of the running of the club on a day-to-day basis there is nobody there."

Fans could associate with a lot of what Wild was saying but it didn't make it any easier to take.

In the space of 12 months Blackburn Rovers had gone from being one of the best run football clubs in Britain to a completely rudderless ship that appeared to be being run from another continent by a family that had little knowledge of Blackburn or football.

Venky's and Blackburn Rovers had become national news for all the wrong reasons. Gone were the good old days of five minutes on *Match of The Day* and a couple of pages on the back of the local paper. By now, most national newspapers seemed to have their own Blackburn Rovers correspondent. As well as the ongoing Kean saga, the week of the anniversary saw the familiar round of bad news in the newspapers. There was the usual transfer gossip that always seemed to involve our best players leaving and someone of little appeal arriving. In this case we were told that Stephen Nzonzi was now an £8 million target for Spartak Moscow, Liverpool were tracking Chris Samba and Rovers were looking at the possibility of signing injury prone 30-year-old Fulham striker Andy Johnson. Just to rub salt in to the wounds, Phil Jones, the player who we handed to Manchester United for £10 million below his true market value, had just gained his third England cap in as many months and the press would have you believe that Fergie had turned him from Bobby Ball into Bobby Moore.

Much more worryingly, Rovers finances were now starting to come under the microscope. When Venky's took over at Blackburn Rovers they paid £23 million for a 99.9% stake in the club and also took on the club's debt. Publicly, Venky's were pretty coy about how they planned to approach the debt. 12 months on and Paul Kelso of *The Telegraph* was reporting,

> "The club owe at least £21 million to Barclays, and it is understood that Venky's agreed to reduce the debt when they took control at Ewood Park. A year later that has not happened though, prompting the bank

to demand more security against its loans as the club face possible relegation. The debt was secured against Ewood Park and all the club's other property assets, as well as Venky's' newly-purchased shares in Blackburn Rovers, and it is understood that an undertaking was also given to reduce the size of the debt. With the club facing possible relegation and no reduction in the size of the debt, Barclays demanded additional security to protect its position. To satisfy Barclays, all the club's centralised television income for this season and beyond has also been provided as security."

Whilst this isn't uncommon at Premier League football clubs, it wasn't great news for the many Rovers fans who had believed that Venky's had cleared the debt at the time of the takeover.

Newspapers started reporting that a Qatar Oil giant had shown interest in buying Blackburn Rovers from Venky's and the words "out of the frying pan and into the fire" didn't cross a Rovers fan's lips. Rovers legend Simon Garner described Venky's first year in charge "a mess" and it was hard to argue with him. The proposed deal with the Qataris would see Venky's recoup all the money they had paid for Rovers and then some. It would also free Blackburn Rovers from the dark cloud of Venky's and considerably strengthen the club's financial position. Venky's were going nowhere. In typical fashion, one day they denied the interest, then they confirmed it, then they were considering it and then they rejected it. The club was not for sale. There was a bit of waffle at the end of it all about passion and fans but by this point I had heard enough from Venky's for one week and I was more bothered about Wigan away at the DW Stadium.

The game against Wigan on the day of the anniversary provided absolutely no respite from the problems of the previous 12 months. Balaji Rao and his brother Venkatesh made a rare appearance at a game but they disappeared at half-time in a limousine. It seemed a long way to come to watch 45 minutes of football. In the end Rovers scraped a 3-3 draw thanks to a Yakubu penalty in the 98th minute. It wasn't enough to drag us out of the relegation places and the Kean Out campaign continued to rage. Shortly after the game it was confirmed that Kean would remain Blackburn Rovers manager and not only that but Venky's were increasing his salary to a reported £1.5 million a year. There had been plenty of niceties and generic statements about the importance of the fans but after 12 months of suspicion and doubt, Venky's had finally revealed their hand. In a poll of 497 Rovers fans on supporter's website *BRFCS* only one person out of all of those polled was against the removal of Kean. A massive 99.8% wanted Kean out and when you rounded that figure up the campaign slogan "100% Rovers 0% Kean & Venky's" told you that feeling towards Venky's was no better. Just 12 months earlier, Venkatesh and Balaji Rao had stepped out on to Ewood Park turf to a rapturous Rovers reception. They had big smiles, big money and a vision to turn Blackburn Rovers in to a major force in football. The fans were happy to embrace their vision and good times were apparently just around the corner. What had gone so badly wrong?

When Venky's London Limited acquired BRFC Investments' 99.9% share of Blackburn Rovers they were required under Rule 9 of the City Code to make a mandatory unconditional offer for the remaining 0.1% of shares. A 19-page document outlining Venky's intentions for the club was drawn up and distributed to remaining shareholders who were then asked to consider Venky's offer. It is all standard stuff for any takeover of this scale and it is not really the legal procedure that is of interest. This was our first chance to really see what Venky's plans were for Blackburn Rovers Football Club. Venky's made a number of assurances and key contractual commitments within the document and many fans came to consider it as Venky's unofficial manifesto for the club.

The Venky board assured that it:

i) Will commit funds on a consistent and systematic basis to future transfer and/or loan activity.
ii) Intends to continue to support the existing management team and staff, and that it is committed to the future development of, and investment in, the club's academy and youth infrastructure.
iii) Will continue to support, promote and extend the club's local community and CSR activities.
iv) Will seek to extend the Blackburn Rovers name and brand into India, the rest of southeast Asia and beyond.
v) Will seek to develop and improve commercial performance across sponsorship, the club's kit deal and general merchandising.
vi) Will seek to enhance the fan experience on match days and to maximise season ticket sales and any remaining match day ticket sales.

vii) Intends to improve the club's media platforms (for example the club's TV Channel) and to become more active in the social media space.

12 months in to the Venky ownership and it was very debatable how many of the above assurances had been met. Point i) is very vague and I would have dismissed it as worthless on the spot. What does "commit funds on a consistent and systematic basis" mean? It is just waffle. If a mother says she is going to give each one of her children pocket money every 19 days she is committing funds on a consistent and systematic basis but the children are still going to want to know how much they are going to get. In the end, Venky's had a net spend of £4.2 million in the January 2011 transfer window and a net gain of £7.9 million in the summer 2011 transfer window - a total net gain of £3.7 million on transfers in their first year at the club. To use the pocket money example again, the mum ended up with more pocket money than the kids. Point ii) didn't really work out as fans had hoped. Departing manager Sam Allardyce explained after his dismissal,

> "I didn't really have any contact with the owners. I spoke with them once on the phone. The rest of the time it was either through John Williams or by e-mail. Other than that, it was little or no contact, which is perhaps a little surprising. If they had come in, done a whole run through of how we went about things, I think they would have found it difficult to find fault with my football structure."

In terms of point iii), as far as I was aware, Rovers continued to meet their basic obligations within the local community although how much credit Venky's can take for this considering the amount of time they actually spent in Blackburn is again a moot point. Point iv) had been achieved to a degree but the club were yet to see any obvious benefit from it. Football remains very much in the shadow of cricket in India. There was news of an under 12's football league based in Venky's home town of Pune called the Blackburn Rovers Junior League but "so what?" was my response to that news. The league was made up of 20 teams and each one wore Rovers home kit for home games and the away kit for away games. Maybe we could uncover the Indian Phil Jones and sell him to Manchester United. Rovers also became the first Premier League club to play in India when they played Pune FC in October 2011. Although certain Rovers players tried to make out that the Rovers welcome in India was akin to Beatlemania, I don't remember The Beatles playing too many gigs in front of so many empty seats. Roversmania may not have been gripping India just yet but, in fairness, we had more fans in India than we did before Venky's arrived. Now we just had to work out how having a handful of new Rovers fans thousands of miles away could actually benefit the club. Point v) was almost as laughable as point ii). Venky's started out by making a number of statements regarding advertising and marketing that were way off the mark as far as Rovers fans were concerned. Venky's were barely through the door before they started talking about renaming Ewood Park. Rovers shirt sponsor Crown got out at the earliest possible opportunity. They made it clear that they had no intention of renewing their three year sponsorship deal, reported to be worth around £5 million over three years. Crown said that the decision had been made after a "revision of their growth strategy" and that there had been no meeting with Venky's about renewing. Rovers were praised for donating their shirt sponsor to The Prince's Trust charity the week before the start of the season but it was like giving all your unwanted clothes to the charity shop because nobody had bid for them on *eBay*. Simon Williams, Rovers head of commercial marketing at the time, told the press way back in February 2011 that Rovers had appointed agents to search global markets for a successor to Crown.

Our one major commercial sponsor WEC Group Ltd, a fabrication and engineering company based in Darwen, went public about their feelings towards Venky's. Group director Wayne Wild wrote an open letter to the owners advising that, "the negative and derogatory publicity that the club is currently undergoing is having a direct impact on our company." Wild got the mandatory meeting with Deputy Chief Executive Paul Hunt but, despite his big title, Paul Hunt already had a reputation for being no more than a Venky errand boy who was sent out to meet and greet the little people. In terms of point vi), credit to Venky's for keeping season ticket prices amongst the cheapest in Britain. Season ticket sales were down in 2011/12 however and Venky's must take a large amount of responsibility for that. Season ticket sales are driven by price and value. Paying the same price as last year to watch a weaker team is clearly going to have a negative effect on sales. There had been no obvious efforts to enhance fans' experience on match day. Poor performances, bad feeling towards Venky's and the continuing employment of a manager that few fans wanted at the club helped to ensure that fans' match day experience was the worst I can remember in my 20-odd years watching Rovers. Reports in *The Guardian* that Venky's had planned to host a summer R&B concert at Ewood Park showed how out of touch they were with their audience. When I saw a picture of Akon in the paper wearing a Rovers shirt I didn't even know who he was. I thought we had signed Claude Makelele. Point vii) is not something I was overly concerned with. I use my mobile to text "where are you?" and the Internet to read the paper. In a study by LEWIS Communications, published in October 2011, Rovers came 18th out of 20 when each Premier League club was ranked on how they engaged with fans across the Internet. If Venky's had plans to utilise social media more effectively there was clearly work to be done.

Venky's also entered into the following contractual commitments with the club:-

i) The principal activity of Blackburn Rovers will continue at all times to be that of a professional football club.
ii) The current President, Vice Presidents and Honorary Vice Presidents of Blackburn Rovers will not be removed from those positions before June 2011 without the prior written consent of those individuals.
iii) The statue of Jack Walker outside Ewood Park will be kept in a good state of repair and will not

be moved to a different location, obscured or have its prominence diluted without BRFCI's prior written consent.

iv) The name of the stand at Ewood Park currently known as the Jack Walker Stand will not be changed without BRFCI's prior written consent.

In hindsight, any fan who wanted a real idea of what Venky's had in store for the club would have been best advised to ignore the assurances and contractual commitments and head straight for the section titled "Cautionary note regarding forward looking statements". The key part of this section read:-

> *All statements other than statements of historical facts included in this announcement may be forward-looking statements. These statements are based on the current expectations of the management of Blackburn Rovers or Venky's (as the case may be), have not been reviewed by the auditors of Blackburn Rovers or Venky's and are naturally subject to uncertainty and changes in circumstances. Forward?looking statements include, without limitation, statements typically containing words such as "**intend**", "**expect**", "**anticipate**", "**target**", "**estimate**", "**goal**", "**believe**", "**will**", "**may**", "**should**", "**would**", "**could**", "**plan**" or words of similar meaning or import. By their nature, forward-looking statements involve risk and uncertainty because they relate to events and depend on circumstances that will or may occur in the future.*

Again, this is all probably standard fare in a legal document of this nature but to me it roughly translated, provided we qualify any statements we make about the future of the club with one of the magic words we don't necessarily have to do what we are suggesting we are going to do. For me, this pretty much summed Venky's up.

It is easy to talk about the Walker Trust years as if everything they touched turned to gold and life was just one long bed of roses for Rovers fans, but even during this golden era mistakes were made. The sale of the club to Venky's is regarded by many as their biggest mistake but there were others. The appointment of Paul Ince was a stinker that ended up costing the club millions. I am all for giving someone a chance but I always thought the appointment of "no badges" was an odd one. In the end, we gave Ince a chance and he failed. Ince has gone on to make some strong comments about his time at Rovers and is currently out of management having left MK Dons and Notts County. In a newspaper article published in the *Daily Mirror* in 2011, Ince was quoted as saying "Sadly, my experience at Blackburn showed that there are double standards out there and that black coaches are treated differently" and "The reasons why I didn't succeed at Blackburn were to do with many of our best players being sold and me having little money to spend". I watched pretty much every game during the Ince tenure and from what I could see he got sacked because he wasted a small fortune signing Keith Andrews, Vince Grella, Robbie Fowler and Carlos Villenueva (on loan) and went on a massive winless streak that ended in a toothless 3-0 spanking at Wigan. Ince was given a fair chance but in the end people who regularly watched Rovers were pretty much in agreement that he was leading us in to The Championship with a team that had finished the previous season 7th.

Rovers' fans never expected the board to get every decision right or massive amounts of money to be ploughed in to the club every year, but the fact is John Williams and his team got a lot more decisions right than they got wrong and we always scraped enough money together when it mattered. There were times when fans would show concern about off-field matters just as they do now. I remember one summer when we sold Santa Cruz for £17 million and Stephen Warnock for £7 million and spent hardly any of this money on replacements. Fans were angry and wanted to know where all this money was going. John Williams came out in the press and answered fans' concerns about where the money had gone with a series of clear and open answers that made total and utter sense and that was drama over. Rovers' fans trusted John Williams.

The new order seemed to believe that they could just come in and win fans over with a bit of waffle sprinkled with fantasy. The majority of Rovers' fans are straight talking, straight forward people and smooth talk and double speak just doesn't go down well. When Venky's took over at Blackburn Rovers a poll in the *Lancashire Telegraph* showed that 52% were in favour of the takeover. Speaking to fellow Rovers fans at the time, my belief is that the other 48% were not against Venky's they just chose to reserve judgement until Venky's had actually done something to judge them on. Rovers' fans wanted Venky's to succeed and the widespread bad feeling towards them 12 months on was not down to any preconceived prejudices from the fans. Rovers' fans had never asked for big ambitious plans. We had always done well enough with a well-executed realistic plan. We never asked for any big plans but when people start talking big and then the results aren't forthcoming it is difficult not to feel that you are being taken for a ride. We could see what was going on out on the pitch and we had a fair idea what was going on off the pitch. Rovers' fans just wanted a bit of candour but a hierarchy of hot air emerged and the problem appeared endemic from the owners right down to the playing staff.

It didn't take long to find this selection of quotes from some of the senior figures at Venky-run Blackburn Rovers.

> "The impression is I've never watched a football match. I've not watched in a stadium but I have been watching the World Cup in India. I have watched hundreds of cricket matches but not live - it's all on TV. To say I don't have any knowledge would be wrong. I am a good listener."
> Mrs Desai

> "The team is in the relegation zone right now, but it is going to come up I am sure of that. We do know that a few people have been generating thousands of mails demanding the ousting of current manager Steve Kean, who is a brilliant manager. But we know the team is going in the right direction and we are very positive about the way the team is performing and the way it is going. On the whole the goal of playing in Europe over the next four to five years is a realistic one."
> Balaji Rao

> "As with other non-UK owners of clubs, our owners watch every game on television and have gone to great personal expense to ensure that all Rovers

games are relayed into their homes. Of course, we hope to see more of them at Ewood in the coming months but I can assure everyone that absence definitely makes the owners' hearts grow fonder!"
Paul Hunt

"It's about giving the lads feedback as a group and there will be bags and bags of positives to give back and very few negatives."
Steve Kean (we had just lost our first three league games of the season!)

"I am struggling to think of any other club in the Premier League with good young players like we have."
Jason Roberts

As bad feeling towards Venky's grew, Rovers fans were increasingly portrayed as spoilt, insolent people that had come to consider Premier League football their birthright. It suited certain people encourage this viewpoint. It was an utter lie. It was the total lack of trust in the new regime that was causing all the unrest amongst fans. A small group of fans had been invited to air their concerns but despite the gesture the fans' words were not acted upon and communication was getting worse rather than better. Essentially, Rovers fans still knew very little about the Indian businessmen that had chosen to run our football club from another continent. What was Venky's true motivation for investing in a football club 6,000 miles from their home in a town they rarely visited? Were they actually as well off as we had originally been led to believe? Most fans had just gone off what we were told at the time of the takeover but it was becoming clear that things were not necessarily as they had been originally reported. Some reports had stated that the Venky family fortune was three times that of Jack Walker's whereas others had claimed that Venky's wealth had been vastly exaggerated, possibly due to the confusion over multiples of rupees, lakhs (100,000 rupees) and crores (10m rupees). Whatever the Venky family's financial power was there was no doubting the scale of the operation they were overseeing. The V H Group was made up of a total of 28 different companies, spanning across 38 countries with a reported 250,000 people employed directly by the group and the same again employed indirectly. Although poultry was Venky's main core business the V H Group covered a wide variety of business interests from making films to selling protein shakes. I found it hard to imagine that members of the Venky family could be micro-managing 28 companies all at the same time. I wondered where Rovers featured on their list of priorities. Prior to the takeover Mrs Desai had stated that Rovers was primarily going to be a way to expose their brand. Earlier the same year the first Venky's XPRS fast food outlet had been opened in Pune. The V H Group planned to open 100 Venky's XPRS outlets by 2013. Of the proposed 100 outlets, 90 were planned for India and 10 for the rest of the world, including one in London. All the outlets would be company-owned and in June 2011 Venky's XPRS London Limited was registered at Companies House. I was seriously starting to doubt exactly how much involvement Venky's had in the overall running of Blackburn Rovers. We knew that Kentaro and SEM had been advising them – were we know meant to believe that Mrs Desai was managing the V H Group's 28 companies all on her own in half hour daily segments? Mrs Desai had still only been to one game in 12 months and her two brothers weren't much better. Why were Balaji and Venkatesh surprised by the reaction they had received at Wigan? The fans were all getting the message loud and clear about every game being beamed in to their house by satellite but were they watching the games with the sound turned down? I trawled the Internet and found footage of the medallion man Balaji Rao showing off his collection of cars. It was like watching a four-year-old show you the contents of his toy box. The disturbing thing was Balaji Rao is not four years old and these were not three inch die-cast metal cars. What was Blackburn Rovers to these people? Was it a new toy, the must-have television channel, a marketing tool or just a get-rich-quick-scheme being managed by someone else? I couldn't work it out but I did still find it odd that the one member of the Venky trio who claimed not to have been previously interested in football was now the one supposedly making all the big decisions? It just seemed too convenient to blame everything on a woman in India. On the pitch, Venky's first year at Blackburn Rovers had been a steady slide towards the wrong end of the table. Off the pitch, it had been a public relations disaster from the start. Why the unfathomable loyalty shown to Kean? Did football even enter the equation?

Chapter 13

On The Pitch
Nov 2011 - Jan 2012

Rovers started November in the relegation zone and would remain there for the rest of 2011. The Kean Out protest continued in earnest. Why wouldn't it? All the problems that had led to the protest (losing games, playing poorly, puzzling team selection, glossing over failure with fantasy, etc) were still there – if anything those problems were even more apparent than ever. Most football fans have seen the unrest that can ensue when a failing manager outstays his welcome by one or two games. We were now about to see the damage that can be caused when a failing manager outstays his welcome by the best part of a season.

Leading up to the game with Chelsea on Bonfire Night 2011 rumours about Sven Goran Eriksson becoming Director of Football were quickly quashed and the focus was soon back on the Kean Out campaign. Rather than taking on board what the fans were saying and acting on it, people in power at Rovers now appeared to be making it their mission to stamp out the protest once and for all. I can't remember another example of a football club turning on its own fans in the way Rovers did but the new order was about to unleash an underhand campaign of action that was far more damaging to the club's reputation than anything the protesters were doing. While influential staff were publicly making light of the protest it was quite clear that club officials were flexing their muscles behind the scenes; smiling for the camera; dropping misleading information in to interviews; watching the mayhem unfold and then playing dumb. This slippery method of action continued well in to 2012 and Kean played a major part in it all. It was so frustrating and exactly the sort of thing that set Kean apart from your average unpopular football manager. When it was announced that there would be a ban on banners inside the ground for health and safety reasons Kean told Alan Nixon of the *Daily Mirror*,

> "The vast majority of the fans are solidly behind everything we're doing. We can't let the small minority get to a stage where it's annoying everyone or getting under their skin."

It had been claimed that there was a risk of a counter protest against the protesters if the official protest was allowed to continue and therefore banners had become a health and safety risk. Do me a favour. The organised element of the protest was growing game by game but acrimony towards Kean wasn't limited to the thousand or so that were actively taking part in marches and sit-ins. While most fans were fully behind the message the official protesters were putting out, there were thousands of fans who were equally against Kean who chose not to march. It didn't mean that they liked Kean. If anything, the organised element of the protest gave the bad feeling towards the manager a focus and stopped anger developing in to something much more chaotic and unsavoury. Protest organisers Glen Mullan and Simon Littler, both lifelong Rovers fans, co-operated throughout.

If fans weren't allowed to bring banners in to the ground there was nothing the club could do to stop protesters flying a banner over the ground. The protest group collected donations and paid for a light aircraft to fly over Ewood Park trailing a banner with "STEVE KEAN OUT" emblazoned across it. The light aircraft circled the ground for around 10 minutes during the first half of the Chelsea game. It was a strange sight and perhaps slightly distracting but this was a consequence of the problem not the problem itself. If the players struggled to focus then this needed to be reflected in their pay. Even Kean looked upwards at one point but he later clarified that he didn't see anything. In terms of the actual game, although Rovers were beaten 1-0 the team played OK and probably should have got at least a point. Chelsea started the day looking to avoid their third defeat in three games. The alleged John Terry race storm was still fresh in the minds and new manager Andre Villas-Boas was struggling to win over the critics. Rovers named an unchanged side for the first time all season. The visitors had plenty of possession but they didn't really go anywhere with it and it was Rovers who had the better of the chances. Yakubu missed two great chances to notch his 100th goal in the Premier League and Pedersen was exceptional all game. Big performances from our Norwegian winger had become a rarity since the departure of Sam Allardyce, This only made it more frustrating when Pedersen showed what he was capable of. Chelsea weren't at their best for large parts of the game but with players like Frank Lampard around eventually Rovers were going to be made to pay for the missed chances. Lampard got the only goal of the game shortly after half time with a knee high header from a Branislav Ivanovic cross. Grant Hanley had an excellent chance to equalise shortly afterwards but Rovers just couldn't find that all important goal. Comedy miss of the day went to misfiring Chelsea striker Fernando Torres and from what I could see Chelsea were some way short of the Spurs side that had visited Ewood Park two weeks earlier. I guess it showed what a difference the manager makes. Shortly after disposing of Villas-Boas, the core of this Chelsea side went on to win the FA Cup and UEFA Champions League.

17. Wolves	P10	W2	D2	L6	Pts 8
18. ROVERS	P11	W1	D3	L7	Pts 6
19. Bolton	P10	W2	D0	L8	Pts 6
20. Wigan	P10	W1	D2	L7	Pts 5

Rovers were now about to enter another international break and the manager was obviously keen to look forward rather than back.

> "This period is massive. You look to the first phase of 11 games and it has been tough. There have been

> a lot of tough games and I feel as though we should have another six points. Now we have got games against teams around us and if our levels are as high as they have been then I am convinced we will pick up points and by the time we get to half way we will be much in a much, much better position."

Yes, if we got to half way we would be in a much, much better position. The problem was getting there. By this stage protesting fans had tried letters, marches, banners, sit-ins and an aeroplane but for whatever reason Kean was still losing games, talking rubbish and firmly entrenched in the relegation zone with Rovers. Maybe the protests now needed to be directed at the owners as well as their UK extension. If that was the plan it would prove difficult to execute with Venky's seldom seen in Blackburn. It was a dire situation and there was little sign of any of it coming to an end. Middle East oil giant Qatar Petroleum was linked with a potential takeover bid but Venky's came out and said they didn't want to sell. If Venky's didn't want to sell, they didn't want to listen, they were barely attending games and they continued to refuse to sack the manager it was difficult to work out what they were able to offer Rovers fans. When Balaji and Venkatesh Rao turned up in the North West for the trip to Wigan a number of travelling fans pointed this out to them. I am not sure what Venky's had been told to expect but if they had been following events closely then the fans' reaction shouldn't have taken them too much by surprise.

In typically disorganised fashion the Rovers team arrived at the game just 50 minutes prior to kick-off and it was hard to argue that this was any way for a Premier League team to prepare for such an important game. Despite the amateurish arrival the players started the game well and the Chuckle Brothers had barely got in their seats before Yakubu had put Rovers 1-0 up. As always, Rovers had brought a strong following to Wigan but the early goal did little to ease bad feeling towards the manager and the owners. In fact the protest seemed to thrive in front of an audience. Rovers' lead didn't last long and our dreadful recent record at the DW Stadium looked like continuing when Wigan scored a second just after the half hour. With Rovers 2-1 down at half-time, Balaji and Venkatesh looked they had seen enough and they headed back to the airport in their limousine. It was later reported that they had been shaken by the level of abuse they had received from travelling Rovers fans. Out on the pitch, there was further embarrassment as David Dunn was sent off shortly in to the second half. The remaining 40 minutes resembled a pumped up under seven's game and there were goals and gaffes a-plenty. It's not often that Wigan V Blackburn Rovers is the first game on *Match of the Day* so it perhaps gives some indication to the entertainment level a game laden with mistakes can provide for the neutral. The biggest howler of the day came from the referee Andre Marriner. Pedersen played a corner to himself; Marriner's back was turned so he presumed someone else had taken it; Pedersen dribbled the ball along the by-line; Wigan were caught on the hop and Hoilett headed home from two yards. Marriner was slammed for the decision and it was hard to argue that the goal should have stood. Wigan scored a third with two minutes of normal time remaining following a mistake by Paul Robinson. There was still time for Robinson to make amends and when Rovers were awarded a corner deep into injury time the Rovers goalkeeper raced up field. Robinson jumped for a 50:50 ball; his head was met with the underside of David Jones' boot and Marriner had no choice but to point to the spot. There was a lengthy delay as the Rovers medical team attended the gaping wound in Robinson's head but none of this seemed to bother the Rovers penalty taker. Yakubu was calmness personified and when the time eventually came he coolly slotted home to give Rovers a share of the spoils. Steve "dignified" Kean gestured angrily towards the travelling Rovers fans at full time and I wondered whether he had been worried how his bosses would react to the welcome they had received from Rovers fans. Shortly after the game the club put out a statement about Kean's position.

> "Following recent media speculation Blackburn Rovers can confirm a revision to manager Steve Kean's existing contract has been completed. An agreement made in the summer has now been formalised. Contrary to some reports there is no change to the length of the contract. The club respects that all contracts are private and confidential and no further comment will be made."

I think I spent the following week in denial. Despite the quite clear statement that Kean had been handed a revised contract, like most Rovers fans, I still felt that he would be sacked if he continued to lose games. I headed for Blackburn Market to purchase a white stairway dust sheet and a can of blue spray paint for my forthcoming trip to Stoke City. Banners may have been banned from the Ewood Park but I saw absolutely no reason why they would be banned from the Britannia Stadium. I had never really put much thought in to how much effort goes into making a good protest banner and unfortunately my lame effort fell some way short of the mark. I had lots of good ideas but in the end "KEAN OUT" was as much as I could legibly fit on the remains of the dust sheet once I had disposed of the 90% I had practiced on. I spent most of the Friday night prior to the game scraping Anti-Kean messages off the hallway laminate as I didn't realise blue spray paint would go through a dust sheet. There was a serious point to all this. Rovers officials were stifling the protest and then putting out the message that the majority of fans were happy. Banners at away games were quickly becoming the only visible way the fans could show that the majority were far from happy. I was about to find out that the ban on banners now applied to away games too. When I arrived at the Britannia Stadium the very friendly steward asked me what my banner said. I thought he was checking them for offensive language. I told him "KEAN OUT" and presumed my banner would be fine. He advised me that Stoke City had been contacted by Rovers and were under strict instruction not to allow any banners that made any reference to Kean in to the ground. In light of this information I told him that my banner said "F-OFF BURNLEY". The steward advised me that this would be fine but he would have to take my first answer. The travelling Rovers steward reported back to base on his walkie-talkie as if he was something out of *Men In Black* and very quickly my jovial mood was starting to turn. I was taken to a store room at the back of the away end where my banner was stored until the end of the game. There were literally dozens of Rovers banners in this room. I didn't for one moment feel any animosity towards the Stoke City stewards. As football fans they were really understanding of the situation. It was quite clear that they were taking instruction from Rovers. As a result of the unnecessarily heavy handed stewarding the atmosphere amongst Rovers fans was not good. The fans were being provoked. It may not have been visible to the casual observer but this was exactly the sort of thing that would cause the problems that became so inaccurately reported at the end of 2011. The game itself was terrible. By this stage that had almost become a given. Formica missed a decent chance just after half time but other than that Rovers didn't pose any real threat to the Stoke City goal until we were 3-0 down. Rochina's late consolation was a fine individual goal but it was another case of too little too late. As Kean walked across the pitch at full time flanked by two bodyguards, the media honed in on the hundreds of angry Rovers fans, many now wearing the yellow and black "100% ROVERS 0% KEAN & VENKY'S" protest T-shirts. It made for an angry looking picture that featured in many newspapers but we had plenty to be angry about. I collected my "KEAN OUT" banner and spent the rest of the afternoon drinking in Macclesfield. The locals treated my banner like an international celebrity. Strangers asking for their photo taken with it made the hours of scrubbing all worthwhile. Under strict instruction from my wife not to bring it back home, when I threw my banner in the bin at the train station after 12 pints of lager I thanked it for a good day out.

I woke up the next day to hear the tragic news of Premier League legend Gary Speed's untimely death. Speed had played over 900 senior games during his career and had started to carve out a career in management with Wales. Rovers would go on to play Cardiff and Swansea in the seven days that followed Speed's passing.

Despite only picking up one Premier League win all season Rovers had won all three League Cup games and now faced Championship opposition for a chance to play the semi-final. Prior to setting off on the long midweek journey to Cardiff, when Kean was asked whether he felt Rovers could win the League Cup, he confidently replied,

> "Yes, definitely. When you get this far, we have got a good tie and we're scoring goals on the road. We're playing a team that is in good form in the Championship so it's going to be a tough tie but we think we can progress."

With starts for Bunn, Petrovic, Blackman and Goodwillie this wasn't really reflected in Kean's team selection and 90 feeble minutes later Rovers were out of the League Cup. Kean was now claiming to have "forfeited" the game because he wanted to focus on the Premier League. This was a sudden turnaround from earlier in the day and if we were going to "forfeit" the League Cup why did we put out such a strong team in the previous round? The 1,000 travelling Rovers fans were furious and many demanded a full refund. Kean blamed the gaffe on a bad choice of words but with every tactless comment the bad atmosphere around the club only intensified.

Burnley fans had christened Kean "Agent Kean". They said that he was employed by Burnley Football Club and had been sent on a secret mission to destroy Blackburn Rovers. I don't know how old the people doing this were but I would necessarily presume that they were children. Burnley fans thought it was hilarious and would post mock updates on the Internet.

> "Keep up the good work, Agent Kean. You are on track to complete the mission by April. Remember – keep selling all the best players and lose as many games as you can. Everybody back home is proud of you!"

I actually found Kean more irritating than Burnley fans so there wasn't a lot I could say in response. By the time the visit of Swansea came round at the start of December Rovers now hadn't won a Premier League game in the previous eight attempts. Swansea would be the first of three winnable home games in just over two weeks for Rovers. The time for excuses was well gone and Kean acknowledged that Swansea, West Brom and Bolton at home were the sort of games that were going to prove vital to Rovers' survival. The poor performances, disappointing results and bad atmosphere was having a noticeably negative effect on attendances. Even a significant number of season ticket holders had started staying away. In a conscious effort to boost the numbers, Rovers offered a special deal allowing fans the opportunity to attend all three pre-Christmas Premier League home games for just £20. There was a good uptake on the deal but there were still many fans who were staying away. The game with Swansea turned out to be the Yakubu show and at last Rovers had another win in the Premier League. Rovers won 4-2 and Rovers' Nigerian striker scored all four Rovers goals. Yakubu was proving to be the one shining light of the Kean reign. Yakubu's goals against Swansea were a fine example of what a lethal poacher he could be. His first goal was as tidy a finish as you are ever likely to see but it quickly became the story of the day for all the wrong reasons. When Yakubu drilled the ball in to the top corner from the edge of the 18-yard box he ran along the touchline and high-fived Kean. Instinctive boos rang out from the home supporters and the media immediately went to town. Rovers' fans appeared to have crossed another line in the footballers' moral code. To me, booing when your team is winning sent out the very clear message that this was now about far more than football. Some people just didn't get it and I felt that others did get it but chose to stick the boot in anyway. Kean told reporters after the game,

> "There must be other issues because I can't fathom why, when we're leading a game, they're chanting, but that's their prerogative. I'm always positive. I think we're in a good run of games and the best thing to do is go on an unbeaten run and climb the table."

With Kean struggling to understand why he was disliked and large sections of the media joining in, it didn't take long for the armchair experts to start parroting what the bigger boys were saying.

> "Fickle and ungrateful. Would they still be booing if that was the goal that kept them up? Disgraceful.Fans with mentality like that need to get relegated to appreciate what it means to support the team over the season."

It is easy not to rise to this sort of comment now but at the time it was difficult for all those that could see what was really going on not to get angry. Of all the people the spotlight should have been shining on Rovers fans were well down the list but again, we were an easy target that couldn't really fight back.

In the build-up to the early Sunday Sky game against Sunderland at the Stadium of Light, Kean was now targeting top 10 again. Sunderland had just disposed of Steve Bruce and the game against Rovers would be Martin O'Neill's first game in charge. Rovers took the lead through Simon Vukcevic on 17 minutes and were unlucky to have a second goal ruled out just before half time. Goal scorer Vukcevic looked a half-decent player but the problem was he very rarely featured. In total he made seven Premier League appearances for Rovers in 2011/12 – the last coming in January 2012. A number of reasons were given for his regular non-selection. Kean said he had a virus. Who knows but whatever happened to Vukcevic it was hard to argue that his signing ultimately justified the decision to dispose of Brett Emerton.

Anybody who felt that Kean was being victimised by supporters probably needs to watch the second half of the Sunderland game again to really appreciate Kean's total tactical ineptitude. For some reason, Rovers decided to sit back for the entirety of the second half and a weak Sunderland side that was chronicly low on confidence was allowed to attack the Rovers goal at will for 45 minutes solid. It looked like Rovers were playing with 10-men. Late goals from David Vaughan and Sebastian Larsson meant that Martin O'Neill didn't have to wait long for his first win and Sunderland were soon climbing up the table.

Reports in the press about Rovers' financial position were now adding to the fans' concerns. The club put out this official statement,

> "There is no financial crisis, and, there is absolutely no danger to the players' and staff wages. Amongst all professional football clubs, finances are regularly assessed and reassessed during the season based on performance, income and costs, and at Blackburn Rovers this is no different."

Tensions were brewing and prominent local businessmen and Rovers fans Ian Battersby and Ian Currie came out in the local press to call for calm. The official protest leaders felt that they were making steps to open up effective dialogue with the club and as a result they postponed any organised protests until after the proposed meeting with Rovers officials. The claims that it was only the official protesters that were unhappy about what was going on at the club were about to be exposed for what they were. Rovers feeble surrender to West Brom the weekend before Christmas meant that the mid-week visit of bottom of the table Bolton Wanderers was now billed as must-win for both clubs. Many in the media were tipping whichever manager lost to get the sack.

Kean said after the home defeat to West Brom, "But I think overall, we can be more than satisfied with our day's work." I was starting to feel that he was losing touch with reality. In the days leading up to the game, the *Lancashire Telegraph* lead with the front page headline calling for the removal of Steve Kean. Sports Editor Andy Cryer included an open letter to Mrs Desai asking the club to now put right the mistakes of the last 12 months. In a pre-match interview with Kean, Cryer posed the question, "Do you not think it would be better if you weren't here?" to which Kean responded, "No, I don't. The lads are 100 per cent with me. I think that shows in their play."

Rovers were 2-0 down to Bolton within half an hour and enough was enough. The anger boiled over and the media were quick to focus in on the angriest faces. Anyone who was saying we should be backing the team needed to realise what was going on here. Rovers lost 2-1 and as angry fans protested well in to the night a much bigger mob was about to go to town on Rovers fans.

17. Sunderland	P16	W3	D5	L8	Pts 14
18. Wigan	P16	W3	D4	L9	Pts 13
19. Bolton	P17	W4	D0	L13	Pts 12
20. ROVERS	P17	W2	D4	L11	Pts 10

Over the next three days, everyone from Michael Owen to Pierce Morgan had their say on despicable Rovers fans. The official protest leaders continued to try and open up dialogue with the club but Rovers officials were milking the scenes at the Bolton game for all they were worth and many outside the club were now buying the laughable suggestion that Kean's safety was in danger if he sat in a room with two Rovers fans to talk about what was going on at the club.

By the time Christmas came I just felt beaten. Kean came out and told the press that he was 100% certain he would remain in his job. For the first time in a long time I found myself believing what he was saying. Venky's weren't averse to sacking people but for whatever reason they weren't going to sack Kean and that was now abundantly clear. I began to accept that Captain Kean was taking this ship all the way down to the bottom of the ocean and there was little anybody could do about it. It was an impossible situation and my head needed a break from it all. Going to football is essentially something you do for fun. What was fun about all this rubbish? Over the following six weeks I read the newspapers and I watched how the story was being reported on television. I went to games, clapped in the right places and went home. I just couldn't invest any more emotional energy in to it.

If you look at the stats we still got battered in our next two games (Rovers had 15 shots, our opponents had 54!) but results did actually start to pick up. Reserve goalkeeper Mark Bunn was in inspired form to help Rovers take a share of the spoils at Anfield. A week later and Rovers went one better with a stunning 3-2 victory over Manchester United at Old Trafford. It was still open season on Rovers fans and it was no surprise when Fergie decided to stir the pot with his usual brand of pre-match tripe,

> "In the case of Steve Kean, when the supporters react that way you say to yourself there's something wrong with society. Every manager knows it's a results industry."

Results industry? Are you sure about that? As for there being something wrong with society I think Fergie needed to take a look closer to home before he started criticising Rovers' fans – and I don't just mean the home dressing room at Old Trafford. It made my day when Manchester United fans booed their own team off the pitch at half time! I know it is disappointing when your Christmas present doesn't live up to expectations but at a time when Rovers fans were getting it from all angles there was something a little bit pathetic about fans of the most successful English team of the last 25 years booing their own team off for being 1-0 down at half time. Funnily enough, I didn't hear anybody else mention it. Grant Hanley's 80th minute winner and Yakubu's brace meant that at 33/1 Rovers became the longest priced winning team in Premier League history and Yakubu joined an elite group of players who have scored 7 goals or more in a month and not be named Barclays Premier League Player of the Month. What made the victory even more remarkable was that Manchester United would have gone top of the league with a point and the win still left Rovers three points from safety. Not only that but many of Rovers' established players had been left out of the side for youngsters like Grant Hanley, Jason Lowe and Adam Henley.

The young team couldn't build on the shock win at Old Trafford and Rovers' lowest home crowd in the

Premier League for three years saw Peter Crouch score two more goals against Rovers to give Stoke City a relatively comfortable 2-1 victory. Leaders of the official protests announced that they were ready to start protesting again and claimed that the club had done everything they could to avoid the promised meetings. By this stage, the mood at Ewood Park was quite different to what it had been towards the end of 2011. It may have just been the back to work blues kicking in but the fire and intensity of the Bolton game appeared to have been replaced by a more subdued atmosphere of helplessness and detachment.

The third round FA Cup tie against Newcastle United created little excitement amongst fans. Few were prepared to risk another £100 day out after the Cardiff "forfeit" fiasco and more Rovers fans actually went to watch old boys Garry Flitcroft and Matt Jansen's Chorley. Rovers lost 2-1 with late wonder goals from Hatem Ben Arfa and Jonas Gutierrez cancelling out David Goodwillie's scrambled opener.

The atmosphere around the club was far from great but bad feeling seemed to have peaked around the Bolton game and tensions appeared to be dying down somewhat. This only made the timing of Jerome Anderson's infamous *Sky Sports News* interview even more frustrating and after two quiet weeks suddenly the soap opera was back on. There was a time when football agents were viewed as a scourge on the game. In many ways I feel that they are now treated with more respect than fans. When Jerome Anderson appeared on *Sky Sports News* on 10 January 2012 I tried to remember the last time I had seen a Rovers fan interviewed at such lengths on the *Sky Sports News* channel. I couldn't recall one but I was keen to see what Jerome Anderson had to say. It soon became clear that any Rovers fan hoping for a Jeremy Paxman-style interrogation would have to wait. Sky anchorman Rob Wotton gave Jerome Anderson the big introduction that indicated to me where this interview was heading. After the big introduction Wotton went on to say,

> "You very rarely appear in public in the media but you are so appalled at the protests at Blackburn and the vitriol against you and your son on the Internet that you have decided to come into *Sky Sports News* today and put the record straight."

Straight away I had to disagree with Wotton's first point – there is plenty of footage out there of Jerome Anderson's media appearances and I like the idea that people can just decide to come into *Sky Sports News* to put the record straight – give me a call! Already I felt that the interview would have been a lot more interesting if a Rovers fan had been posing the questions. Jerome Anderson told Wotton that it had been Rovers who had initially contacted him. He pointed out that it had been the Trustees and the board that had collectively decided they wanted to work with Venky's. In reference to the subsequent changes at board and management level Jerome Anderson stated that "those decisions were made purely by the new owners". Exactly what makes new owners with little knowledge of English football pick SEM clients Kean and Jensen to take over from the existing manager and his assistant? Jerome Anderson wasn't questioned further on the recruitment process that saw Kean appointed Rovers manager. I am presuming that, as Kean's agent, Jerome Anderson played a part in that process but what did that involve? From what John Jensen had said Jerome Anderson had been instrumental in bringing Jensen to Rovers, what part had Jerome Anderson played in Kean's promotion and who handled contract negotiations? These are the things that Rovers fans wanted clarification on but the questions weren't being asked. Jerome Anderson moved on to the January transfer window of 2011,

> "I received a call from the owner of the club saying look we have got one or two issues at the moment that are causing me concern would you be kind enough to help us through this difficult period which was the January transfer window, so I basically slept at the training ground for the month of January and helped the club in so many different areas."

By this stage I had given up any hope of Wotton asking any of the questions I would have asked. Jerome Anderson's take on the January transfer window was an interesting one.

> "When I left the training ground at the end of January the place was absolutely rocking. Some of the more experienced players said they were so excited about the future, not for many, many years had the club looked to bring in players like Rochina and Formica and Jermaine Jones and again that was job done."

I was interested to know who were these senior players that were "so excited" to be playing alongside an American who had been frozen out at Schalke, a player that had never played for a club outside South America and a 19-year-old from Barcelona B? When Jerome Anderson said that Rovers had not looked to bring in players like this for many, many years, unless he was referring to the players' relative obscurity, I couldn't really understand what he meant. Benni McCarthy had won the UEFA Champions League, Roque Santa Cruz had played over 150 league games for Bayern Munich, Craig Bellamy had been named PFA Young Player of the Year and Michel Salgado was one of the most decorated players in world football. Jerome Anderson stated that he did not receive a penny for any of the renegotiations and assistance. Maybe David Cameron's Big Society was working? He then turned his attentions to Rovers fans,

> "Wouldn't it be wonderful if the supporters really got behind the manager and team? Sometimes people forget these are young players, and young players need support when they're coming through. To go on the football pitch with fear is the worst thing you can do, and that's probably why some of the best results have been away from home."

Of the protests, he said,

> "Are there other things going on that we are not aware of? Are there groups of people that say they are supporters but actually don't want Venky's to succeed for whatever reason or for the manager to succeed? But what the world of football can't

understand is where is this coming from? It does seem to be well organised and from people who say they are supporters but who are hell-bent on making sure Venky's are not successful as owners and Steve Kean is not a successful manager."

A lot of people from Blackburn took exception to Jerome Anderson's comments. Certain people at Venky-run Blackburn Rovers have been highly critical of local figures commenting on Blackburn Rovers affairs but from the fans point of view, a lot of these people were making more sense than the people who were actually running the club. Leader of Blackburn with Darwen Borough Council Kate Hollern was spot on when she told the *Lancashire Telegraph,*

"There are no ulterior motives or dark forces at work. Fans are simply just rightly frustrated and angry at how the club is currently being run. We simply want greater transparency from the owners, better communication, a visible presence from them in Blackburn and proper leadership to sort this mess out. This is not just about results on the pitch. Blackburn Rovers FC is at the heart of the local community. The club is vital to the area's well being. We are just concerned that their future is safeguarded."

As far as I was concerned, not only had the timing of Jerome Anderson's interview been dreadful (a week before a winnable home game at a time when the public frustrations were showing signs of calming down) but also the interview itself did nothing to make me warm towards him. Jerome Anderson's lawyers contacted the

Lancashire Telegraph and a temporary freeze was put on comments on the website. It wasn't the first time Jerome Anderson had flexed his legal muscles.

> "I think that the important thing from today, Rob, is to inform everybody who is interested, and I would hope that would be a lot of Blackburn people, of the actual facts and the truth so that people can make their own judgements, vent their own feelings based on the truth."

Based on the information available, that is exactly what Rovers fans were doing.

The week following Jerome Anderson's interview Nick Harris published a letter on the *sportinintelligence.com* website from three former Rovers Directors - John Williams, Tom Finn and Martin Goodman. The letter clearly showed the three Directors had grave concerns about the direction the club was going in. Williams, Finn and Goodman had all since left the club and many of the points they raised in their letter remained cause for concern for Rovers fans. The week the letter was published John Williams' son and Head of Marketing Simon Williams left Rovers. Alan Nixon was also now reporting in *The People* that there had been an inside plot to remove Kean. According to Nixon the plotters were foiled when the internal memo sent to Mrs Desai urging her to sack the manager landed back on the Kean's desk. If details of the memo were known they were not revealed at the time.

In between all this Rovers managed to pick up a second Premier League win in two weeks with a 3-1 win over Fulham. Rovers' chances didn't look great when

Yakubu was sent off for a high challenge on Danny Murphy after 20 minutes. Goodwillie was sent on in his place and the young Scot had arguably his best game in a Rovers shirt. Pedersen gave Rovers the lead on the stroke of half-time with an excellently taken low, curling free kick and David Dunn doubled Rovers' lead a minute after the break. Damien Duff got another goal against Rovers to make it 2-1 and with over half an hour still to play the signs didn't look good for 10-man Rovers. The Fulham onslaught never came and on 78 minutes Mauro Formica fired home Stephen Nzonzi's clever through ball to seal all three points for Rovers.

As Rovers fans had been saying all season, wins were the only way to turn this around and while two wins in five games was hardly title winning form it was a step in the right direction. Next it was off to Goodison Park for what David Dunn described as Rovers best performance all season. Rovers started the game brightly and were unlucky to go behind on 23 minutes when Marouane Fellaini used his hand to set up Tim Cahill's opener. Rovers didn't lose hope and eventually got an equalizer through Goodwillie on 72 minutes. Goodwillie's three goals in January may have been three of the scruffiest tap-ins you are ever likely to see but in terms of his overall performance he was really starting to win me round. There was a late onslaught from Everton but in the end Rovers held out for a well deserved point.

17. Bolton	P22	W6	D1	L15	Pts 19
18. ROVERS	P22	W4	D6	L12	Pts 18
19. Wolves	P22	W4	D6	L12	Pts 18
20. Wigan	P22	W3	D6	L13	Pts 15

The three months between September and Christmas had undoubtedly been as bleak as I have known at Rovers. The club was still riddled with problems both on and off the pitch but eight points from a possible 15 since the defeat against Bolton meant at least there was now some glimmer of hope we could avoid relegation.

CHAPTER 14

A Year of Kean

At 10pm on Tuesday 20 December 2011, close to 500 Rovers fans congregated outside the players entrance at Ewood Park to demand the immediate removal of manager Steve Kean. Kean had become the public face of the new way of doing things but the new way of doing things wasn't working and the fans now wanted change. Rovers had just gone bottom of the Premier League following another toothless defeat, this time to local rivals and statistically the worst Premier League team of 2011, Bolton Wanderers. As an impassioned chorus of, "we want our Rovers back" rang out behind the Jack Walker Stand, Deputy Chief Executive Paul Hunt was inside penning a 2,500-word letter to Mrs Desai advising her that the manager had lost the players and the fans and that action must now be taken to save the club. Rovers' rookie manager had been in the job for 12 months and if opinion towards previous manager Sam Allardyce had been divided, Rovers fans were almost unanimous in their feelings towards Kean. 99.8% of

Rovers fans were against his continued employment and any fan not on the impromptu protest was more likely to have been absent through an overwhelming feeling of helplessness rather than what Kean himself often portrayed as fan support of his leadership. There wasn't just one reason why Rovers fans wanted Kean out – there were a whole host of reasons and the list was getting longer by the day. I am a grown man with a mortgage, a wife and a kid. At close to midnight, a week before Christmas, I didn't really want to be marching round Ewood Park protesting about the manager of a football club. This was not the organised campaign of hatred and vitriol it was reported to be; this was the spontaneous reaction of proper football fans who cared passionately about their club. I am a proud local man and I had had enough of what was going on at Blackburn Rovers. Whoever was the main decision maker at the club was destroying Blackburn Rovers and it was hard not to see Kean as their weapon of mass destruction. I had waited patiently for 12 months and I had had enough of failure. Forget what the media had to say. For every half-baked reason they could give for keeping Kean, I could give you 10 why he should be sacked. I didn't care how thick his skin was and I had certainly seen enough of our streetwise manager not to be buying into the "dignity" and "positivity" lines. It was no longer an option to sit back and wait for things to get better. Rovers weren't bottom of the league by accident: it was a consequence of all that was wrong at the club. Venky's were adamant that they were here for the long haul so they needed to start putting their mistakes right. The removal of Kean was now the only way forward as far as Rovers fans were concerned.

Wind the clock back one year to December 2010 and it would be fair to say that the manner in which Kean had been catapulted into the Rovers hot seat had done little to endear him to the average Rovers fan. His predecessor Sam Allardyce may not have been every fan's dream ticket but there were few who doubted his Premier League pedigree and even fewer who were happy to see him replaced by a total novice. Within a month of Venky's arrival at the club, Allardyce and his assistant Neil McDonald had been shown the door and within 24 hours of their departure Kean had landed the role of caretaker manager. While the rest of the football world was still trying to work out what had just happened, Kean was telling the press that he would be delighted to be considered for the job full-time and Mrs Desai was making it public that our caretaker manager of just 48 hours would now have final say on transfers. Premier League history is littered with internal managerial appointments that have failed spectacularly – Chris Hutchings at Bradford City, Steve Wigley at Southampton and Les Reed at Charlton are three obvious examples that spring to mind. At the time of Kean's promotion he told the media that he was in regular contact with Allardyce but subsequently it became clear that relations between the two were severely strained. "Sam's got the hump with me but I can sleep at night," Kean told the *Daily Mail*'s Matt Lawton in January 2011. Allardyce felt that somebody had said something derogatory to get him removed from his post. The back-stabber jibes were hard for Kean to brush off. When Kean was made caretaker manager the day after Allardyce's departure the fact was that he still hadn't managed a first team game of professional football in his life. He oversaw his first game the following Saturday but an uninspiring home draw against bottom of the table West Ham did little to win over the sceptics and those fans who did manage to make it to Ewood Park that day wondered why the club's best player and biggest asset Phil Jones had been dropped to the bench. With heavy snowfall across the country there was a strong case to say that the game shouldn't have gone ahead at all and I struggled to understand why Rovers had been so keen to press on with the fixture at this difficult time. Shortly after the game our eager caretaker manager flew out to India for a one-to-one with Venky's. I began to fear that Kean's appointment was not the short-term stopgap that most Rovers fans still thought it would be. Newspaper reports of large bets being placed on his appointment in Glasgow and London did little to allay my fears and soon after Kean arrived back from India it was announced that the 43-year-old Glaswegian had been made full-time manager until the end of the season. Upon his return, anyone unimpressed by Kean's appointment was about to see an example of his man-management skills. One of the first things Kean did was strip club captain (and second-biggest asset) Chris Samba of the club captaincy and make it known to the public that Samba had been looking to leave the club for 12 months. It was about as subtle as a sledgehammer and I was not so sure the manager should be dropping this kind of information into press conferences. For me, the 10 days after Allardyce's departure had given Rovers fans a good idea of what we could expect from our new manager – questionable team selection, dropping points, trips to

India, ill-chosen media declarations, out-going transfer speculation and widespread unrest. In the space of just over a week, a man with over 700 games in professional football management had been replaced by Steve Kean and once it was clear that this was not a joke, I found myself asking the question, "Steve who?"

A year later, in December 2011, I had a much better idea of who Steve Kean was and I was no longer buying in to the notion that he was some kind of great undiscovered managerial talent. I was now aware of Kean's wholly unspectacular football background, stretching all the way back to his post-school playing days in Glasgow. Kean's short playing career had been limited to no more than a handful of games at a relatively low standard and he had then gone on to work with his old pals Mark McGhee and Chris Coleman at Reading and Fulham. By the start of 2003, Kean's achievements in top-level football were still negligible and he had undoubtedly been helped along the way by his impressive list of friends and former associates. Prior to his arrival at Rovers Kean's most notable achievement had been to occupy the role of assistant manager to Chris Coleman at Fulham, Real Sociedad and Coventry. Looking at their record at the three clubs in question, I am not sure it would have made sense to replace Allardyce with Coleman, so to replace him with Coleman's assistant was even more difficult to fathom.

Kean had been brought to Rovers in 2009 by Sam Allardyce, following the departure of former first team coach Karl Robinson to MK Dons. Kean was now working under Allardyce and McDonald and was largely responsible for training the first team.

Essentially, the difference between the role of first team coach and manager is as broad as the difference between a P.E. teacher and the Headmaster of a school. Shortly after arriving at Rovers, Kean had been linked with the vacant managerial position at Kilmarnock. I feel that this would have been a logical first step into management for Kean. Kean was managed by SEM, the same company that had helped advise Venky's before and after the takeover and many felt that it was Kean's association with SEM that had been a key factor in him landing the manager job at Rovers. Questions about the links between Venky's, SEM and Kean would not go away and when Kean appeared on *Sky Sports' Goals on Sunday* programme on 27 February 2011 presenter Ben Shephard asked,

> "One of the things that certainly seems to have complicated it, from the perception from the outside, is that you are managed by the same people that are now advising the Venky's and advised them on the purchase of the club. From the exterior it kind of looks very convenient that they put their man in at the club. What do you say to that?"

Kean went on to talk about "Jerome Anderson (SEM Chairman and Chief Executive) who I respect (sic) greatly" and explained how SEM were given the task to find an owner by Blackburn Rovers and had been brought in by the previous regime at Blackburn Rovers to find a buyer. Shephard wanted more and when he pressed Kean about how it looks from the outside Kean interjected by saying,

> "If I was an outsider and I wasn't involved in it, I would go, well that – exactly that – well that looks a bit contrived, that looks a bit cosy."

It was difficult to understand the thought process behind the decision to replace Allardyce with Kean and equally difficult to understand the recruitment process that had followed Allardyce's dismissal. It wasn't even clear whether any other candidates had actually been interviewed and to use the words of Kean himself, yes, a lot of Rovers fans did feel that it looked a bit contrived and a bit cosy. It didn't really help matters when Mrs Desai was quoted saying "He is a good thinker; that is his biggest strength."

Although the decision to appoint Kean made little sense the great thing with football is, while past achievements may give some indication of what you are going to get, once in the job the manager will almost always be judged by the fans on his team's results. Translators, physiotherapists and even electricians have all risen to the top in football management – maybe Kean could now make his mark from a similarly unlikely starting point. There were clearly much better qualified managers out there but once it was clear Kean was going to be given a chance, if he could quickly show that he had the ability to win games and move the club forward (or even sideways!) there were few who would begrudge him a place at the top table. Allardyce was respected but he was not loved. If Kean felt he was worthy of his opportunity, here was his chance to grab it. Kean did need to hit the ground running however and unfortunately he didn't. Rovers picked up just one point from winnable home games against West Ham and Stoke and the boo's at the end of Kean's second game in charge reflected the frustrations of the entire club. It wasn't just the fans who had failed to take to Kean. At this point, the most scathing criticism of him was coming from the media and his managerial peers. He did manage to pick up his first win in the third game of his stewardship and in fairness, over the following four weeks there were signs of progress. The football was undoubtedly easier on the eye than it had been under Allardyce and by the end of January 2011 Rovers were seventh in the league. Fans were not happy with how Kean had climbed into the manager's chair but if he was able to show that he could do a better job than Allardyce then the majority of fans were willing to take him to their hearts. The popular misconception is that Rovers fans disliked Kean and Venky's from the start and nothing was going to change this. Rovers fans couldn't have been more welcoming towards Venky's and after a tricky start a large section of fans were singing Kean's name by the time West Brom came to town at the end of January 2011.

Prior to Venky's arrival, the Rovers' board had a great track record in guiding new and unfashionable managers through the pitfalls of Premier League management. John Williams and Tom Finn were there for Kean if he had wanted to use them but it appeared that he was very much part of a new order that essentially bypassed board members and worked with agents, advisors and the owners. If Kean wanted to be part of a new order that did it their way, he had to prove that this way was better, or expect criticism. After the home win against West Brom in January 2011,

Kean targeted three more wins and then he and the owners could sit down and work out how far the club could go. The big problem was, by the time Kean got three more wins, eight months had passed and we were five games into the following season. It is just a fact of football that if you consistently fail to win games, especially if you don't have any good times to fall back on, everything that you do will be scrutinised to the highest degree. Rovers went on an 11 game winless streak (the club's longest in the league for 25 years) that stretched from the end of January 2011 to the final day of April 2011. Kean's record at the start of 2011/12 was no better than it had been in 2010/11 – in fact it was worse. By the time Rovers were beaten by Bolton on 20 December 2011 Kean had been in charge for 38 Premier League games, of which Rovers had picked up just seven wins and a total of 32 points – nailed-on relegation form. There had been a couple of high profile wins, notably the televised game with Arsenal in September and the win against Wolves on the final day of 2010/11. These two games went some way towards winning Kean credibility with the casual television viewer. The frustrating thing was for every game Rovers won under Kean there were then four more that we didn't.

There was a lot of speculation about the exact nature of Kean's role. Some felt that Kean was a "yes man" who was simply carrying out orders for the boss; others were saying that Kean had final say on all football decisions. The feeling amongst many is that Kean was not the main decision maker at the club but simply the man who was sent out to front up to the media in exchange for a handsome pay packet. Both Michel

Salgado and Keith Andrews have publicly questioned whether Kean had that much of a say but I am going to judge Kean on what he himself has said on the issue. Kean said that he had final say on all football decisions. In that case he has to shoulder his fair share of the blame for the major mistakes made in 2011 with contracts, transfers and team selection, as well as the apparent problems with team performance, individual player performance and unrest amongst members of the playing staff.

Kean inherited the core of a good squad – certainly one that could challenge for a mid-table place given a few minor adjustments. The problem was that the wrong adjustments were made. I felt that poor judgment was shown in handing out new contracts to senior professionals who were of debatable long-term value to the club. Nelsen, Roberts, Dunn and Salgado had all seen better days and it just seemed logical to let their existing deals run their course. After blowing a small fortune re-signing a load of 30-somethings Kean tried to claim it was like signing new players. Dishing out new contracts to some of the more vocal members of the squad may have made Kean's job easier but few fans saw Nelsen, Roberts, Dunn and Salgado having much of an impact at Rovers beyond 2011. Serious questions have to be posed when players are handed new contracts in January and then aren't featuring in the first team squad by the end of the year. Of even more concern, in the case of Roberts and Salgado, was that the players concerned claimed they weren't being picked for contractual reasons while the management claimed they weren't being picked for football reasons. I didn't see what Roberts and Salgado had to gain from making this up. Either way it comes back to the question – "surely it was a mistake to hand them a new contract?" Members of the first team squad had been openly critical of the owners following the departure of Allardyce and McDonald. By the time the pay rises had been doled out most were telling anyone who would listen that Kean and Venky's were the way forward. To add salt to the wounds, while new contracts were handed out to a group of senior players who went on to have little impact in 2011/12, Kean crucially stalled on contract negations with one of our best young prospects, Junior Hoilett. It may have been Kean who gave Hoilett his big chance to play regular first team football but at a time when the club felt the need to issue new deals to SEM client Nick Blackman and veteran striker Jason Roberts, Kean went on record to say that Hoilett's contract was not a priority. Was Kean awarded a pay-rise for making these kinds of decisions or was he awarded a pay rise for taking the flak for these kinds of decisions?

Equally damaging to the club's long-term chances of staying in the Premier League were the worrying developments in the transfer market. Again, Kean was always ready to talk up his role when it was put to him that he was just a "yes man", so he must also accept his share of the criticism for the mistakes that were made in the transfer market. Few Rovers fans were under any illusions that Phil Jones would remain at Ewood Park forever, but would he have stayed for another season if we had a more high profile manager? Also, when the time did come for Phil Jones to leave we were well within our rights to expect him to be sold to the highest bidder. Kean had been very vocal in saying that Rovers' summer transfer kitty would be our "biggest ever". Why then did we end up signing David Goodwillie, Bruno Ribeiro and Myles Anderson? Upon their capture, Kean infuriatingly likened these three players to Wayne Rooney, Denis Irwin and Chris Smalling. Even if these signings were being forced on Kean, to come out with this sort of rubbish was just adding insult to injury. By the time Christmas came, Myles Anderson and Ribeiro had never played a competitive game in the first team and Goodwillie just looked totally out of his depth. Never mind the new Rooney, Goodwillie still had some way to go prove that he was better than Kalinic, the man he had replaced. Kean's words came to mean nothing. Petrovic and Vukcevic were also signed in the summer and they too went on to make little or no impact. Although Yakubu had proved to be an excellent signing, there were fans who felt that Scott Dann was now the fifth-best centre-back at the club behind Samba, Givet, Hanley and Nelsen. Even after the sale of Phil Jones, Rovers officials were still trying to claim that if a few minor things were changed in training Rovers could finish higher than they did in 2010/11. Scott Dann could train every minute for the rest of his life but he will never be as good as Phil Jones. By the same token, I could train from now until the year 2040 and I will never reach the levels that Dann has reached. That is why Phil Jones is in the England team, Scott Dann is not in the England team and I am limited to kick-abouts down the park. Trying to cover up the clear downsizing that was going on at Venky-run Rovers by talking about tweaking things in training was an insult.

With few permanent signings other than Yakubu going on to show that they were better than the players

Kean had inherited from Allardyce, it became even more important that Kean got the most out of the players that were already at the club. I honestly cannot think of one established outfield player who improved as a footballer during Kean's first year in charge. Robinson played well in goal, but I think that had more to do with how busy the rest of the team was keeping him. Credit to Kean for giving chances to Hoilett, Lowe and Hanley and they all made steady progress but certainly not enough to compensate all Kean's other failings. As for the established players, you can go through them all one by one and you will struggle to find one who played better under Kean than they had done under Allardyce. It wasn't just individually, but as a team Rovers were lacking in so many games in 2011. Not only did it become difficult to know who would be playing, but it also became difficult to work out who would be playing in what position. The odd injury may have dictated who he played at the back but the team had few injury problems up front and in his first season Kean appeared to be picking random combinations of Roberts, Mame Biram Diouf, Kalinic, Hoilett and Santa Cruz by the game. Even form seemed to count for little. Kalinic didn't help himself by getting a three-match ban for a silly sending-off, but after he and Benjani got match-winning braces either side of the New Year, neither really featured again for weeks. Dropping a goal scorer became a regular pattern that fans began to pick up on and I really couldn't understand what the criteria were when it came to team selection.

Once we did get a team out on to the pitch, we seemed unable to force the tempo of a game when it mattered. Rovers' fans were willing to see a phasing out of Allardyce non-football at the expense of the odd win here and there provided we weren't triangular passing ourselves into The Championship. For all Kean's talk of entertaining football I would say we saw free-flowing, attacking football resulting in Premier League wins no more than four times. Kean's public claim that he had a squad full of players that was behind him and full of great team spirit was so flawed that I don't really know where to start. I can name you a full team of players who were either reluctant to commit long-term to the club, left the club under a cloud or were not being selected when they were physically fit to play. I am struggling for a goalkeeper (Phil Jones can play there – he plays everywhere else!) but after that it is a stronger team than team Rovers put out against Bolton for Kean's 38th Premier League game in charge.

Phil Jones, Salgado, Givet, Samba, Nelsen, El-Hadji Diouf, Andrews, Hoilett, Benjani, Roberts, Kalinic

This is basically the core of the Premier League team that Kean inherited from Allardyce and they all had their issues at Rovers during 2011. For Kean to claim that the squad of players was 100% behind him was quite frankly embarrassing.

As all these problems became apparent and Rovers slipped further down the league, Kean wasn't helping matters by declaring that we were going to finish in the top 10. Even at the end of November 2011, with Rovers in the relegation zone, Kean was still saying it. I am not prepared to play the "did he mean it or didn't he mean it" game again. If a 44-year-old man comes out and repeatedly says something in public I am going to presume he means what he is saying. If he doesn't mean what he is saying he has to ask himself why he is saying it. At this point many non-Rovers fans may be thinking that, other than the manner of Kean's promotion from first-team coach to manager, all this is standard fare for any run-of-the-mill, failing football manager. Bad managers have been losing games, picking the wrong players and making mistakes in the transfer market for decades. Those fans would be right, so having covered Kean's more redeeming qualities I am now going to make a start on his bad points.

When Kean took the position of manager in December 2010 he said that the main two differences between his role as first-team coach and that of manager would be the media side of the job and the level of contact he would now have with the owners. For me, Kean failed monumentally in the first but ultimately he excelled in the second. There are different ways of approaching communication through the media and the fact that 12 months after taking to the microphone there was a massive campaign against Kean indicated to me that he had got the media side of things badly wrong. Kean's relationship with the owners was always going to be of far more consequence to his long-term employment and as a fan it became difficult to work out what the purpose of his media work actually was. I think that the purpose of a football manager's media duties should be to inform people what is going on, create a good impression of the club and put across what you are all about as a person and guardian of the sort of job that interests people enough to want to ask questions about what you are doing. I am not sure that Kean, assisted by the club's press officer Paul Agnew shared my philosophy and if he did I had to strongly question how he went about it. As well as the bold predictions that he became notorious for, Kean would say players weren't for sale when nobody was asking if they were, use words that the media were always going to create a story from, use spin to cover up every bad performance, drop misleading statistics in to conversation and wholeheartedly support every baffling decision that came out of the club. You may argue that it is an employee's job to wholeheartedly support every baffling decision his employers make, but Kean went way beyond the call of duty. Again whether, he meant what he was saying or was simply doing a job as an employee of a private company, for anybody who still considered that private company to be a football club it was equally hard to take. Even without including any of his embarrassing likening of Rovers players to well-known international stars, the list of cringeworthy Kean quotes is extensive. I have tried not to just use the ones that make him look stupid but here is a sample of 10 of the more notable quotes Kean made prior to the campaign for his removal from the club.

> "I don't know if they have taken reference from Edwin van der Sar, Louis Saha, Karl-Heinz Riedle, Lee Clark, other people I have coached – Andy Cole"
>
> *Kean on why the owners may have shown such strong support towards him.*

"You have to respect people that brought you to the club. Sam brought me here and showed a lot of confidence in me."

Kean on respect.

"If we can get solid, reliable foundations and then sprinkle a little bit of magic on top of that then fantastic."

Kean on trying to sign a marquee player.

"I can understand the scepticism because the owners are not based here, but I think the fans are starting to see they are in it for the long term. The investment they are going to put in is real. They are very wealthy people and enthusiastic about taking the club forward."

Kean on Venky's.

"He is always welcome here when he does come here, the same as any other agent who has an appointment here to see myself or a player. We always make that facility available. We are a very warm and open club and will continue to do that."

Kean on his agent Jerome Anderson.

"We've got a good group and a good vibe, and you don't take five positive results out of seven if the group is not together."

Kean on team spirit having drawn three games against sides that were ultimately relegated.

"We would have finished top six on our first half results but we were bottom on our second half results."

Kean on... not sure what his point is there really. Half-time team talks maybe?"

We are not going to be able to invent 10 games where we can go on an unbeaten run because there are not enough games left."

Kean on... again, not sure what.

"The overall message is that there is going to be investment in this transfer window and the chair lady says we don't have to sell anybody"

Kean on the summer transfer window 2011.

"It was difficult with Phil because he got the opportunity to go to Manchester United and he wanted to play Champions League football now. We're not there yet but I'm sure we will be in the next three or four seasons."

Kean on why Phil Jones left Rovers.

Hopefully this very small sample of *Keanisms,* as they are known to anyone who lives in Blackburn, helps to explain why Rovers fans were becoming so frustrated with Kean. For me, he was treading a very thin line between spin and claptrap and he needed to rein it in. If there had been the odd few fans that were willing to give Kean another chance at the end of 2010/11, by the time the 2011/12 season was under way there was little vocal support for his management. The problem was most Rovers fans just didn't believe him. If you are going to make big statements and then not deliver on them what do you expect? After all the big talk about what he and the club were going to do, the reality was, whatever words were being used in Kean's communication through the media, the club was quite clearly going backwards.

Bad feeling towards Kean certainly wasn't helped by his appearance in court in August 2011. When Rovers fans displayed a banner saying, "Taxi for Kean" I am not sure if he understood. Two days after the opening day defeat against Wolves at the start of 2011/12 Kean was banned from driving for 18 months after admitting drinking and driving. Details of the case made extremely uncomfortable reading. Kean had been stopped by police doing 90 mph on the M6 near Knutsford, six hours after the 1-1 draw with Manchester United in May 2011. When stopped, Kean told officers that he had not been drinking despite telling reporters earlier in the week that he planned to share a post-match glass of wine with Fergie. Kean was breathalysed by the roadside and was found to be almost twice over the legal drink-drive limit. He told the officers that he was shocked and stunned. Later that night, Kean confessed to the police that he had been witnessed having one bottle of beer. By the time Kean arrived at court three months later he was now happy to admit to drinking two and a half glasses of wine with Fergie. A medical report explained that with the rate of alcoholic units being broken down between the time of the game and Kean being stopped around 9pm, he would have only registered five microgrammes in breath having drunk what he claimed to have done but he gave a breath sample of 11 times that. Kean then claimed that his drink may have been spiked while drinking in a pub with Rovers fans. Kean said he didn't drink whisky or vodka. He drank beer though so you would imagine the beer would taste different if it had whisky or vodka in it. Kean asked for an adjournment because one of his key defence witnesses, *Sky Sports'* Jeff Shreeves was busy at a press conference at Arsenal's training ground and couldn't make it. The application was dismissed and in Judge Nicholas Sanders, it appeared we finally someone who had the power to stand up to Kean's babble.

> "There is no evidence of lacing of drinks. No one has come forward and said: 'Yes, I put 17 vodkas into his beer.' There is another explanation – and that is Mr Kean had more to drink than he has admitted."

Sanders went on to add,

> "It is relevant that when he was stopped by the police and asked if he had anything to drink, he replied not and this was clearly untrue."

Not only was Judge Sanders able to question Kean's ability to tell the truth but he was actually able to do something about it. Kean was banned from the road, fined £1,800 and told to pay £720 costs. It was a small price to pay. Just 40 miles down the same stretch of motorway Plymouth Argyle goalkeeper Luke McCormick caused the death of Arron Peak, aged 10, and Ben Peak, aged eight, while driving under the influence of excess alcohol. Later that year Rovers fans had to watch the media create an image of Kean as some sort of vilified saint. "A man of great dignity" was the common phrase that was used. Strangely, there was no mention of the unsavoury drink-driving episode. Kean may have been doing his fair share of charity work – notably his fine work for the Save Our Squirrel campaign – but drink driving is just not acceptable.

The breakdown in trust between the fans and those in authority at the club was a major factor in the protests that started in September 2011. The *Keanisms* didn't stop once the protest got under way. In fact, they became more regular and if anything they were now so out of touch with what Rovers fans could see was actually happening that they were becoming more likely to provoke anger than sniggers.

> "We are disappointed there was a little bit of a demonstration, but only a couple of hundred people turned up. That is one per cent so that tells me 99 per cent of people are happy and can see what we are trying to do here."
>
> *Kean on the protest that is backed by the vast majority of fans at the club.*
>
> "I don't know if it is a large section of the crowd and to be fair, I'm not really paying any attention to anybody who is staying behind."

Kean on the importance of the fans.

"I try to reply to all of them."

Kean on the 500 letters he receives every day, from all around the world. That's a lot of replies.

"I'm always very open and honest with anything I'm asked."

Kean on being honest.

"We are in a position where we have forfeited going through and having the chance to reach a cup final."

Kean on the fans' pointless 10 hour round trip to Cardiff.

"I talk to people in the village and they can see what we're trying to do. They can see the way we're trying to play football, and they tell me 'keep going'."

Kean on the village and losing games.

"I live in the area but I don't go out in Blackburn because I can't. You just never know who you might run into."

Kean on the village and losing games

"I was advised that it would be in my interest to have somebody with me at all times."

Kean on his bodyguard.

"Kevin Gallagher's never been a coach or a manager and, to my knowledge, Jack hasn't either. Their comments were not helpful. It would be better if Jack could just keep the roads gritted so we can all get to the training ground."

Kean on gritting the roads in another MP's constituency

"I know that every player at the club now wants to be there..."

Kean on all the good players leaving the club.

Was Kean dumb or was Kean clever? Kean was being advised on public relations by Paul Agnew. Surely Agnew had worked in the field of public relations for long enough to be aware that if Kean dropped references to bodyguards and personal safety into conversations with journalists they would pick up on these words and turn them in to a story. They weren't just said once either; they were said on a number of occasions. I can't find any examples of Kean dropping it in to conversation that he had a driver so why the regular references to his bodyguard? "The chap who protects me is a seventh dan in karate, but he is not big or butch or anything. He knows how to handle himself." Protect Kean from who? The protesters? The fans wanted him sacked not assassinated. Playing out a public war through the media that centred on the supposed threat to the manager's safety posed by good, honest, hard-working football supporters showed the depths that the club had sunk to. It was so frustrating. Duncan White of the *Daily Telegraph* summed up the feeling of Rovers fans when he said,

> "The fans could see with their eyes plain before them that Blackburn were playing really poorly and they just got fed up of being lied to basically and being told that everything was rosy and going well and the big transfers were round the corner and then they get let down. Kean was complicit with the owners in that."

Unfortunately, for every reporter who could see why the fans were so frustrated there was another who was now ready to paint Kean out to be the victim. What their motivation was I really couldn't tell you but Rovers just wasn't Rovers any more.

Whoever was actually running things Kean was certainly facilitating their failings. Overpromoted Kean continued to big up Venky's at every opportunity and it became hard to know where Kean ended and Venkys's began. I could see how the relationship helped Kean and I was starting to take an educated guess on why it helped Venky's but I really couldn't see how it helped Blackburn Rovers. In October 2011, Kean told the *Lancashire Telegraph,*

> "Venky's, as a family, have shown great support to me as a young manager and we share a special relationship. They share a personal relationship with the players. That is quite unusual. They have the passion to drive the club ahead. It won't just last overnight. We know they are in here for the long haul. They will drive us to the top end of the game. In four or five years, we shall be in European football. We might not be in the Champions League but maybe in the Europa League. The media in England laughed at this. But we believe."

The love was nauseatingly two-way. Around the same time as Kean came out with that Balaji Rao said,

> "The team is in the relegation zone right now, but it is going to come up I am sure of that. We do know that a few people have been generating thousands of mails demanding the ousting of current manager Steve Kean, who is a brilliant manager."

Was this some sort of sick joke that I just wasn't getting? It appeared that one man was living the dream while 20,000 others had to endure the nightmare. Kean's travels across the globe had become a feature of his time at the club. His monthly trips to India were beginning to grate with Rovers fans. What was wrong with the phone? Couldn't Venky's send someone to Blackburn if they really wanted to know what was going on? I couldn't believe it when I read that Kean travelled to India seven days before our relegation showdown with Wolves at the end of 2010/11. Kean wasn't slumming it in "cattle class" on these flights, by the way. "It's an 11-hour flight, but I have a flat bed on the plane. I just get my pyjamas on and go to sleep" Kean told reporters in 2011. Again, other people may have been pulling the strings here but in Kean they had found someone who appeared more than happy to play the willing servant, mouth-piece and beneficiary. It wasn't just India – every time I picked up the paper Kean was in another country. I had to question the justification for a lot of these trips. Was his visit to Canada really necessary? Kean wanted to talk to Hoilett's dad about a new contract. I failed to see how a home visit from Kean was really going to sway the decision-making process and I have been proved right.

It was becoming increasingly evident throughout 2011 that Kean wasn't working for the fans; he was working for the owners and that relationship was rock solid. Kean may have bent over backwards for Venky's and anyone with a microphone but I can't remember a less approachable manager at the club. Kean's poor relationship with the fans may have been a major inconvenience but it didn't appear to pose too great a threat to his employment status.

Kean had become a master at setting himself a target, not hitting it and then conveniently moving on to his next target. When the 2010/11 season wasn't going to plan he said we could push for Europe further down the line. When the summer transfer window wasn't going to plan he said "judge me in September". When September came and Rovers had no points, he said judge me when my new signings have played a few games. When his signings had played a few games and Rovers were still bottom of the league he told us that the squad was worth more money than it was six months ago. What? When Rovers picked up no points from tough home games against Manchester City, Spurs and Chelsea he said judge me on winnable fixtures against Wigan, Stoke, Swansea, Sunderland, West Brom and Bolton. When the team picked up just four points out of a possible 18 from those six games he told us the January transfer window was coming up and he was going nowhere. In fact he was given a new and improved contract. Venky's loyalty to Kean was incomprehensible. As all those around him (Sam Allardyce, Neil McDonald, Chairman John Williams, Chief Executive Tom Finn, Finance Director

Martin Goodman, assistant manager John Jensen and eventually Deputy Chief Executive Paul Hunt, amongst many others) left the club Kean's position appeared to get ever stronger as Rovers edged closer towards The Championship. To compound the misery, all this was now the fans' fault and Kean had been cast as the victim by large sections of the media. Kean was lapping it up. "I have got a lot of support from some very experienced managers. No disrespect to MPs, local journalists or ex-players, when I get experienced managers telling me I am doing a 'marvellous job' I listen to them." I felt as though I was going insane.

Chapter 15

January Transfer Window 2012

For large parts of the previous two transfer windows the majority of Rovers' fans had been happy to take Steve Kean's transfer declarations at face value. When we were told that our summer spend would be "substantial" we naively believed that £30 million worth of playing talent would be on its way in rather than on its way out. Rovers' fans had been starved of major investment in new players for so long that Kean had a captive audience. Even when Venky's first transfer window had failed to live up to its big billing, Rovers fans were still prepared to accept that January had just been a dry run for the big summer-spend. People will only believe for so long and by the time Venky's third transfer window came round unfortunately Rovers fans no longer believed. As it happened, Venky's appeared to have gone mute anyway – at least as far as communicating directly with the fans was concerned. We hadn't really seen or heard from them since Balaji and Venkatesh walked out of the Wigan game in November. Unsurprisingly Kean was more than happy to do the talking for everyone. It had taken a while but I was quickly learning that when Kean said things like, "Yakubu will go on to be a great player for us for years to come. I don't know why it didn't work out for him at Everton." It didn't necessarily mean that Yakubu will be a great player for us for years to come and that Kean didn't know why it didn't work out for him at Everton. Kean had done so much talking in 2011 that even he had lost track of some of the more notable statements he had made. By the start of the transfer window Kean found himself having to clarify, "I don't think we ever said we were going to get into Europe this season."

12 months earlier Kean had said in his programme notes prior to the Liverpool game,

> "As for Rovers, the hopes and aims for the new year are two-fold. Firstly we want to achieve a top half finish in the Barclays Premier League this term. Then, looking ahead to next season we want to push things forward towards the top six. To the outside football world that might sound ambitious. However, given the investment we anticipate in this (and the summer) transfer window, we feel it is realistic."

Talking the talk and failing to walk the walk was now typical Kean behaviour as far as I was concerned. While we were going from one disaster to the next on the pitch, if there was a positive to cling to, Kean's knuckles would be white around it. Kean had been talking up this transfer window since November. Personally I felt it was just a delaying tactic to deflect attention away from our dreadful league form. At the time we were bottom of the league and four points adrift of safety with over a third of the season gone. When the fans wanted to know why we had picked up just three points from our last seven games Kean appeared to be more interested in focussing on a transfer window that most fans didn't want to see him here for anyway. I wouldn't mind but it was just the same old same old in terms of who was coming in and how much we had to spend. Kean told reporters at the end of November,

> "Once we get the budget we can identify the players we want to bring in to the club. There are always areas of the pitch you are looking to strengthen in. We are scoring goals with Yakubu but you are always looking to add goals to your team and you are always looking for different options in the midfield. We have always said we are looking to bring a midfielder in and another striker if we can. We would like someone who can give us a different dimension in midfield. Someone who can give us good legs, passes the ball and can continue the service. What has been shown is if we can give good service, we have players who can create and score goals. On the flip side we have to close the door a little bit so it is an all round midfielder who can pass and close it up a little bit as well."

Once again it appeared that Kean was covering all eventualities however it did look like it was the midfielders and strikers who needed to be more on their toes than the defenders. Weren't previous Kean signings Formica, Rochina, Petrovic, Vukcevic, Goodwillie and Slew all midfielders and strikers?

By mid-December Kean was happy to tell reporters,

> "I don't want to say the figure but I am aware of the funds I have. Without going into specific positions we will be looking for a bit of experience. When you look at the make-up of the squad we have enough young players, and I think it is important for the profile of the squad to have a bit of experience. That is what we will be trying to do."

On the morning of the Sunderland game on 10 December 2011 Nick Harris of the *Mail on Sunday* led with the headline "Blackburn fear their players won't be paid as bankers demand £10m deposit". Harris wrote,

> "Blackburn Rovers' owners have been told by their bankers, Barclays that they must deposit £10million in the club's account by New Year's Eve or the bank will not extend the credit needed to pay the players' wages beyond the first month of 2012."

Harris went on to say that Venky's were understood to be angry at the Barclays ultimatum and that Barclays in India were well aware that Venky's had ample finances to cover the overdraft. Harris claimed that an agreement had been in place between Venky's and the bank that Rovers' Indian owners would inject specific amounts of capital in to the club at certain times. According to Harris that hadn't happened, hence

Barclays demand for a £10 million payment to stop Rovers exceeding their fixed overdraft. The implication was that although failing to make the payment would not result in the club going bust, within a couple of months it may become difficult for Rovers to meet their monthly wage commitments.

Predictably, senior figures at Rovers rubbished the claims but the clubs aims and objectives for the upcoming transfer window noticeably changed after Harris' piece in the *Mail on Sunday*. Nobody actually cleared anything up they just denied anything negative that was thrown their way. Good old positive energy will see you through anything if you are deluded enough. There were further worrying stories about the state of the club's finances. Shortly after the embarrassing loss that left Rovers bottom of the Premier League at Christmas, Alan Nixon of the *Daily Mirror* reported that Venky's had made a pre-tax loss of £18.6 million during their first financial year at the club. Even more shocking than the alarming multi-million pound loss was the fact that this loss occurred during a period that in which Formica and Rochina were the only permanent additions to the first team squad. I wasn't the only person who was really struggling to get my head around where this loss had come from. I have now had the benefit of looking through the "Blackburn Rovers Football and Athletic Plc Annual Report and Financial Statements for the Year Ending June 2011." Filed in December 2011, the 27-page report includes company information; a report from Deputy Chief Executive Paul Hunt; a statement from Finance Director Karen Silk (she had only actually been appointed in the role earlier that month); the business review (see below); the profit and loss account; the balance sheet; cash flow statement and further information about the club.

	2010/11	2009/10
Turnover	£57.6m	£57.8m
Wages & Salaries	£49.9m	£47.4m
Other Operating Expenses	£11.9m	£12.1m
Operating profit/(loss) – before player trading	(£4.2m)	(£1.7m)
Interest Payable	£0.6m	£0.6m
Profit/(loss) – before player trading	(£4.8m)	(£2.3m)
Player Trading	(£13.8m)	£0.4m
Profit/(loss)	(£18.6m)	(£1.9m)
Net cash movements in/(out)	(£7.7m)	(£2.5m)
Closing Net Debt	(£26.3)	(£21.0m)
Finishing Position in the Premier League	15th	10th
Average League Attendance	25,008	25,427
Wage to Turnover %	86.6%	82.0%
Number of live TV games	7	13

The things that stood out about the figures here were the £4.2 million operating loss (before player trading); the £18.6 million loss (after player trading) and the £5.3 million increase in closing net debt. Player amortisation accounted for £7.8 million of the £13.8 million loss on player trading. When a player is bought (e.g. for £3m on a 3 year contract), the club categorises the player as an asset on the balance sheet and releases the £3m cost over the period of the contract, i.e. £1m per year. In fairness to Venky's the amortisation charge for 2011 is therefore largely out of their control however the remaining £5.9 million lost on player trading and the

£5.3 increase in club debt was a concern considering the players that were brought in and those that were re-signed. Wages had gone up by £2.5 million with £671,451 of the increase being made up of compensation for loss of office for former directors. Worringly for Venky's their share value had now gone down from £23 million when they bought the club to just £17 million. This was some loss of value in just over six months. Football finance commentator Nick Willis commented,

> "The valuation of the club at the time of purchase was £23m - this can be arrived at in several ways, usually a combined measure of the value of current net assets plus expectations of future profits. The Venky's shares only had a book value of £17m as at June 2011 because the club posted a large loss for that year, therefore the net asset position deteriorated. One interesting point is that the position would have been even worse, but the club converted £10m of debt into shares as part of the takeover - a debt for equity swap. If they hadn't done that the net asset position at the year end would have only been £7m - not far from being technically insolvent in such an unstable business as football."

The fact was, Rovers had been treading a financial tightrope for years and the club couldn't afford to make the mistakes that had been made after the takeover. For the first time, we saw the huge financial implications of the poor management, lack of leadership and bad decision making that had become commonplace since the arrival of Venky's. I'm not sure if anybody had explained it all to Kean yet,

> "The finance side of the club is dealt with by the directors. Hopefully the numbers can come back saying we can be active at a good level. Money has come into the club with Phil Jones and Nikola Kalinic going, and I would like to think we can keep the majority of the squad together. We want to keep the squad together and build on that, add faces rather than take them away, and that is very important for the next two to three years. I am optimistic I will get that backing. We will not be talking about a final figure. We will just be discussing areas where we want to strengthen. I think we should be doing it that way because in the past names got out – not through our end – but maybe through the players being so excited about coming to Blackburn Rovers and when they don't materialise it ends up being a negative feel rather than being close on a number of occasions."

So that is how the Ronaldinho and Beckham stories got out? If you didn't laugh you'd cry. By the end of 2011, Nick Harris was back to reveal more bad news for Rovers fans. Harris reported,

> "Rovers have not paid Barclays any of the £10 million the bankers wanted by December 31 to allay fears of a funding crisis – and it is inevitable that Rovers will embark on a player sell-off in this month's transfer window to raise cash instead."

No doubt helped by the fact that Rovers managed to pick up a few unexpected points with a team of untested youngsters over the festive period, now that the club's reported financial problems were out in the open the emphasis had clearly shifted from who was coming in to who was going out. Everyone had become an asset and the only players that appeared to be safe were those with low sell-on values and low wages. The two players attracting most outside attention were Hoilett and Samba. Samba played one more game for Rovers in 2012 before getting his big move to Russia but more about him later. Hoilett's contract saga had been rumbling on for almost as long as he had been a first team regular. For months Kean had been telling anyone that was still listening that Hoilett was ready to put pen-to-paper on a new deal at Ewood Park. By January 2012, even Kean was ready to accept that Hoilett's immediate future may lie elsewhere. Kean told the *Lancashire Telegraph,*

> "If he would like to commit his future to the club we have always said from day one that we would like to get it tied up. He has probably taken the opportunity to look elsewhere. I don't know where he is on it. If we can get to a point where he wants to sign then great; if not, if there is a bid that comes in then we would obviously have to consider that, and the fact that he hadn't signed. But no bids have come in."

Depending on whom you believed the proposed stumbling block was an £18 million sell-on clause Rovers wanted to insert in to the contract and Hoilett's father (also his agent) wanting certain assurances on where the club was going long-term. Whatever the stumbling block was, it had been six months since Hoilett was handed his first contract offer and he still hadn't signed. Rovers had always been keen to point out that even if Hoilett left in the summer we would still receive a hefty compensation package for him. Even this now looked in doubt. The compensation rules for players transferring from one country to another are markedly different from those for a player who transfers between clubs in the same league. Provided it was re_invested in to the team, Rovers fans had been hoping for a fee similar to the £4 million Chelsea had paid to Manchester City for Daniel Sturridge but now that Hoilett was attracting interest from Germany and Italy that fee could be as low as £670,000. Kean blamed the previous regime for not handing Hoilett a longer contract two years earlier but I felt that Kean needed to be more aware of his own failings before he started criticising the previous, much more successful administration. There was reported interest from Bolton, Spurs and Stoke but there was no January move for Hoilett and he ended up seeing out the final six months of his contract at Rovers.

If Rovers wanted to ease the wage burden and get some quick money in then it looked like they had to look elsewhere. Michel Salgado and Jason Roberts had both been frozen out of Kean's plans since December. Kean had been quick to blame most of our defeats in December on defensive absences but bizarrely he refused to pick Salgado ahead of stand-in right back Jason Lowe – even though Salgado himself claimed to be fit. Maybe Kean knows better than two times UEFA Champions League winner and four times La Liga winner Salgado and if Kean said he needed to rest then he needed to rest. Why would anyone possibly believe that Salgado had been left out because further appearances would trigger a revision to his existing contract? Jason Roberts had the same issue but again it took the player himself to clarify the situation. Roberts publicly stated,

> "Contractual issues have not allowed me to be selected. It is about contractually a few more games would give me a longer contract and obviously there are decisions to be made there."

I wouldn't have minded so much but it had been Venky's who had overseen these two contract extensions less than 12 months ago. Salgado ended up seeing out the rest of the season at Rovers but he didn't play another game for the club. Reading took Roberts off our hands. Roberts did really well at Reading and there is no doubting that he is an excellent Championship player. I particularly liked the "overhead kick" he scored on his debut. Only Roberts could take a penalty, shank it, shin the rebound, trip over the keeper and end up on the floor at the same time as the ball was hitting the back of the net. I notice they didn't let him take the next penalty.

Keith Andrews was the next unhappy player to leave. During his time at Rovers Andrews had been targeted by some sections of the crowd. In fairness there were few that felt his replacement Petrovic was better and while Andrews was some way short of being Zinedine Zidane nobody ever doubted his commitment to the cause. Publicly, Kean said that keeping hold of

Andrews was still an option but personally I couldn't see Andrews being in any rush to play for Rovers. When Andrews finally went to West Brom he delivered this parting shot,

> "There had been a lot of interest throughout January but I don't think the way Blackburn dealt with things helped because it was very hard for me or other clubs to get a straight answer out of them. There was sheer relief at having finally cut my ties at Blackburn. Even if the window had shut without me having got a move somewhere, I would have looked to have gone out on loan because I couldn't stay there."

Even players that had only just arrived at the club were now reported to be on their way out. Formica was attracting interest from Greek side Olympiacos. According to reports in the press, Argentinian Formica had been feeling homesick having struggled to settle in England. Homesickness can be a terrible thing but somebody might want to check a map of the world before they start telling Formica that they had found a cure in Greece. In-form Yakubu was attracting interest from a host of club's and newspapers were even reporting that Scott Dann now wanted out. Dann had arrived at Ewood Park with a big reputation but for me he had failed to deliver. He claimed to be finally finding his feet at Rovers. The next challenge was to find the rest of his body. In the end neither Formica, Yakubu nor Dann left in January but it was hard not to feel that the only players who saw out their contracts these days were kids on short deals, or players like Vince Grella.

It was getting hard to keep up at Rovers. Paul Clement had replaced John Jensen as Kean's assistant back in October 2011. Just three months in to his short-term contract, it was announced that Clement would be leaving Rovers to hook up with Carlo Ancelotti at Paris Saint-Germain. Rovers received a compensation package and Clement was quickly replaced by Steve Bruce's former second-in-command Eric Black. I don't know whether it was coincidental or not but Black's arrival seemed to signal an upturn in form at Rovers. Black wasn't the only January arrival but it was far from easy going.

There had been reported interest in £1 million-rated Giorgios Fotakis from PAOK Salonika; summer target Vedad Ibisevic was back on the radar; as were Robbie Rogers from Columbus Crew and Australian international Brett Holman. I didn't fancy our chances of landing Ibsevic after what had gone on in the summer and none of the other names on the list filled me with much joy. Newspapers were also reporting that our bid for Fulham's Andy Johnson was turned down and Real Madrid squad player Esteban Granero had said he would rather wait around for an offer from another club than spend the rest of the season on loan at Rovers. Midway through the window and Kean was still predictably up-beat despite the slow progress:

> "It's slow everywhere but we've been very, very busy over the last eight or nine days. Clubs are deciding to be slow in responding. We're actively trying to improve the areas I think need improving and I'm confident we'll get people in. We're active – there's things out there that clubs are sitting on

> before we've moved anyone (sic), so that's as positive as we can be."

Later that week it was reported in the *Lancashire Telegraph* that Joao Souza was back at Ewood Park to help sporting director Simon Hunt and director Vineeth Rao in their search for new additions to the Rovers squad. Weren't we the lucky ones! Venky's Brazilian mate Souza had played a key role in helping Rovers try and sign Ronaldinho 12 months earlier and had also been instrumental in helping in the summer capture of Bruno "where are they now" Ribeiro. I know people who have been barred from pubs for less than that. I didn't hold out much hope for Souza's latest recruit, Anthony Modeste. Looking at his record it was a case of Modeste by name, not even that good by nature. Striker Modeste had 16 goals in 98 top-flight games in France and had not featured for his parent club Bordeaux since October. For me, it said a lot about what Kean thought of the strikers he had signed earlier in the year. As for Souza, I hope he wasn't getting paid too handsomely for landing us with some of this garbage. I wanted to see money being spent on permanent signings that would actually play games in the first team. I didn't want to see money being lavished on "advice" and agents – particularly when a lot of that advice was either really poor or not being listened to.

By the time deadline day came round it was sort of a case of "whatever happens, happens" for me. Rovers' fans were powerless but to just watch on. There were reports linking us with Swiss international Scott Sutter from Young Boys of Bern, QPR squad player Bradley Orr and Martin Olsson's twin brother Marcus. Would any of these players get a game over the next six months? In truth, I had no idea. I knew nothing about Sutter so I had to suspect that there was every chance he could turn out to be the new Ribeiro, Petrovic, Myles Anderson, Vukcevic or Goodwillie. 29-year-old Orr was struggling to get a game at QPR having played out most of his career in England's lower leagues. Marcus Olsson had been on trial previously at Rovers and nothing had come of it so I wasn't holding out too much hope for him this time around. In the end Stutter didn't come and we ended up signing Orr and Marcus Olsson. Orr spoke of his excitement to be joining a Premier League team but at this stage few at the club, other than Kean, were too excited by his capture. Kean said of our eventual three signings,

> "We said we wanted three or four bodies in and we have managed to get three in. The ones we have got in, it has been tough getting them in, but we have new faces, which is always good. The plan was to bring in experienced players and we tried hard. We tried a number of different avenues to sign players with more Premier League experience but we got flat no's, we got don't come back, don't enquire again. It has been that type of window where clubs have been trying to keep their squads together and it has been really difficult to get players in. The players who are playing in teams, clubs are fighting tooth and nail to keep them. We tried for a few that have started in other teams and it was 'don't be silly, we are not selling'. So went and got Marcus, Anthony and Bradley and are very happy with what we have got."

Undoubtedly the most bizarre activity of the January transfer window had to be the Ryan Nelsen to Spurs saga. Leading up to transfer deadline day most Rovers fans were under the impression that 34-year-old Nelsen was fighting to save his career. Kean had already come out earlier in the month and said,

> "I would be very surprised if the way his knee is that Ryan would think about moving to play anymore because he is in some discomfort. I don't think that is even in his mind at the moment."

Since signing a new contract 12 months earlier, Nelsen had only played one game since April 2011 but this didn't stop Kean bemoaning how much he was missed every time we shipped a load of goals. I had to imagine that if he was fit he would have been playing. When it was announced late on transfer deadline day that Spurs were interested in him I thought it was some sort of joke. An announcement was made by Rovers that Nelsen's contract had been terminated and two days later he signed for Spurs as a free agent. Either Spurs had a good doctor or Nelsen had made a miraculous recovery. Spurs' assistant boss Kevin Bond said that Nelsen had "been fit for weeks" and that he would be involved immediately for Spurs. Despite walking straight in to the Spurs squad for the trip to Anfield the following Monday, Kean still maintained that Nelsen was "a long way from being match fit". Yes, Nelsen was a long way from being match fit because he hadn't played any matches. Dear me, and still Rovers fans were cast as the bad guys for not backing Kean.

For fans of pretty much every other club in the Premier League, February 1st signalled the end of the transfer window for 2011/12. That just wouldn't be Rovers would it and the Christopher Samba transfer saga rumbled on regardless. Having signed for Rovers from Hertha Berlin in 2007 for £450,000, Congolese international Samba had gone on to establish himself as one of the most solid central defensive performers in the Premier League. Still only 27, Samba had been attracting interest from a number of clubs for some time. In fairness to Samba, the interest never seemed to detract from his level of performance under the guidance of Mark Hughes and Sam Allardyce, or even Paul Ince. I don't want to sound like a broken record but, publicly at least, it was the arrival of Kean that seemed to act as a catalyst for the breaking down of Samba's relationship with Rovers. Appointed club captain by Allardyce at the start of the 2010/11 season, one of the first things Kean did when he arrived in the Rovers hot-seat was to unceremoniously strip Samba of the club captaincy. Very diplomatic. Despite putting in a transfer request Samba was persuaded to sign a new contract just six weeks later. Key to this new contract was a series of promises and assurances that, by the summer of 2011, Samba felt had not been met. Samba was again absent from the squad at the start of the 2011/12 season but when no firm offers were received for his services he was quickly re-instated to the team. By the time the January transfer window came around, Samba had clearly had enough of life at Rovers. Throughout the season he had not been shy in stating that he felt the team was not good enough and there were few that could argue that Rovers was the same club he had joined in 2007. At the start of January 2012 Samba gave an interview with French newspaper *L'Equipe* making it clear that he no longer saw his future at Rovers. Samba told *L'Equipe,*

> "I tried to maintain my level of performance but I sense that it is time for a change. The club doesn't evolve at all. I'm resigned. I've always put the interests of the club before my own. I've invested a lot, always tried to lead by example, but things have not gone as I was told. I hope people will understand me."

Many fans were critical of Samba but I could see exactly where he was coming from. He wasn't saying anything that wasn't true and nobody could argue that he hadn't given Venky's a fair chance to prove themselves. At the time of signing his new contract the club had been linked with Ronaldinho and Beckham. 12 months on and many of our established high earners were being shown the door, Rovers were entrenched in a relegation battle and, with all due respect, we were now signing players like Marcus Olsson and Bradley Orr.

Kean insisted that Samba was not for sale but every neutral's favourite manager was kidding himself if he felt that Rovers held the cards here. Kean's baffling decision to start a public war with Samba looked doomed from the start. Samba didn't really cover himself in glory during this period and that has probably soured how some Rovers fans feel towards him. Again, though, I could sympathise with a lot of what he was saying. I'm a lifelong Rovers fan and I now felt little connection with the club – what chance did anyone else have? As the transfer window reached its final week, Samba told *The Sun*,

> "Blackburn need players who are 100% for the club — and I'm not. The only way to solve this is for them to let me go. It will be very difficult for me to play for this team again. I'm at the end of the road here. I'm not going to change so, for their good and mine, they must sell me now. When a couple don't get on they get a divorce — and that's what me and Blackburn have to do. I signed a new deal last January because Venky's told me they had big plans. Names like Ronaldinho were mentioned and they promised there was going to be a lot of investment in the team. It hasn't happened. They don't understand football in this country and they don't realise how much I've given to Blackburn and that they have broken promises they have made. I stayed because I believed them but they weren't honest with me and now I know I made the wrong decision. I share the frustration of the fans who must have believed the owners too."

Was Samba really saying anything that the majority of Rovers fans weren't? Samba made his last appearance for the club in the 2-1 home defeat to Stoke at the start of 2012. Various reasons were given for his absence in subsequent games but he was still employed by Rovers so many felt that unless that changed he should have just knuckled down until he got his move. By the end of the transfer window Rovers were yet to receive any acceptable offers for Samba. There had been a couple of feeble bids from relegation rivals QPR and reported interest from Spurs and Paris Saint-Germain but ultimately Samba remained a Rovers player. There was no public reconciliation between player and manager in the days that followed the closing of the transfer window and it was clear that Samba would play no further part under the management of Kean. As had now become common under the leadership of Venky's and their UK extension Kean, it was another sad end for a Rovers legend.

Just as it looked like Samba would linger on the sidelines until the summer, news started to emerge that former Chelsea manager Guus Hiddink was now interested in bringing Samba to Russia. Hiddink had just been appointed the new manager of Russian Premier League outfit FC Anzhi Makhachkala and although the English transfer window had closed for business at the end of January the Russian transfer window didn't close until the back end of February. Hiddink didn't have long to move and within days of expressing an interest in Rovers ostracised former captain he got his man and Samba became a FC Anzhi Makhachkala player. In many ways it was a strange move for Samba. Although Anzhi had UEFA Champions League ambitions, bags full of cash and a squad that included players like Samuel Eto'o and a number of Russian internationals, Samba's new home was a far cry from the cut and thrust of the Premier League. The Anzhi players weren't even based in Makhachkala. The club's players lived and trained in a village near Moscow and flew in for home games – flying about 1,250 miles 15 times a season. Many Rovers fans are under the impression that a lot of Rovers players live and train outside of Blackburn and only really visit the town on match days but at least they are not based 1,250 miles away. Samba was believed to be on good money and personally, I wished him all the best. I didn't really see that he would cross paths with Rovers in many UEFA Champions League games in the future.

If Rovers had needed to find a few million quid to see off the bank then the sale of Samba was no doubt a welcome solution for the boardroom number crunchers. Not only had we got a big earner off the wage bill but we had managed to get a decent injection of money for a player who wasn't playing anyway. As the transfer window was now closed, there was little immediate pressure to re-invest the Samba transfer cash back in to the team. Despite the eventual inevitability of Samba's departure, Rovers fans still wanted to know whether this was now the end of the big money departures at Venky-run Blackburn Rovers. When quizzed about whether there would be further big name sales at the club director Vineeth Rao told the *Lancashire Telegraph*,

> "There are no plans like that there, that is ridiculous. There are no plans to sell any more key players, why would there be? Our immediate focus is on staying up in the Premier League. We hope Chris Samba will be the last key departure. There are no plans to sell any more key players because we want to improve the squad."

With all the posturing truisms it had all become a little too much like BBC's *Question Time* for me. There was further confusion over exactly how much Rovers had been paid for Samba. The player himself claimed that the fee was £12 million. Other sources claimed that the eventual transfer fee was nearer the £7 million mark. I had got to the point where I was past caring. Realistically, whatever the transfer fee was I couldn't see it being spent on high-class replacements. Around the same time that Samba was sold to Anzhi for however many millions, Dundee United confirmed that they had received the late payment for David Goodwillie and Rovers announced that they would be laying on free coaches for the upcoming relegation six-pointer to Wolves. All aboard the pop and crisp bus for a party. Not.

Chapter 16

On The Pitch (February 2012 – May 2012)

Despite all the problems of 2011, unbelievably by February 2012 Rovers were still very much in the fight for Premier League survival. The defeat to Bolton the week before Christmas and the media onslaught that followed represented an all-time low in my years following the club. Fans who had watched us struggle in the old Third Division felt the same. By the time Newcastle United came to visit Ewood Park on 1st February 2012, although many of the same problems continued off the pitch at least we were now starting to show signs of improvement on it. Twelve places above us in the Premier League, visitors Newcastle had become one of the only teams I can remember to sell four of their best players (Andy Carroll, Kevin Nolan, Jose Enrique and Joey Barton) and then improve. However, with Demba Ba, Cheick Tiote and new signing Papiss Cisse all away on African Nations Cup duty this was as good a time as any to come up against the season's surprise package. Yakubu was still suspended following his sending off against Fulham and with David Goodwillie out through illness, loan signing Anthony Modeste started for the first time. Goodwillie had been a bizarre signing (of his 117 league games for Dundee United 50 of those had actually been as a substitute) but January 2012 had been by far his best month in a Rovers shirt. As well as three goals he had also chipped in with a couple of good performances in the Premier League. Shortly after his equaliser against Everton, however, Rovers' young Scottish international was substituted and he went on to make just five more appearances, all as a second half substitute, between February the end of the season. Not for the first time, a striker scoring goals seemed to result in him falling down the pecking order. Loan signing Modeste wouldn't have to worry too much about the consequences of scoring goals - he never scored any. Modeste featured in nine games for Rovers. Not only did he fail to score himself but the team scored just one goal whilst he was on the pitch and conceded 15. Whatever his loan fee was it was too much. He quickly showed that despite his big, powerful, athletic build, he was lacking in all the qualities that set good strikers apart from an Olympic 400-metre runner. Worryingly, the game against Newcastle would turn out to be his best game in a Rovers shirt. After going behind to a Scott Dann own goal early in the game Rovers carved out chance after chance to equalise. The David Dunn penalty miss just before half-time was actually more difficult than some of the chances Rovers missed from open play.

A number of the missed chances fell to Modeste. One in particular in the second half when he was clean through on goal showed a lack of composure you seldom see in top level football. Credit to Tim Krul in the Newcastle goal who had an excellent game but this turned out to be a real opportunity missed by Rovers. We failed to score from 23 attempts and Newcastle rubbed salt into the wounds when Gabriel Obertan made it 2-0 deep into injury time. Rovers needed the Yak back and quickly.

On average, the Premier League sees a game with eight or more goals once every 120 matches. When Rovers play Arsenal at The Emirates it is nearer one in two. Understandably when Pedersen cancelled out Van Persie's early opener with an exquisite free-kick on 30 minutes there were few who predicted that this would be the end of the scoring. Arsenal quickly made it 3-1 and when Givet was sent off just before half -time you didn't need to have the foresight of Mark Lawrenson to work out what was going to happen next. Arsenal ran out 7-1 winners with Robin Van Persie netting a hat-trick. In truth it could have been double figures and the second half was little more than ritual humiliation. Weeks earlier Arsenal fan Jerome Anderson had told Sky viewers all about supporting your team. I wondered if he had mixed emotions watching this mess unfold. It was hard to fault Paul Robinson for any of the goals but I am not so sure the same could be said of Scott Dann. According to *Sky Sports News* big clubs had been interested in Dann all summer. Hats off to whoever had convinced Rovers fans that this made him a top player. The twisted testicle injury had been an unfortunate setback but now that everything was in the right place I just don't think he was that good. I genuinely don't mean this as a criticism of the man himself – he may well be a top guy -but if you want to look through all the goals Rovers conceded in the Premier League in 2012 the fact is Dann was at fault for a lot of them. What was most disappointing is that this is a player who was constantly linked with a move away from Rovers. I know quite a few fans who would have happily driven Dann to Aston Villa in person if we hadn't lost Nelsen and Phil Jones, with Samba also about to leave. The Arsenal game was the last time Rovers fans would see our best remaining defender Gael Givet play for ten weeks. Once again it wasn't just losing that was irritating Rovers fans but the inability of the club's management to get our best players out on the pitch every week.

Kean apologised for letting the travelling supporters down. Shortly after his apology he advised that Samba would be out of the QPR game with a hamstring injury. There was further embarrassment for Rovers when it was announced that the Indian national side's proposed visit to the training ground had been cancelled. All India Football Federation general secretary Kush Das explained,

> "Blackburn have told us that this is not the right time to visit the club. They are going through some management problems at the moment."

The bad atmosphere around the club was having a noticeable effect on attendances. Rovers failed to post an attendance over 21,000 in 2012 until the visit of

Manchester United in April. Despite the importance of the "must-win" home game against QPR, more and more fans were staying away in protest at how the club was being run. Rovers were now three points from safety and the seven goals conceded against Arsenal meant that we would have to beat QPR by two goals and hope Bolton didn't win in order to climb out of the relegation zone. Yakubu was back and within 15 minutes of his return he had put Rovers 1-0 up with his 13th goal of the season. In many ways the game was a lot like the Wolves game on the final day of the 2010/11 season. The early goal eased the nerves and Rovers were 3-0 up by half time. It had been a bit of a horror show from QPR. The fact that many "experts" considered them too good to go down because they had handed out ludicrous contracts to players like Joey Barton, Bobby Zamora and Djibril Cisse was yet another case of the lunacy of the Premier League. Whatever the scoreline, Kean was as unpopular as ever and only a three-month run of good results without dropping in any references to bodyguards was really going to change this. With Fabio Capello having resigned from the England manager's post earlier in the week, "Keano for England" replaced the usual "Kean Out". QPR finally woke up in the second half and it was inevitable that Rovers would come under pressure at some point. A mistake by Bradley Orr let Jamie Mackie in for QPR's first on 71 minutes. Orr had actually looked OK for Rovers since making the switch from QPR reserves. At this point I remembered the £5 bet I had put on Yakubu to score the first goal and Rovers to win 3-1 at 70-1. Rovers were winning so I saw nothing wrong with wanting the score line to stay 3-1 for the next 25 minutes. I have lost enough bets to know not to spend the money until you have got it but I must admit I could almost taste crispy duck when Jamie Mackie scored a stunning goal from long range to make it 3-2 in the 93rd minute. A mad minute followed but Rovers held on for a vital three points. It wasn't enough to take us out of the relegation zone and walking home one or two fans expressed their frustration with how the second half had panned out. I was disappointed not to be collecting £350 but I was realistic enough to realise that this could well be one of the last times I saw Rovers win a Premier League game for some time. Paul Merson said that Rovers had been lucky to come away with a win. We had been the better side for large parts of the game so I am not sure what he was talking about.

The international break was a good time to assess where the official protest now was. 2012 had brought about a different approach to the campaign for change. The club's underhand attempts to discredit the protest at the end of 2011 left a bitter taste with many fans. Personally, I still strongly suspect that there were people at the club who were so keen to protect their own position that they were happy for the spotlight to be shining on the fans. As a normal paying fan I struggled to understand why Rovers, rather than putting out statements that Steve Kean was a brilliant manager, dropping references to bodyguards into conversations with journalists and enforcing strict bans on anti-Kean banners home and away, hadn't just replaced a manager who was clearly out of his depth in the Premier League. In fact it was the failure to remove Kean that really made me question what was going on behind the scenes at Blackburn Rovers. In one of many conversations with representatives of the club, press officer Paul Agnew had told the protesters that they should be targeting the owners if anything – not Steve Kean. How aware of this Venky's were when they gave Agnew a promotion at the end of the season I am not entirely sure.

The official protesters had been disappointed at how their attempts to put across the frustrations of the fans had been portrayed at the end of 2011. The suggestion by sections of the media that this was anything more than normal fans who were unhappy with how the club was being run was damaging and wholly inaccurate. Rovers is a family club and this was very much reflected by the make-up of the official protest group. When Jerome Anderson questioned the protest organisers' motives on Sky he was so far off the mark that it only served to antagonise further the 99.8% of normal fans who wanted his client Steve Kean removed. These people were Rovers fans first and foremost and all they wanted was what was best for Blackburn Rovers. They had co-operated fully with club officials but by the start of 2012 it was clear that both Steve Kean and Venky's were here to stay and anyone who dared to challenge how the club was being run was likely to face heavy criticism from influential voices in the media. In truth many expected the protests to fizzle out. I know that my stomach for a fight was seriously waning. Testament to the commitment and sheer bloody-mindedness of those involved in the protest the democratically elected BRFC Action Group was formed and the protest got stronger. As well as further demonstrations prior to games, the 24 hour sit-in and a number of media appearances members of the group were soon looking at opening up dialogue not only with the club but also the Premier League, the Football Association and members of Parliament.

The Fans' Forum was still the only group with an official link to the club but they too had grown frustrated with the owners, prompting this statement in February,

> "When Venky's invited a group of Fans' Forum members to join the club's trip to Pune in early October we had high hopes that this represented a commitment to improved communications with the fans. During our meeting with Balaji Rao we were led to believe that this was the opportunity for a new start. Since we returned we have had no communication from the owners and we are disappointed expectations set at that meeting have unfortunately not been followed through to date. Nevertheless our relationship with the management team at Ewood Park continues to be good and it is clear that they are committed to continuing to work together with us. We hope that through local management we can develop clearer communication links with the club's owners in Pune and will continue to provide a voice for all Rovers fans. The Forum recognises that many fans feel remote from its work. As a result we plan to open up our pre-meets, which are held prior to the meetings with the club and set the agenda for those meetings. In addition vacancies on the Forum occur from time to time and we would welcome new applications for membership."

A small section of fans remained critical of the Fans' Forum following the Pune trip back in October. I felt that it was time for criticism of the Pune Nine to end. These were proper Rovers fans who had been let down by the owners just like everybody else. The Fans' Forum remained the fans' best line of communication with the club. There was nothing to be gained from cutting off this line of communication and I for one was happy with the work they were doing.

In a further development it was now emerging that Rovers fan Wayne Wild, director of Darwen-based WEC Group Limited (one of the club's commercial sponsors), was launching the Blackburn Rovers Supporters Investment Trust (BRSIT) along with finance expert Daniel Grabko. The aim of BRSIT was to sell 10,000 shares at £1,000 each in a bid to raise enough money to buy the club. When asked about BRSIT Wild explained,

> "At some point, and maybe soon, we believe Blackburn Rovers will be put up for sale. We believe the best ownership model is to be entirely owned by the supporters through a trust. We are seeking to engage with the current owners to advise them of our plans and we ask that they consider our proposals seriously as a credible and respectful way to pass on ownership of the club. At this stage we are asking Blackburn Rovers supporters if they would be willing to buy a share in their club. The more fans to buy a share, the stronger and more credible our bid will be. The aim of the trust is to establish a truly democratic ownership model, which can be independently monitored and held to account by

> the people who really matter - Blackburn Rovers supporters."

BRSIT was soon receiving support from fans, businessmen and prominent local figures. Blackburn MP Jack Straw was one of those publicly backing the scheme,

> "The work has been done by Wayne Wild but I am supporting it. I think if you can find agreement with the Venky's and we are able to raise sufficient funds, which is a big if, then it is a sensible approach. It is going to be very hard to get it off the ground but I applaud Wayne Wild's efforts and those of everyone else involved."

Whatever those at Rovers had hoped would happen following the media campaign against the fans, the protest hadn't gone away: instead, the protesters had got smarter. It was clear for all to see that Rovers was not being run as well as it had been under the Walker Trust. As long as this remained the case the fans would continue to challenge the new regime.

The Saturday afternoon late kick-off against Manchester City was exactly the sort of non-contest you expect to see when a team featuring players like Radosav Petrovic comes up against a squad valued at half a billion pounds. Manchester City bossed the game from start to finish and with just 31% possession and two shots Rovers were totally outplayed. Mario Balotelli's goal on the half-hour meant that Rovers had now set a new top flight record of 26 games without a clean sheet from the start of the season. Paul Robinson made a string of fine saves and although he was at fault for the second of Manchester City's three goals he was the only Rovers player who could draw any credit from his performance. Steve Kean's claim that Rovers should have had a first-half penalty was a largely pointless comment in my view but Manchester City doing the double over Rovers didn't worry me too much. It was time now to get a few more points against the teams around us.

16. Wolves	PL26	W5	D7	L14	Pts22
17. QPR	PL26	W5	D6	L15	Pts21
18. ROVERS	PL26	W5	D6	L15	Pts21
19. Bolton	PL26	W6	D2	L18	Pts20
20. Wigan	PL26	W4	D8	L14	Pts20

Prior to the Aston Villa game at Ewood Park, just in case anyone had missed any of his previous reminders, Kean once again made a veiled reference to the win at Old Trafford,

> "From our point of view we are delighted we have got five tough away grounds out of the way and have picked up five points from these grounds."

I wasn't entirely sure what relevance this comment had to the upcoming home game against Aston Villa. If it meant that we now had done the hard bit and the rest would be relatively straight forward then I remained doubtful. The build-up to the Aston Villa game was another painful reminder that Blackburn Rovers was changing beyond recognition. Before Christmas the

Lancashire Telegraph had led with a front page story calling for Steve Kean to be sacked. Two months later they were now running the "Shout Blackburn Rovers to Safety" campaign. Whether this was a commercial or editorial decision I am not entirely sure. From what I could see Rovers fans had backed the team all season. It was just the manager, owners and other key figures behind the scenes that the fans struggled to take to their hearts. BRFC Action Group had hoped to meet with club officials prior to the game and in exchange it was agreed that the planned pre-match march would be postponed. According to members of the BRFC Action Group senior figures at the club would not agree to details of the meeting being minuted so the peaceful protest went ahead. Once fans arrived at the ground, there was a noticeable change in the methods being deployed by Rovers staff. Many fans felt the stewarding was somewhat over-zealous and complained about children being body searched. Having been told that "Kean Out" banners were a health and safety hazard, I was disappointed to see that same didn't appear to apply to "McLeish Out" banners in the away end. Rovers' first-half performance was as poor a 45 minutes as I had witnessed all season. I could overlook poor performances away at the top sides like Manchester City but against Aston Villa (a team that finished the season 16th) this was not acceptable. The only comfort I could take from the first-half non-show was that Rovers were only 1-0 down at half-time. To the team's credit they were infinitely better in the second half and by the time David Dunn headed home a late equaliser Rovers were actually deserving of a point. That goal seemed to signal an upturn in form for

Rovers. Not only did we go on to record two clean sheets in a row but Steve Kean managed back to back Premier League victories for the first time in 50 games. Rovers were the better side for large parts of the 2-0 victory away to Wolves and also in the 2-0 home victory over Sunderland. Hoilett was key to both victories and Kean was still adamant that he would not give up hope of Hoilett signing a new deal. I found Hoilett a frustrating character. He was clearly a player of talent as his goals showed. The contract saga irritated me greatly however and even though he was good on the ball he would have to do a lot more if he wanted to become a regular in a better team than Rovers. Following the win over Wolves Rovers climbed out of the relegation zone for only the third time all season. The short spell at the dizzy heights of 16th in the Premier League prompted some of the most bizarre pieces of journalism (see Chapter 17 for full details) I have ever seen. A handful of journalists were now saying that Steve Kean should be made Manager of the Season. Although Venky's hadn't been seen at a game for months I still struggled to accept that Kean hadn't played a significant role in many of the problems that we had seen on and off the pitch since their arrival. Beating Wolves and Sunderland was now considered a major achievement and off the back of a largely non-existent "feel-good factor" Rovers took the opportunity to launch the sale of season tickets for the 2012/13 season. Cue tumbleweed. You couldn't argue with the price: it was the product the majority of fans had a problem with. As well as the ongoing PR campaign to boost the reputation of those who had clearly contributed to the club's demise, a major charm offensive was now under way to coax more money out of the pockets of the fans. The appearance of press officer Paul Agnew and Deputy Chief Executive Paul Hunt on *BBC Radio Lancashire* provided little reason for me to warm to the new order at the club. I think that *BBC Radio Lancashire's* coverage of the Venky's story has been excellent. More than any other part of the media, print or broadcast, they have acknowledged that the fans are right to be concerned and have incorporated this into their reporting of events. Maybe it helps that they are based in Blackburn and can see with their own eyes that the fans' frustrations are totally valid. They can't get it right every time and I must admit to being disappointed with this early warning from the presenter,

> "All I ask of you is this evening is to be polite. I don't want any bad language. I want everyone to get on nicely."

I have listened to countless *BBC Radio Lancashire* phone-ins and I can't recall obvious examples of Rovers fans not being able to adequately police their own conduct. What was the purpose of this comment and was it something that the presenter had decided to say himself or was it being encouraged by the same people who kept making reference to Kean's bodyguard? Paul Agnew started off the show by saying that the only time he can recall similar criticism of the club was the last time we were relegated in 1999. I am not sure if he was deliberately trying to mislead people or had simply forgotten the season in question but I am happy to argue that the events of 2011/12 had been quite different to anything I had seen in 1998/99. I don't recall major protests against the employment of Brian Kidd; I don't recall the *Lancashire Telegraph* calling for Brian Kidd to step down; nor do I recall so many questions about the role of the owner at the time. I was growing tired of being disrespected. Paul Hunt said that Michel Salgado (frozen out of the first team picture long ago) trains every day: interestingly there was no mention of where Salgado actually trained. When the issue was brought up about holding a minuted meeting with protesters, considering the email to Mrs Desai that was later published in the national press, I particularly liked this part of Paul Hunt's response,

> "We are transparent – we have got nothing to hide really to be fair."

We may have won two games in a row but I decided to leave the 2012/13 season ticket for now. This was a matter of principle. Rovers continued to state that season ticket sales had been encouraging but they didn't give a figure and by the final day of the Early Bird promotion (eventually extended to August!) Paul Hunt was ringing fans personally. Many fans also received a recorded telephone message from David Dunn. Two days after the victory against Sunderland, over 10,000 fans watched Rovers beat Burnley in the first leg of the Youth Cup semi-final. Rovers won the second leg and, although we were beaten by Chelsea in the final, the attendances at these games showed that the passion for the club was still there. Unfortunately there had just been a complete breakdown in trust.

16. ROVERS	PL29	W7	D7	L15	Pts 28
17. Bolton	PL28	W7	D2	L19	Pts 23
18. QPR	PL28	W5	D7	L16	Pts 22
19. Wigan	PL29	W4	D10	L15	Pts 22
20. Wolves	PL29	W5	W7	L17	Pts 22

By the time Rovers played Bolton at the end of March, now six points clear of the relegation zone with nine games to play, several "experts" were predicting that Rovers were safe from relegation. Few who had endured the majority of the previous 29 games felt that we were out of the mire just yet. Rovers duly went on to lose the next five games in a row. There was no shame in losing out to late goals from a Manchester United team that eventually finished second in the Premier League on goal difference but the other four defeats had relegation written all over them. Bolton were one of the few sides that were worse than us but two headed goals from David Wheater meant they did the double over Rovers for the first time in my life. Although we had a good shout for a penalty turned down by referee Andre Marriner at 0-0 Rovers just weren't good enough on the day. All eyes had been on the Reebok stadium following Fabrice Muamba's heart scare (the Bolton midfielder had collapsed during a game at White Hart Lane the previous week) but once the decision had been made to go ahead with the fixture I felt that it was the manager's job to focus the player's minds on the task in hand rather than to keep referring back to it.

By now Kean jive-talk was so regular that it has proved a real difficult task editing it all and even I am still sometimes shocked by how much babble he is able to talk. Shortly after the Bolton game not only was Kean warning Fergie off Grant Hanley but apparently he was also winning round the fans,

> "We get positive feedback, we get mail and emails – yes me personally – day in, day out. I get support from Blackburn fans and supporters from all over. But a hell of a lot of Blackburn fans send messages of an admission they were a bit negative. It is great we are going in the right direction and that is always nice to read."

If Kean received any fan mail after 3-0 defeats at Swansea and West Brom then you have got to wonder how many were written by Burnley fans just having a laugh. By now people were really starting to question how much stomach for the fight Rovers actually had. Losing, picking the positives out of defeat and then shining the spotlight on the fans had become an all-too-common pattern. The fact that Dunn and Pedersen, two players who hadn't strung five good games together since Allardyce left, were now forerunners for the Player of the Season award showed that the fans weren't the problem here.

The 3-2 defeat against Liverpool was one of the most embarrassing losses I can remember for a long time. Again, on the face of it there is no shame losing to Liverpool but let's not be under any illusions that this was a good side. With players like Doni, Flanagan, Coates, Henderson, Shelvy, Spearing and Carroll in the team, forget what shirt they were wearing, this was a mid-table Premier League outfit at best. Despite several of Liverpool's better players being rested for the upcoming FA Cup semi-final, the visitors still managed to race into a 2-0 lead after just 15 minutes. At this point it looked like being another long night for Rovers' fans but on 26 minutes the game was turned on its head when Flanagan played a weak back pass to reserve team 'keeper Doni. Hoilett intercepted Flanagan's poor effort and as he raced through on goal Liverpool's second choice goalkeeper (standing in for the suspended Reina) dragged him down. The referee awarded a penalty and Doni was sent off. With still over an hour to play, Liverpool were forced to bring on their third-choice 'keeper Brad Jones. As Yakubu waited to take the penalty suddenly things started to look up for Rovers. Brad Jones had other ideas and his first touch for Liverpool was to save Yakubu's penalty. Having played together at Middlesbrough, it turned out that Brad Jones was one of the few 'keepers who had worked out how to dive the right way for a Yakubu penalty. Rovers' Nigerian striker made amends shortly after with a well-taken header to make it 2-1 and the impetus was now all with Rovers. Right on the hour mark, Rovers were awarded a second penalty when Brad Jones pushed Yakubu over in the box. There were calls for a second red card but the referee deemed the push only a yellow card offence. Yakubu made no mistake this time and there now looked like being only one winner. With only three Premier League goals all season, Liverpool's record signing Andy Carroll was poor for large parts of the game. As well as a glaring miss at the start of the second half he almost made it 3-2 to Rovers with a looping header from a Paul Robinson clearance. Both teams carved out chances but just as Rovers were ready to settle for a point, it was Carroll popped up with an injury-time winner to condemn Rovers to another embarrassing defeat.

16. QPR	PL34	W8	D7	L19	Pts 31
17. Wigan	PL33	W7	D10	L16	Pts 31
18. Bolton	PL32	W9	D2	L21	Pts 29
19. ROVERS	PL34	W7	D7	L20	Pts 28
20. Wolves	PL34	W5	W8	L21	Pts 23

By the time Norwich arrived at Ewood Park on April 21st Rovers were now three points from safety and, with five Premier League defeats in a row, once again we were amongst the favourites for the drop. Not only had we stopped picking up points but, with the exception of Wolves, the teams around us had now started winning games with alarming regularity. Since Rovers had last added to their points tally, Wigan had recorded wins against Liverpool, Stoke, Manchester United and Arsenal; QPR had beaten Liverpool, Arsenal and Swansea and even Bolton had picked up three points against Rovers and Wolves. Some of these results were quite frankly bizarre but we couldn't blame our league position on other team's winning.

Having lost many of the club's best players, it wasn't clear why players like Gael Givet, Ruben Rochina, Simon Vukcevic and even David Goodwillie were now being used so sparingly. In April 2012 Goodwillie was sentenced to a 12-month probation order and to carry out 80 hours of unpaid work following an incident outside a takeaway in Glasgow in 2010. The *Scottish Sun* also reported,

> "David Goodwillie is being sued for £400,000 by his former agent. Mark Donaghy claims the Scotland striker breached the terms of their contract when he used another agent to sign for Blackburn from Dundee United in the summer. Donaghy says his cut in the lucrative £2.8million deal would have seen him rake in around £400,000."

I hope that Goodwillie was professional enough not to have let either of these things affect his football. Prior to the game against Swansea, Givet had been involved in a well-publicised spat with Kean. It was rather worrying when Kean said,

> "We need guys who want to play even if they are injured or their heads are not quite right, but I would rather keep the conversation between myself and Gael private."

Whatever was going on off the field, it was difficult to argue that Dann and Hanley were the best two centre-backs at the club. Hanley was much improved but we had still conceded two goals or more in our last five games. It was the same old problems as far as the fans could see. Rovers' director Vineeth Rao dismissed claims during the week that investment bankers Goldman Sachs had been instructed to broker a deal with potential buyers. In the build-up to the game against Norwich there was another march, the biggest to date, with over a thousand Rovers fans taking part in the peaceful community march from the town centre to Ewood Park. BRSIT, the supporter-led scheme that was aiming to raise enough funds to put a credible offer in for the club if it came up for sale, was up to a million pounds in pledged funds and Rovers legend Simon Garner was now involved in promoting the cause. With a noticeable lack of former players publicly backing the fans it was fitting that Blackburn Rovers' all-time leading league goal scorer, after-dinner speaker, football pundit and painter and decorator, Garner should be the first high-profile name to come forward. Anyone can be born with the ability to kick a football but it takes something extra to step forward and show your support for the fans when your peers appear reluctant to get involved. Garner showed that he had a little bit more about him than your average ex-player.

Although there was much said about the effects of the protests on the team, Rovers results on the weekends that the fans protested were very good. In fact, if we had shown the same form throughout the season we would have actually stayed in the Premier League. The game against Norwich was another example. Once Formica got the first goal just before half-time the points always looked safe. Hoilett added another wonder goal to his impressive collection of solo strikes shortly after the interval and Rovers ran out 2-0 winners. By now Wigan were showing the sort of form that you would normally come to expect of title contenders. QPR were unable to string two wins together but they were on a long run of winning one and then losing one. By the end of the weekend Rovers were three points from safety with three games to play. Kean, now being paid the salary of 20 doctors, remained positive and Rovers fans remained realistic. We had to beat Wigan at home and hope for a win at either White Hart Lane or Stamford Bridge – and even then we weren't guaranteed to be safe. In truth most Rovers fans had been preparing for relegation since 2011. Spurs away would be the last desperate throw of the dice – or so we hoped.

The Rovers performance against Spurs in the live 4 o'clock Sunday Sky game was appalling by any standards. Considering the importance of the game it was one of the most disgraceful team displays in the history of the Premier League. By 6 o'clock I didn't feel as though I had watched a game of football. I couldn't really work out what I had just watched. With no shots on target, no shots off target, no cards and one corner, Rovers became the first Premier League team since 2004 not to have one attempt at goal in an entire game. Spurs ran out comfortable 2-0 winners and even people in the Sky studio finally started to accept that Rovers fans were angry for a reason. The Spurs performance may have been the worst performance of the lot but I could name a dozen games during the 2011/12 season that were almost as bad. During the week Kean continued to claim Rovers could beat Wigan and Chelsea to stay in the Premier League. He assured the fans that he wouldn't walk away if Rovers went down. I imagine that the win at Old Trafford and draw at Anfield probably got a mention somewhere down the line. There was newspaper talk of an intruder at the training ground and with the deadline for the early bird season ticket offer now up, Paul Hunt was "encouraged" by season ticket sales for the 2012/13 season,

> "It has been an encouraging response from supporters and we are very pleased with that. There is no denying that since we launched the early bird in March it has been a challenging time for the club.

> I would like to offer a huge thank you to all who have opted to take advantage of the early bird discount."

Unsurprisingly there was plenty of waffle but no number. With Rovers game against Wigan being played on the Monday night, mission unlikely quickly became mission seemingly impossible when our closest relegation rivals QPR beat Stoke with a late winner on the Sunday to go six points clear of Rovers. Even if Rovers were able to beat Wigan and Chelsea we were still likely to face the drop. Kean reiterated that he would not walk away regardless of the result. Dignity is defined as "conduct, or speech indicative of self-respect or appreciation of the formality or gravity of an occasion or situation." I struggled to see what was dignified about what Kean was doing.

In order to stay in the Premier League Rovers needed to beat both Wigan and Chelsea with a positive goal difference of five goals. In our last seven Premier League games we had won one, lost six, scored five and conceded fifteen. We were entering miracle territory. When Rovers fans turned up at Ewood Park for the Monday night May Day bank holiday game against Wigan there was a real air of inevitability about what was going to happen next. Following 18 months of lies, false dawns, bad decisions and football coming a distant second to money-making, Rovers fans were in no mood to happy clap the team for another 90 minutes. For many fans, the season had left such a mark that regardless of what division Rovers ended up in next season this would be the last time they would visit Ewood Park until Venky's and Kean were gone. For me, the game was a clear indication that, almost without exception, every single Rovers fan was vehemently opposed to what the new regime at Blackburn Rovers had turned the club into and what they stood for. Kean was seen as the visible figurehead of this regime. "Kean Out" was sung at every opportunity; a chicken managed more minutes on the pitch than Bruno Ribeiro and Myles Anderson put together and Antolin Alcaraz scored the late goal that sent Rovers in to The Championship. As the referee's whistle sounded to signal full-time a handful of angry Rovers fans ran on to the pitch. Flanked by his bodyguard Phil Moulton, Kean hung around on the touchline. Despite the widespread feeling of anger towards Kean at no stage was any serious threat posed to his safety. Although the usual suspects were quick to condemn Rovers fans, in the latest twist to the story increasing sections of the media were now claiming that they understood why the fans were angry. Rovers fans had stopped caring long ago how the media were choosing to report the justified indignation towards the Venky regime and boos rang out around Ewood Park. After 11 years in the Premier League, Rovers' longest run of top-flight football since the Second World War, the "adventure" was over and Rovers were back in the second tier of English football. Far from being over, the nightmare was about to enter a new chapter.

In January 2012 Alan Nixon revealed that "Steve Kean survived a plot to sack him by senior staff within the club." The day after the defeat to Wigan, Nick Harris of the *Mail on Sunday* published an e-mail on *sportingintelligence.com* written by Deputy Chief Executive Paul Hunt. Sent on 21st December 2011 (the day after the 2-1 defeat to Bolton Wanderers that left

Rovers bottom of the Premier League at Christmas) the email was originally intended for Mrs Desai but eventually found its way to the press. In the email Paul Hunt offers his 10-point plan for survival. Whether the points made were in order of importance only Paul Hunt could tell you but here they are:-

1. Promotion to CEO

I am aware that that when we met in April, we said we would look at this within the first year. I believe now is the right time to promote me to CEO. The "Deputy" title is confusing to staff, supporters and media. I am confident that I now have the knowledge to be able to deliver strong progress. We have a great club, good team and an excellent range of staff that I feel can take this club forward, given the right support from the owners. Naturally, with extra responsibility I would like extra salary and I would be happy with a relatively modest increase with the promise of a good bonus and increase in salary in the summer that would reflect the improvement in position. I am currently the lowest paid senior club official in the Premier League.

2. Owners to invest in the club

As you are aware Barclays have asked for the owners to put £10m into the business. This needs to happen and I am confident that this could only be a loan as we would increase the value of the club significantly. With all the speculation in the press the playing staff value and overall club value is depreciating on a daily basis. By putting an end to this the owners would be protecting their investment, putting their trust in the executive team and the club. The position with the finances is a cause for grave concern. Auditors KPMG have put as many obstacles as they can in the way of signing off the accounts due to their concerns. We continue to try and work with Barclays but they are very quickly losing patience as we cannot give answers. We have been forced to agree to additional spending against our wishes (Christmas hampers, sponsoring the Princes Trust event etc) and I am fearful that the situation will only get worse.

During January we need additional funding to pay wages etc. Scottish club Hearts did not pay their players in November and have effectively breached their contracts. By law (supported by FIFA) the players can now annul their contracts, seek other clubs and still chase the club for payment of their wages. Clearly, the club will not receive any fee for any transfers. You may also be aware that HMRC (tax authorities) have been chasing Portsmouth Football Club for a debt they owe. HMRC have made a technical mistake in law and therefore cannot claim the money they are owed. They will make sure of course that the next football club that falls out of line, won't be so lucky. We need to make sure that this club is not Blackburn Rovers.

3. Manager to change and report to the CEO

Publicly I have been asked to support the manager and I always have as I personally like Steve. I have supported him from the start and have been desperate for him to do well. However, I am now of the opinion that it isn't working and he is ready to go. He has lost the crowd and as a result of this evening's game has lost the dressing room as well – the players no longer want to play for him. It is a shame and disappointing but we must act now to save the club. The board should be asked their opinion in who should be the new manager. The board has over 60 years football experience between them, it would be a travesty not to rely on that experience for the biggest decision the club will make this season. The new manager should now report into the board who then recommend and endorse his wishes to the owners. Allow the board to protect the owners from the media, supporters etc.

4. Trust the executive – bring us in

Give the executive team at Ewood Park the latitude and authority to run the club. Everything at the club needs to come through either myself, Simon Hunt or Karen Silk – both Karen and Simon are excellent appointments. We have vast experience and with Vineeth as well, I am sure we have a winning team. The owners must learn to trust us. I am enjoying working with Vineeth and although he has little experience in football, he is quickly learning. I am trying to establish him with all the other staff too and am introducing him to the Heads of Department on an ongoing basis. I don't really think for one minute that the owners will allow this club to go into ruin but without knowing this for sure, we need to be prudent. However, if we had more information on your plans, strategy and thoughts going forward (after assisting you in formulating that strategy of course) then we can support and deliver growth. Without knowing the plan, we will of course be guarded and suspicious. With our fiduciary responsibilities as directors, if the club goes under, the directors (including Vineeth, Mahesh and Gandhi Babu) are all potentially personally liable for that failing and the courts could take our houses from us. My family do not deserve this.

5. PR just from Ewood

Another big issue is the PR and the fact that a lot of it in the past has come from India, without our knowledge. ALL press statements need to come from Ewood Park with me as the spokesman. That way we can control all the output and protect the owners. I will take on an experienced PR consultant who will advise the board/owners. It will be someone who will be aware when any negative stories are about to hit the press. We must now remove the club from being headline news for the wrong reasons. A full PR strategy needs to be instigated from January 1st that re-engages the owners with the supporters – the owners need to trust us in this regard as we know our customers. As owners you are not protected. Use the board (and manager combined) as a buffer zone to the media, the bank, the fans and we will protect you. I want to tell the media that what they are printing is not true but the truth is that I do not know. It is clearly evident that neither yourself, Bala or Venky currently feel comfortable coming to Ewood Park. If we as an executive team had more say, day to day running and authority, we would be able to support you and take all the criticism ourselves. The damaging story in the Mail on Sunday has caused players, staff and the supporters much concern. We need to invest time in stopping leaks leaving the club.

6. Regular visits to India

To be able to understand the strategy and to assist the owners, the executive team of myself, Simon Hunt and Karen Silk must visit India once every two months as a minimum. This way we can be together on all issues and help to craft them with our experience. I am happy for the new manager to be a part of that delegation and would welcome his input. I am very concerned that I have not met with you properly during the six months I have worked at the club. You have asked me to deal with things locally but to be able to do this, as I have asked before, I need a greater understanding of your aspirations so I can deliver on them. If you keep me informed and learn to trust me, I can be your mouthpiece.

7. Regular visits to Blackburn and Premier League games

The owners must attend games in Blackburn as often as possible and I would suggest that at least one of the owners is present for at least a quarter of the games. The staff needs to meet you and get to know you too – whenever I have met the owners, I feel warm and strong and you instil in me the fight to face challenges and win. The supporters also need to meet you and we need to get the message of solidarity out there as quickly as possible.

8. Hire and Fire

The executive team at Blackburn Rovers must be allowed to hire and fire staff. We will of course ask for the owner's opinion for senior positions but we must be allowed the latitude in this. In Simon Williams we have someone who is against the owners and spreads the word wherever he can. I am disappointed I was not allowed to remove him from post in the summer, when he and the rest of the staff were expecting it. We must act soon in this regard and look to review other positions and then give the staff great morale.

9. Lost revenue and brand equity

We are losing fans/customers at an alarming rate. I am very concerned that fans are voting with their feet and not attending, not purchasing and not engaging with the club. Research shows that only 5% of ex season ticket holders will ever return. We are losing sponsors and suppliers. I am concerned we will lose Umbro if we continue to manufacture Rovers shirts in India for the RoverStar programme.

Their contract specifically disallows this and we are putting at risk £800k of annual revenue. The Blackburn Rovers and Venky's brands are both suffering terribly. Whilst there are negative goings on such as protests, complaints, media stories, unhappy fans etc, then both brands are losing brand equity and consequently, losing value. I am also concerned that the Premier League will intervene soon as they may take the view that their brand is being tarnished by association too. It is all reparable of course but we must start to act now by building bridges with fans and the media as above.

10. Support is necessary / Final thoughts

I am disappointed that we have not managed to progress as I would have liked over the past 6 months. I for one was very excited to be given the opportunity and wanted to assist the owners in delivering strong progress for the club. However, we have been too busy fire fighting (protests, media intrusion, finance issues) to do this so far. As you know, I like to be proactive but the current climate only allows us to be reactive. I feel impotent as I am not asked by yourselves about my opinion on matters. I joined the club to make a difference, not to sit by and simply action instructions. I appreciate that my advice will not always be acted upon but I am disappointed that I am not asked. I have a great deal to contribute and have great experience. I won't get it right every time but will always do my best and learn from any mistakes. My concern is for the staff. They have put up with a lot recently and are still supportive. They live in the community and are being asked questions by their friends and family but cannot answer them. They are also being challenged at the games and when they come into contact with fans. Most are junior or part time staff who are feeling under pressure. I am concerned that they are going to become too stressed and will look to get jobs elsewhere. We have some great staff and cannot afford to lose them. I may be speaking out of turn here, but I am also concerned that no one reports everything to you, that is, everyone tries to report positive news and are not overly forthcoming when negative news needs to be told. By not having the full details, anyone would find it difficult to make decisions that encompass all the facts, all of the time. I am sure that if you were exposed to the full story, no matter how negative sometimes, that you would do the right thing. I need to be able to report a little more readily to you and on an infinitely more regular basis. Please don't view this as me questioning the owners unjustly. Please be reassured that I do question things, it means I am doing things right for the club and the owners by not accepting things lightly. This is how I work and how I must continue to work to get the best for Blackburn Rovers. With my experience of Blackburn now and my previous experience at three other prominent clubs, I do feel as though my suggestions come from a position of strength and can make a huge difference to life at Blackburn Rovers. I would very much appreciate an opportunity to speak with you on these points by invitation to India. Without instigating these points it will get more and more

> difficult to deliver progress for the club. I call on the owners to act, to play their part in the investment that puts all our minds at rest, and then allows me and the executive team to initiate all of the above points for the greater good of Blackburn Rovers. I look forward to hearing your thoughts. With very best wishes for a bright future, Paul.

Rovers had been the only club not to list a Chairman and Chief Executive in the official Premier League Handbook for 2011/12. On 10th May 2012, the day after the e-mail was made public, it was confirmed that Deputy Chief Executive Paul Hunt had left the club. Venkatesh Rao stated that Paul Hunt's departure had nothing to do with the leaked e-mail but "some staff have to go to bring the budget down." The owners' baffling loyalty towards Kean continued.

The Chelsea game on the last day of the season was a largely pointless affair. There was a debut for goalkeeper Jake Kean and rare appearances for Adam Henley and Josh Morris. Chelsea won 2-1 and Yakubu got his 17th Premier League goal of the season. A late goal at The Britannia Stadium from ex-Rovers trainee Jonathan Walters meant that Bolton Wanderers and Steve Kean's SEM stablemate Owen Coyle would also be joining Rovers in The Championship. I was reminded of my £100 bet on Rovers to be relegated. With promotional offers I ended up collecting £850. I got no joy out of Rovers' failure. I spent the money on flyers and T-shirts to help promote the book.

17. QPR	PL38	W10	D7	L21	Pts 37
18. Bolton	PL38	W10	D6	L22	Pts 36
19. ROVERS	PL38	W8	D7	L23	Pts 31
20. Wolves	PL38	W5	D10	L23	Pts 25

Everybody was familiar enough with the ramblings of Steve Kean to know exactly what this statement meant,

> "The rebuilding starts straight away. In any type of rebuild you have to fight for the players you have got under contract because the clubs will be swarming around and trying to take the service of some of our players. It is about making sure you can keep the majority of the squad together. I will be going out to speak to the owners and will be continuing the talks we have already had and build as competitive a squad as we can. I do it every season. When I go out and speak with the owners, we will talk about what went on last season and the rebuild programme will stay within the club. We will move forward."

The sale starts now, in other words. As for the end of season meetings, there was only one thing Rovers fans wanted from Kean's meeting with the owners and that was the immediate termination of Kean's contract. The emergence of a video clip showing Kean talking to Rovers fans in Hong Kong in the summer of 2011 should have been the final nail in his coffin. In the clip Kean claimed that he discovered Phil Jones, predicted that Rovers would finish in the top half of the Premier League and would also win the Carling Cup in 2011/12. He also labelled former Rovers manager Sam Allardyce "a fucking crook" – prompting Allardyce to threaten legal action. Predictably, even after yet another embarrassing episode involving Kean, he still kept his job. The owners' refusal to sack him only left further questions about exactly what was going on at Blackburn Rovers Football Club. Many were now seriously calling in to question exactly who was advising who in these meetings in Pune. Venky's were portrayed as clueless cricket fans when it suited and then hard-line business people. To me, they just came across as rabbits trapped in the headlights. Having relied on advisers before, during and after the takeover I struggled to accept that they were now making all the big decisions. Venkatesh Rao's appearance on *Sky Sports News* shortly after the decision to retain Kean was truly bizarre,

> "The fans are like a family it is like your family crying, your brothers and sisters crying...... sometimes you go wrong so your parents get angry and they get violate you this is so many things good bad ugly same with the fans so they are our parents and I am sure we will rectify ourselves and whatever our parents tell we will listen."

If Venkatesh claimed to be listening, the personnel changes at Rovers over the summer were further evidence that whoever was making the decisions clearly was not listening. In the video that emerged from the Hong Kong trip interestingly Kean told the Rovers fans that he would report back to Paul Agnew about sorting out the Fans' Forum. Why would he report this back to the club's press officer? Paul Agnew stated that Kean had leaned heavily on him since being appointed manager in December 2010. When the dust had settled on a shambolic 18 months, personally Kean and Agnew would have been the first two employees I would have got rid of. Agnew was promoted to the position of Operations Director and given a place on the board. Just a few years earlier when promoting his book about Tom Finney, Agnew, a former journalist, public relations adviser and Chief Executive at struggling Preston North End, had told how he "went to bed on stories of Tom Finney as a boy." He was now happy to declare,

> "As a Blackburn Rovers supporter from the age of six, there were two big dreams. One to play for the club or to have a role in the running of it. This a great chance for me and it is up to me to prove I am up to a very serious under taking."

Football secretary Anthony Bloch was replaced by Ian Silvester formerly of Leicester City, Leeds United and Liverpool. The role of football secretary is a key role that involves the preparation of player contracts, registration documents, transfer documents and work permits as well as liaising with FIFA, UEFA, Football Association, Premier League and Football league on various aspects of football administration. This was Rovers' third football secretary in 18 months. Shebby Singh, a former Malaysian footballer and television pundit on the *ESPN Star Network* was appointed Global Advisor at Rovers. What the role involved I guess only time would tell. It appeared this was another new appointee who enjoyed reading books and shortly after arriving at Rovers Shebby Singh told the *Lancashire Telegraph,*

> "The autobiography about Ronnie Clayton: 'A slave to soccer' was my inspiration. I read this book when I was 11 years old. It left an impression on me, all I wanted to do for the rest of my life was to be a footballer. That is it. I think I have achieved a lot of what Ronnie achieved in this book. As an 11-year old reading a book that you thought was a story book and then realise it is a true story. This book is awesome. It is about being a professional footballer, the big games, the big crowds. Playing for the national team. This is simply wonderful and that was it from 11 years old I just wanted to play football."

By now, following Rovers was like watching a vandal draw biro scribbles on to a work of art. Agnew's friend and colleague from his Preston North End days Derek Shaw was soon appointed Managing Director. As hundreds of Rovers staff worried about the effect relegation would have on their jobs, Mrs Desai said of the additions to the board,

> "We are keen to build up a good image for BRFC among the fans, media and general populace and we feel sure that Derek and Paul can work in close cooperation to achieve this. It's a new start, a new era and we are very excited."

Shortly into the start of the new era the predictable exodus of players started. Yakubu left for China after just 10 months, Hoilett never did get round to signing his new contract and the *Lancashire Telegraph* reported that Pedersen, Blackman, Petrovic, Slew and Linganzi may all now be surplus to requirements. I fully expected other first team regulars to follow. It was reported that Rovers had lost out in the bid for Category One academy status. Goal.com reported,

> "Newcastle, Blackburn and Palace are believed to have all been awarded Category Two status. This will have considerable financial consequences and inhibits the academies' capacity to produce future first-team players to follow in the footsteps of star graduates like Andy Carroll, Steven Taylor, Phil Jones, Victor Moses and Nathaniel Clyne."

Failure to get Category One status was a major blow that wasn't really softened by the signing of Danny Murphy, Nuno Gomes, Leon Best and Dickson Etuhu – four players with an average age of almost 32. In the case of Best (a player who averaged 12 league games and 3 goals a season over the previous three seasons) he could well pick up £1million in wages before he plays a league game for the club. How this odd spending spree is being funded and the financial consequences of failure to get promotion back to the Premier League are not entirely clear. Shortly after relegation to The Championship Dan King of *The Sun* reported that Venky's had cleared debts of over £20 million with Barclays and ended the club's 12 year relationship with the bank. It is now believed that Blackburn Rovers do their banking through the Bank of India.

Chapter 17

The Media

Mark Clattenburg's whistle sounded to signal the end of Blackburn Rovers' 11-year stay in the Premier League. Newspapers and television networks from London to Mumbai were on hand to offer their final thoughts on a story that their bosses could only have dreamt of. How much of the reported story you chose to believe probably depended on whose version of events you were listening to and whether or not you actually cared about the long-term well-being of Blackburn Rovers Football Club. For me, not only had the story become an unreliable mix of fact, fodder and backtracking but it had also become a showcase of all that was good and bad about the British media.

Just two years earlier and a youthful Rovers team that included academy graduates Martin Olsson, Phil Jones, Junior Hoilett and Grant Hanley completed a rare win at Villa Park to seal yet another season in the top 10 of English football. The style of football may have been grim but it was an achievement of note all the same. The media weren't that interested. In fact, many were still scratching around at Upton Park looking for West Ham players to take to the World Cup. Allardyce's comments that England would regret not taking the standout English goalkeeper of the 2009/10 season, Paul Robinson, went largely unreported.

Like most things at Rovers, everything changed at the start of the 2010/11 season and the arrival of Ahsan Ali Syed triggered a very noticeable increase in column inches and television air time. Whatever forces determine what is newsworthy and what is not appeared to have reached the decision that the Blackburn Rovers story was infinitely more interesting now that Indian business people were involved. Over the next 18 months Rovers became major news and people who hadn't been seen at Ewood Park since Alan Shearer left for Newcastle United soon became Rovers experts again. Suddenly everyone with a press pass and access to a television was involved in the story. It is a shame that some of the weaker articles published did end up damaging not only the reputation of Rovers fans but equally the profession of those that were writing them. The press as a whole was actually pretty sympathetic towards the fans' plight but it is always going to be the more outspoken articles that people are going to remember. The work of the *Mail on Sunday's* Nick Harris in publishing the previous board members' letter to Mrs Desai, the leaked Paul Hunt email and bringing certain aspects of the Ruben Rochina transfer to the public's attention is to date the only real solid breakthrough in uncovering what is going on behind the scenes at Ewood Park; the *Daily Telegraph's* Henry Winter brought positive attention to the protest when many of his peers were still sitting on the fence or turning their noses up at real fans; the *Daily Mirror's* Martin Lipton has been as passionate as anyone about highlighting the problems that exist at Rovers and *The Guardian's* David Conn has been writing interesting, well-informed, thoughtful articles about Rovers for years. It is people like this that make it difficult to make sweeping generalisations about the media and as a Rovers fan I think their input could be vital to what happens next. There will be others in the national media that have played their part (and I am not just talking about all those who started sticking up for the fans three games before the end of the season) but it is impossible to name them all here. The good journalists know who they are and I am pretty sure that the bad ones will eventually find out who they are.

Alan Nixon of the *Daily Mirror* had been one of the few national journalists to be consistently reporting on Rovers prior to the takeover and he became an important part of the story. Nixon clearly wasn't feeding off the same scraps as the other journalists and he was often the first to break key news regarding the takeover and many of the subsequent transfers. When he linked Rovers with players like Luis Fabiano and Ronaldinho let's just say I didn't rush out and have these players' names put on my shirt but once you worked out which bits to ignore, he became one of only a handful of journalists who could actually add to the fans' understanding of what was going on. I find it hard to imagine that Nixon could have been accurately guessing a lot of the stuff he was putting out so whoever was feeding him his information appeared know a lot about developments behind the scenes.

Interestingly, despite all the departures at Rovers, Nixon's information remained a step ahead of other journalists throughout the story. For me this significantly narrowed down where he was getting it from. When I look at the people who were left at the club by July 2012, wherever Nixon was getting his information from, as a Rovers fan, I had serious doubts about what the motivation was for putting it out there. That was the main problem with the reporting of events for me. A lot of people were chipping in to have their say but what was their motivation? In many cases, I began to seriously doubt that their number one motivation was the long-term well-being of Blackburn Rovers.

I eventually grew tired of the travelling circus that attached itself to my town's football club. Although some of the early reporting of events had been interesting and informative, within 12 months some rather ill-informed and unhelpful attitudes towards Rovers fans were starting to creep out. The key turning point seemed to be the start of the Kean Out campaign. Prior to this and even as late as the Phil Jones transfer, journalists were almost unanimous in their criticism of Kean and Venky's. The protest was perfectly justified and anybody who made the effort to look into it would have seen that this was the case. By the time the generally peaceful protest got underway Kean and Venky's had been sowing the seeds of failure for the previous 10 months. While the majority of television personalities were quite open in their disdain towards the protesters, the better journalists remained consistent throughout. It wasn't long before a handful of newspaper journalists were echoing what was being said on television. Before you knew it people in the paper were saying it, people on the television were saying it, people who read the paper were saying it, people who watched television were saying it, then somebody else wrote about it in another paper and it became the commonly-held view that Rovers fans were a disgrace. It was like watching a fire take hold. It is quite easy for a journalist to attack a group of fans when they know that those fans don't have a right to reply. As a passionate Rovers fan I am now more than happy to name and shame a few of the worst offenders. I was literally lost for words when I read this garbage about protesting Rovers fans the week after the Swansea game.

> "Of course, if most of those waving the placards and posing for the TV had had a life, they'd remember it wasn't so long ago that fighting relegation from the top flight would have been a pipe-dream for Rovers. When I was a teenager, they were old-school Third Division material. League One, in new money. Duff, in other words. A small club from a smoky old mill town, homespun and eternally hopeful, like 90 per cent up and down the land. Also-rans whose hopes only became reality because a local tycoon decided to sink millions into them rather than buy yachts and Caribbean islands. Blackburn Rovers only ever punched so far above their weight because Jack Walker stuck a golden horseshoe in their glove. Yet somehow, a shower of ungrateful, attention-seeking muppets have decided that glory is their birthright. When the truth is they don't know they're born. Do they have any idea what it's like to follow an

> Accrington or an East Stirling? Course they don't, silly question. They're just the same as thousands more like them lucky enough to have been born into an era when their club is playing at a far higher level than their dads and grandads could have imagined. They see relegation as beneath them, like someone asked them to clean pub toilets with a toothbrush."

You would be forgiven for thinking that this had been written by a Burnley fan on the back of a toilet cubicle door. No such luck. This is actually part of a published article written by a paid journalist from a national newspaper. When the writer signs off by saying "Where were you when you were shit?" you are really seeing that, in the hands of Bill Leckie of *The Scottish Sun,* this was journalism that had sunk to whole new depths. Everyone is entitled to their opinion but to my mind, if you have a loud voice and want your views to be taken seriously, you have got to be able to stand up to questioning from the people you have chosen to attack. If anybody wants to speak to me about anything I have said in this book, feel free to get in touch. If you can convince me to change my mind about anything then I will. I politely emailed Leckie about his article and asked him for a quick chat about some of the points he had raised. I wondered whether Leckie, co-author of a book about life in Scotland's lower leagues, had been one of the lucky few football fans to have witnessed Steve Kean's one and only appearance for Alloa Athletic. It was a shame that Leckie didn't want to engage in conversation on a subject that he clearly had a lot to say about. Leckie has a reputation in Scotland for being a big mouth that hides behind his pen and it looks like we were seeing another example of it. Although Leckie's bizarre tirade against Rovers fans was the most blatant example of anti-Rovers bile that I came across, he certainly wasn't the only journalist taking pot shots at Rovers fans.

Shortly after Kean's 19th league defeat of 2011, David Anderson of the *Daily Mirror* wrote a story under the headline "Why Blackburn boss Steve Kean doesn't need enemies with 'fans' like these". In the article David Anderson slammed Rovers fans and even posed the question, "How many of the points Blackburn have dropped this season are directly related to their own fans?" I found it hard to imagine this sort of stuff being thrown at the Liverpool fans who had wanted Roy Hodgson removed or the Bolton fans who had hounded out Gary Megson. Little effort was made by David Anderson to acknowledge why the fans were so angry; nor did he do anything to point out Kean's contribution to 12 months of failure. Considering some of the provocation that was coming from Kean (see most of the previous 16 chapters for details) I genuinely do believe that he would have faced far worse at many other clubs. I will accept that some fans did cross the line during the Bolton game but for every Rovers fan with a vein popping out of their neck there were easily a thousand others that the story makers chose to ignore. It felt as though the story had already been written and Rovers fans were just providing the pictures. Not only have the media tricked people into believing that Newcastle fans somehow love a goal scorer more than the fans of any other club; and that big attendances equal more passion but it was quickly becoming "common knowledge" that Steve Kean was a very nice man and Rovers fans were the lowest of the low. Some of the articles appearing in the paper at the time may have only been throwaway comment pieces because Rovers was the latest hot topic on the conveyor belt, but I am not sure how much consideration was actually being taken about how damaging these comments were. It wasn't the 20 fans shouting a little louder than is socially acceptable who were the problem here and it only made all Rovers fans even angrier when they continued to be wrongly portrayed.

The *Daily Mail*'s Matt Lawton did an interview with Kean shortly in to 2012 that was so nauseatingly rose-tinted that I will forever struggle to take Lawton seriously. The interview read like a cross between an episode of *This Is Your Life* and a victim's account of a serious crime. When I read the headline "Unable to walk down the street for fear of attack from his own fans, Steve Kean is... under siege" I didn't know whether to laugh or cry. Was Kean frightened he was going to get slapped with a handbag or attacked with a school satchel? Or were we were talking assassination attempts here? Some Rovers fans did start to raise questions about whether certain journalists actually believed in what they were writing or whether a PR campaign was now underway to rebuild the reputation of Kean and Venky's. The same words were being bandied about every time. It was almost as if you weren't allowed to mention fans without saying "vitriol" or make reference to Kean without saying "dignity". Personally, I started to wonder what sort of idiots were actually buying this rubbish. Then special friend to the stars of ITV2 Piers Morgan decided to get involved. I don't know if these people genuinely didn't understand what was going on at Rovers or they were just being deliberately provocative but the problem is, for every person who will take the time to read a balanced, well researched, thoughtful article by *The Guardian*'s David Conn there will be hundreds more who are hanging on Piers Morgan's every Tweet.

If anything, the pro-Kean/anti-fans articles became more regular throughout the season and there was almost an infantile "Ha, told you so!" element to some of them in the end. It was actually slightly embarrassing. When Rovers managed to pick up seven points from three games in March 2012 Martin Hardy of *The Independent* did a full page spread on Kean that I wouldn't eat my chips off. Testament to how powerful the words of the media can be were these comments left by a fan of another club underneath the article,

> "Blackburn really don't deserve Steve Kean. I think we're all agreed on that! I hope Blackburn have got the common decency to pay up his contract in full at the end of the season, and to release him from the living hell in which he finds himself so that he can go and get a job that is more appropriate for a man of his skill and expertise."

When I read it a second time I realised that the guy was serious. Had this fan missed the point here? Rovers' fans had been campaigning for Kean's contract to be paid up for the majority of the season. The same week, *The Guardian's* Paul Wilson and the *Daily Mirror's* Brian Reade claimed that Kean should be named Manager of the Year. It was a strange thing to say considering Kean's awful record and the fact that there were 19 better managers than him in the Premier League (even Terry Connor)! I am prepared to forgive Paul Wilson because in fairness he has written a number of good articles about Rovers. I am not so sure about Brian Reade. There aren't too many examples I can find of Reade actually writing about the situation at Rovers so why wait until this point to unleash his wisdom?

> "If Steve Kean keeps Blackburn up but doesn't win Manager of the Year, there is only one course of action open to the man who does. Decline it, on the grounds that the adversity Kean has overcome, and the manner in which he has overcome it, has done more for their profession's reputation than one man winning any amount of trophies could ever achieve. I can't remember a manager in this country having to endure the sustained level of abuse Kean has faced this season. Before Christmas, it reached its ugly nadir when Blackburn lost 2-1 to Bolton. Thousands of fans held up copies of the local paper's front page editorial which told him to go, their voices and faces riddled with hate for a man who was simply trying his best."

Whether he kept us up or not there was absolutely no way on earth Kean should be considered for the title of Manager of the Year. What was most disappointing in the case of Reade is that this is a man who has written a book about the damage owners can do to your football club. To me it just echoed the contempt certain sections of the media had for the 99% of Rovers fans who felt Kean was not up to the job. It also showed remarkably poor judgment considering the likelihood that Rovers would be relegated. I emailed Reade about his comments and the reply came back that it is a game about opinions. Personally I can't help but feel that some of these journalists would be best advised to stick to writing about the "Big Four" until they were ready to move on to more complex subjects - like one of the other 88 clubs that help make up the top four divisions – but that's just my opinion. Or even better, rather than taking misguided cheap shots at good honest fans, why didn't they write us a story about who attended the meetings Kean travelled to Pune for every month.

A lot of these articles were so out of kilter with what I could see with my own eyes, whilst some were no doubt written by individual numpties looking to make a name for themselves, I struggled to accept that this was always the case. As defined by Wikipedia,

> "Public relations (PR) is the practice of managing the flow of information between an individual or an organisation and the public. PR provides an organisation or individual exposure to their audiences using topics of public interest and news items that do not require direct payment. The aim of PR by a company often is to persuade the public, investors, partners, employees, and other stakeholders to maintain a certain point of view about it, its leadership, products, or of political decisions. Common activities include speaking at conferences, winning industry awards, working with the press, and employee communication."

When football sold out it sold the lot. PR is an important part of any business in the commercial world and Blackburn Rovers is no different. Press officer Paul Agnew was the man largely responsible for handling Blackburn Rovers' PR needs and he became very unpopular with Rovers fans. Having been at the club since the late 1990s Agnew was another minor character who rose to prominence following the arrival of Venky's. Although his name began to feature more and more, many fans didn't really know what he did beyond putting the club programme together. In 2008, Agnew visited the Fans' Forum and answered questions about his role at Rovers. He explained that he was not directly employed by the club but instead his company Paul Agnew Public Relations (PAPR) was on a year-by-year contract. He confirmed that 75% of PAPR's work involved Rovers. He said he was very active in courting journalists from the national media. To give an example of what he did, he said there had been story reported by a Manchester based journalist from the *Daily Mail* (Ian Ladyman) about a player revolt at Rovers. Agnew claimed that there was no truth in the story and the club spent some time refuting it using player interviews over the following few months. As well as his work on the matchday programme, a large part of Agnew's job was to get good news in to the media and keep bad news out. In theory, a relatively straight forward task, so what went wrong? Agnew's comment on *BBC Radio Lancashire* in 2012, that "these days it's very difficult with the advent and Twitter, Facebook and whatever" perhaps indicate that this is not a man who is at the forefront of the global communication revolution. Whilst his company PAPR were able to offer websites "with bells and whistles" Agnew came across as a man who was very much old school in his approach to PR. In the leaked email to Mrs Desai written at the end of 2011, Deputy Chief Executive Paul Hunt highlighted that PR was an area that Rovers need to improve on. Hunt wanted to stop stories like the *Mail on Sunday's* article about problems with Barclays getting out. Personally, I would have been more keen to stop some of the garbage that was being written about bodyguards and threats to the manager's safety. Not only were Rovers not stopping these stories, they appeared to be encouraging them. For me, Agnew has to shoulder a large amount of the blame. Having made a name for himself as a journalist and publicly stating that Steve Kean was heavily reliant on his help with media matters, he will have been aware that certain words trigger certain reactions. Bearing in mind that Agnew had previously confirmed that he had been active in courting journalists from the national media exactly what was he doing to discourage damaging and inaccurate stories about the fans? After the end of the 2011/12 season Agnew was promoted to the Blackburn Rovers board. Many fans began to question whether his role was to create positive PR for Kean or Blackburn Rovers. Jeff Weston, a football agent with SEM and PR expert for 34 years, was one of many figures who appeared to encourage negative views towards Rovers fans. While PAPR may have been able to utilise links with the *Accrington Observer*, the *Burnley Express* and *Lancashire Telegraph*, SEM was able to boast professional links with organisations like Sky and the *The Sun*. For me, PR has a lot to answer for.

From a Rovers' point of view the story was pretty clear – the new owners had come in and, acting on the advice of a number of wealthy private companies, had undertaken an intense period of cost-cutting that had ultimately turned a mid-table Premier League side in to a Championship side. Rovers fans gave the manager and new owners ample opportunity to prove themselves but after 10 months of poor performances, strange decisions and misleading statements a carefully considered period of peaceful protest was decided upon. The protest wasn't born out hatred and vitriol; it was born out of a genuine concern that Blackburn Rovers Football Club was heading for total ruin. This isn't propaganda; this is what happened. Evidently, nothing did change and the club ended the season relegated to The Championship. For whatever reason, a lot of the ex-footballers in the television studios didn't want to see it like this and a different story was often reported. The real damage to the reputation of Rovers' fans was not being done by national newspaper journalists – it was being done by a small group of opinionated middle-aged ex-footballers whom I prefer to call "sofa monkeys" rather than "experts." A lot of them remind me of those chimps of the *PG Tips* adverts and I often wonder if you would get any less insight from a chimp in a suit drinking a cup of tea. Whether the "sofa-monkeys" were being directed by people behind the camera, the version of events according to a lot of these self-styled experts was:-

- Blackburn Rovers had been punching above their weight for too long in the first place.
- Allardyce was no longer around to mastermind the team's Premier League survival.

- Kean was a very dignified man worthy of a place at a club like Blackburn Rovers.
- Blackburn Rovers wasn't a big enough club for the Premier League and was about to go back where it belonged.

When we did end up going down, one season after many had predicted, it was more to do with the organised campaign of hatred against all-round good guy Kean than the sale of players with over 1,000 Premier League games to their name, dreadful signings, delusional public declarations, general tactical ineptitude and the quite apparent shambolic running of the football club. Now, I am all for a game of devil's advocate but the sofa monkeys were so wide of the mark with this one that it was untrue. Unfortunately, the input of a lot of these people is treated with far more respect than it deserves and the sad fact is, if enough people say something often enough on national television, eventually people start to believe it and repeat it.

There were loads of them at it – Charlie Nicholas, Ray Wilkins, Phil Thompson, Iain Dowie – it was a problem that was endemic across an entire organisation – in this case, Sky. Never mind a couple of paragraphs, I could write a whole book about the guff aging ex-pros have come out with on Sky over the last 18 months. No offence to 1970s West London poster boy Gerry Francis but I just had to cringe every time he came on *Sky Sports* and somebody asked him a question about Rovers. In a way I felt for the guy because, just like I wouldn't be happy being put on the spot about QPR, Francis was clearly well out of his comfort zone when he continued to be asked questions about events at Blackburn Rovers. A lot of the time Francis just ended up trotting out the same old lines about patience and sticking by the manager. I had to look where his eyes were going to check he wasn't reading it off an autocue. In the case of Gerry Francis, I actually don't mind him and even though he was consistently off the pace when it came to Rovers insight at least he did it with a bit of diplomacy. If only his Sky counterpart Paul Merson could have done the same. A couple of years ago, I didn't really have much of an opinion of Paul Merson. Unlike Merson himself, I tend to shy away from having too strong an opinion on things I don't really know that much about. 12 months on and now that I am more familiar with Paul Merson the television personality, I can certainly see why he has lost so many bets. If you ever want a good laugh take a look at his weekly predictions on the *Sky Sports* website. He makes Mark Lawrenson look like Nostradamus. I am not going to be too hard on somebody for not being able to read the future but in Merson's case it is his apparent inability to read the present that I find most disturbing. Merson had been tipping Rovers to go down since December 2010. There was no real reason given – just various strange facial gestures punctuated with big words like "shocking", "scandalous" and "monumental". Rovers didn't go down when Merson first called it but as is often the case with most self-styled experts there is no period of re-evaluation and reflection - it is just straight on to the next set of failed predictions. By the time the 2011/12 season came round, Rovers actually were now a good shout to go down. Merson predictably called it again but his comment three games in to the season that, "Blackburn are solid at the back, but will they do enough at the other end?" showed that the world's latest Blackburn Rovers expert was still some way from getting his badge for worthwhile Rovers insight. Merson's take on the protest was astounding. Apparently it was fine for him to take cheap shots at Rovers but when paying customers decided they weren't happy it suddenly became a different story. When commentating on the Swansea game in December 2011, Merson said,

> "People behind the goal now it is embarrassing. Steve Kean should get a few of his mates and go and sit outside their workplace on Monday and start calling for them to get the sack."

It sounds like something a five-year-old would say. I wouldn't mind but posing as an expert, Merson then went on to call Givet "Yuvay" (Givet had played over 70 games in the Premier League at this point); he got Steve Kean mixed up with Scott Dann (clue - one is a man in a suit with no hair and the other is a man in a football kit with black hair) and Jeff Stelling had to remind Merson what Yakubu's first goal was like. You get the feeling that a lot of Sky's expensively assembled cast of experts would struggle to find the toilet if wasn't for Stelling. Three weeks later and football's answer to Shakespeare was at it again. Referring to one angry Rovers fan as a "fatty" and the rest "scandalous" Merson claimed that Rovers fans would rather see their team lose 5-0 than draw 0-0. I wouldn't mind but he says this stuff as if it is fact. Personally I'd have paid double to watch a 0-0 and so would all the other Rovers fans I know- but who are we to question the wisdom of Paul Merson? I have absolutely no problem with people criticising my club if they know what they are talking about but I really can't see what qualifies Paul Merson to have such strong and damaging opinions on Blackburn Rovers Football Club.

I feel that Sky took the lead with the underhand campaign against Rovers fans but there were people in the BBC studios weren't without their moments (or muuuuuuuuurments as one of the worst culprit likes to say!) I love *talkSPORT* but even they have had their fair share of digs at Rovers' fans over the last 12 months. Presenters like Adrian Durham, Danny Kelly and Alan Brazil are as informative and entertaining as any sports broadcasters around. If they have a dig at Rovers fans I know that there is probably a bit of thought and a reason behind it. I don't have a problem with people criticising my football club as long as I feel that their argument is balanced and fair and there is some element of knowledge behind it. When Everton manager David Moyes criticised Rovers fans after the Bolton game I was happy to listen to what he was saying. I have listened to Moyes talk about Rovers for 12 years and I have always found the majority of what he has said interesting, accurate and fair. I acknowledge that a handful of Rovers fans were out of order that night. The media hysteria that followed Moyes' comments was what made me angry. I genuinely don't have a problem with criticism or acknowledging mistakes. My real bugbear is people who know nothing about anything clambering on the bandwagon to chip in with their opinion about absolutely everything. There are loads of them at it and it was so unnecessary, ill-informed and damaging.

Where has the anti-Rovers feeling come from? I couldn't tell you with any certainty but I do feel that some people have power, some people have money and some people have popularity. When you see agents appearing on television, ex-footballers becoming advertising tools and commercial television networks facilitating them all, are we not just seeing a trade-off of power, money and popularity? Are there other things going on that we are not aware of? I honestly don't know. A high percentage of those with strong anti-Rovers opinions seem to be wealthy television celebrities who are paid to travel around the country watching Premier League football games – many of them are actually managed by Jerome Anderson's SEM. Do middle-aged millionaires really want to be spending large amounts of their time in Blackburn? Probably not. Do they really want to be taking digs at the Chairman and Chief Executive of the company that gets them on these shows? Probably not. It also has to be recognised that Sky and the Premier League are ultimately commercial entities. Behind everything they do is the need to make as much money as possible. The new £3 billion Premier League domestic television deal isn't going to pay for itself. Not only do big city clubs with big grounds generate more money on match days but it is pretty much fact that a 40,000-seater stadium full to capacity looks better on television than a two-thirds full Walkersteel Stand – making the Premier League a much more attractive commercial package. Even if they are not doing it deliberately, once you are playing for money, you don't cheer for the horse that wins you £10 over one that wins you £20 – that's just human nature.

Essentially, Sky is what it is - a massive private corporation that is doing its thing and making lots of money. You could argue that if people didn't like it then they don't need to buy in to it. I don't necessarily agree that only Sky subscribers are affected by the actions of Sky but as long as they continue to make lots of money from sport I don't see there will be any major changes to how they go about their business any time soon. The role of the BBC is a totally different matter and I think they need to have a serious look at how they broadcast football. The radio coverage is good. I prefer *talkSPORT* for the banter and comment but for me *BBC Five Live* has the edge when it comes to live games. What really disappoints me, especially when it comes to a lot of the football that comes on the television, is that the BBC's sports department still seems intent on branding itself as Sky on a budget. Surely the BBC is capable of better than this? I can honestly say that, provided it stays below £150 a year for at least the rest of the decade, the television licence fee is one of the few direct debits that I don't mind paying. With the exception of the football coverage I actually really like the BBC. I just think that their television football coverage is basically rubbish. When Sky came along at the start of the 1990s, the tactical analysis and razzmatazz was new and exciting. It wasn't the ex-footballers playing with draughts on a table that people were tapping in to, it was the fact that Sky's coverage was different to everything else that was around. Having ex-footballers sitting on a sofa talking you through condensed highlights of games they didn't go to isn't different anymore - nor is it relevant. I think that the BBC's television football coverage is boring, self-indulgent, wasteful and unnecessary and I imagine it is one of the principal reasons that more and more youngsters are turning away from football. When the BBC launched *Match of the Day 3* on *iPlayer*, presenter Jake Humphrey opened the show by asking guest pundit Lee Dixon, "So what happens here?" Dixon said, "We basically just talk rubbish for about 10 minutes." "So how is it different to *Match of the Day 2* then?" was Humphrey's reply. Humphrey and Dixon may have just been having a joke but I felt they had hit the nail on the head. Ex-pros talking rubbish - that's all modern television football coverage is to me.

Back in October 2011, a week in which the BBC announced 2,000 job cuts, my 37-inch TV almost wasn't wide enough to house the BBC's weekly panel of football experts. I don't mind my television licence fee going to Lee Nelson or George Alagiah but really, do I have to fund the public "rehabilitation" of Joey Barton? Wasn't this the same bad boy turned good that I had witnessed publicly assault Morten Gamst Pedersen less than 12 months earlier? At the time of Barton's many media appearances, I emailed the BBC and asked them, in a world of cuts, how long before they gave us the option to watch football without the pointless input of one pundit – let alone four? That would be a great red button feature. The reply came back,

> "We try to get a range of views on the week's events in football and we feel that hearing from two or three ex pros or current players helps provide with extra insight into certain footballing issues."

A range of views? Extra insight? Most of these pundits are essentially different models of the same person and I could tell you before they open their mouth what valuable insight is going to come next. People like Mark Lawrenson and Alan Hansen have been coming out with the same lines and been getting paid fortunes for the best part of 20 years – not to mention all the public money that has been wasted ferrying them to and from London every week prior to the BBC's move to Salford. I don't know why the BBC still thinks these people are worth the money. There are one or two ex-players at the BBC who have the ability to inform, amuse and entertain (Jimmy Armfield and Robbie Savage are the only obvious ones that spring to mind) but in the main the rest, and not just the ex-pros, are as bland and pointless as water soup. I couldn't comment on the ability of the people who work behind the scenes (the cameramen, make-up artists and the like) but a lot of those that I can see and hear are terrible. Which BBC football correspondent do you think came out with this one?

> "Aaaah, here we are at Anfield, the theatre of so many inescapably beautiful moments over so many dramatic years, but not the 'Theatre of Dreams', as their adversaries on the green sward today would have it. Liverpool v Manchester United; the aristocracy of the top flight, pledged once more in mortal combat. The crowd vociferous, Benitez demonstrative, Ferguson dismissive, and the officials keeping watch betwixt the vengeful forces not without some moments' worry. The weather is as if Thor himself has taken up residence by the Liver

birds, and his hammering can be heard above the din and opprobrium of the baying masses gathered in the howling wind and lashing rain brought by him to rent them asunder. Nevertheless, the cut! The thrust! The United back pair of Ferdinand and Vidic were as the Pillars of Hercules, seemingly able to stem the tide from reaching the Atlantic Ocean of Van der Sar's goal emanating from the wizardry of Gerrard and brutal strength of Robbie Keane. At the other end, Hyppia was like an insurmountable Everest, blocking Ronaldo's ascent to the peak he so desires, and after 70 minutes without a shot on goal, it's 0-0!"

Steve Claridge? Mark Bright? Martin Keown? Come on, you knew it was Stuart Hall by the time you got to the second sentence. Stuart Hall may not be everybody's cup of tea but at least he can string a sentence together without reaching for a cliché. It is becoming more and more common for broadcasters of his ilk to be replaced by monosyllabic ex-footballers telling you that the goalkeeper has just done a "worldy" or the fans are "shocking." No matter how popular football is, eventually people will just get turned off by this. The rise of punditry brought a lot of middle aged ex-players back from the dead in the early 1990s but I am afraid it has now become baggage that a non-commercial broadcasting network can no longer justify. I have absolutely no doubt in my mind that if the BBC started showing games with no pundits and the option to watch games with or without a commentator, not only would the BBC save millions but the games would be more enjoyable for a large proportion of those paying for the pleasure of watching them. We live in a totally different world to the one that saw the rise of football punditry. If you want to know what an ex-player thinks of a football game just turn on your laptop. The energy and relevance of the early days of *Sky Sports* has eventually turned in to five middle-aged men squeezing on to camera shot and taking turns to point out the obvious. Real work may be slowly corroding my brain but I am not quite there yet and I refuse to accept this rubbish. For me, and this applies to all forms of media in sport, the aim of what they are doing should be to inform, amuse and entertain otherwise we might as well just be watching the game without them. I appreciate that with commercial networks there is the underlying need to persuade, promote and sell and how much has this been a factor in some of the attitudes that have been encouraged towards Rovers fans remains a sticking point.

Chapter 18

What Now?

The one shining light throughout this mess has been the passion, commitment and sheer bloody-mindedness of the fans. Widely criticised for large periods of the 2011/12 season for daring to challenge the strangle hold the money men have on the game, Rovers fans have never let up in the fight to free our football club from those that hold power at Blackburn Rovers. When the fans were universally condemned for refusing to back a regime we didn't believe in we carried on protesting. It may have come as a shock to Premier League machine but not all football fans take their lead from middle-aged men in television studios.

Our club's rapid decline has been the result of far more than just not being good enough on the pitch and that is what the fans cannot accept. Steve Kean and Venky's are disliked by 99.8% of Rovers fans. Think for a moment what that actually means. We are not talking pockets of disparate minorities. We are talking about almost every single Rovers fan there is. From 80 year old men who have been attending games since before the Second World War to groups of teenage friends who don't know who Mark Atkins is.

Much credit has to go to the group of fans that came forward at the start of the 2011/12 season to take part in the protest marches, not least the protest organisers. Despite many attempts to discredit the protests, mainly from people within the club and certain sections of the media, I witnessed the protests first hand and they were peaceful, well organised and fully justified. People power is the one thing that I still think terrifies the establishment as it is normal people that are essentially funding the Premier League's private members party. When Steve Kean talks of "activist groups" it conjures up images of balaclava wearing teenagers with Kaleshnikovs strapped to their back. I think we are far enough along in the book for you to know exactly what I think of what Steve Kean says. These are normal football fans with families and full-time jobs who just want to protect Blackburn Rovers' proud 137 year history. The protest movement has quickly evolved into the fully elected BRFC Action Group. Now an official affiliate of the Football Supporters Federation, BRFC Action Group has made great strides since its formation at the start of 2012. With the help of prominent local figures including Jack Straw, former Blackburn with Darwen council leader Sir Bill Taylor and Councillor Maureen Bateson MBE, BRFC Action Group managed to secure meetings with Chairman of the Premier League Peter Scudamore, the Football Association and they have even visited the Houses of Parliament. Testament to the challenges normal fans face if they want to put the brakes on the Premier League gravy train, the same day that members of the BRFC Action Group went to Parliament to discuss reform of football governance rules Peter Scudamore announced that the Premier League's television deal for 2013 to 2016 would be a massive £3 billion - a 71% increase from the previous deal. Football agents and their clients across the world will have been too busy working out how to lay claim to their cut of the new TV deal to worry too much about the snail like progress being made in the Houses of Parliament.

Although it has been BRFC Action Group that has become the most high profile supporters' group there are many other Blackburn Rovers supporters groups and communities that continue to work tirelessly for the cause. Some fans have expressed concern that the various different groups could have a divisive effect. I think it is good that all these different groups exist. Whereas people used to be grouped together by location, advances in technology mean that we are now more likely to be grouped together by shared interests and ideals. I would urge Rovers fans to look into the work these different groups do and to get involved.

The Fans' Forum has grown in prominence and numbers since the start of the 2011/12 season and continues to maintain a line of communication with the club. Let's hope that the club starts to listen properly again to what the Fans' Forum is actually saying. In July 2012 the newly appointed Global Advisor Shebby Singh met with members of the Fans' Forum and answered their questions for over an hour. In the meeting Shebby Singh acknowledged that without the fans the club is nothing. Members of the Fans' Forum expressed the view that the current broken relationship with the fans could only be fixed properly with a change of manager. Steve Kean remains his post at the time of writing.

Several members of the Fans' Forum will be better known for being part of Ewood Blues - the group of Rovers fans that provides coach travel to away games from the Aqueduct pub. Whether Rovers have been playing mid-week games away at Portsmouth or pre-season friendlies in Scandinavia there will have been few games that Ewood Blues have not had some presence at. Going to games and having a good time is essentially what football is all about to most people and that is the spirit of Ewood Blues.

There are a number of excellent Rovers sites on the Internet. I have dipped in and out of them all from time to time but BRFCS is the site that I always return to. I think that the BRFCS message boards are second-to-none when it comes to discussing Rovers.

There was a time that I prided myself on being part of the biggest group of all – the normal football fan who just wants to go to games and have a laugh. I have now come to accept that this is all that the members of the various groups and communities are – in many cases they are just prepared to go the extra mile to ensure that this continues to be the case. An example of the lengths some of these fans will go to in order protect the proud history of Blackburn Rovers Football Club is the work of BRFCS forum members in ensuring that the 64 year old tradition of burying the coffin every time Blackburn Rovers are relegated was upheld after our latest relegation. Sixty-four years ago, upon Blackburn

Rovers' relegation from the old Division One to Division Two Blackburn Rovers fans gathered in the cellar of the Trades Hall, Bamber Bridge to lay a coffin in a symbolic burial of their dreams, marking the sad passing of their team's time in the then Premier League. Thus began a quirky custom that was also adopted by neighbours Preston North End. Over the years, the custom developed into something far less sombre than the funeral element suggests. Gradually, an ever-growing procession of milk floats, carnival style, and mock mourning (a comic priest delivering a few last words) were incorporated into proceedings, usually followed by a convivial gathering in the nearby public houses and fundraising for charity. Unfortunately, mainly due to police and local licensee disagreement on how events could take place safely and happily (following public order issues after Preston North End's burial event last year), it looked like the long-held tradition would disappear for good until a handful of Rovers fans stepped forward to organise the event themselves. The "funeral" was a great success and provided much needed light relief from the stresses and strains of the eighteen months that had gone before.

I understand why some fans still feel that having all these different groups could have a divisive effect. I think that the initiative led by Sir Bill Taylor to bring all the groups together to regularly discuss their progress is a logical and worthwhile development. Initially named "Blackburn United," the meetings now fall under the more appropriately titled "Rovers Supporters Groups and Communities." On announcement of the initiative Sir Bill Taylor, told the *Lancashire Telegraph,*

> "The group has the support of all three local MPs, Blackburn Council Leader Cllr Kate Hollern and Ewood councillor, Cllr Maureen Bateson. Both the Mayor and Deputy Mayor are supportive of the group's intentions. Graham Jones MP was in attendance. The aim of Rovers Supporters Groups and Communities is not to impinge upon the work of any of these hard working groups but to work alongside them all to coordinate all their efforts. As individuals Rovers fans are comparatively powerless compared to the wealth and strength of the current regime running the club. Our strength is in the depth of our passion and commitment towards what we hold preciously and dearly. We only wished that Venky's would simply talk and listen to us in a mutually respectful manner."

The Rovers Supporters Groups and Communities continue to meet regularly and good progress is being made. Essentially the people involved are still all part of the biggest group of all – normal football fans who just want to enjoy going to Rovers knowing that the club is in safe hands – and that is why the different approaches will work if they continue to be co-ordinated correctly.

So what is the alternative to the shambolic reign of Venky's? Unfortunately, at no point during their eighteen month reign have Venky's made any indication that they are ready to sell the club. If Venky's do decide to sell, BRSIT, the initiative that plans to bring Blackburn Rovers into community ownership is working tirelessly to put together a realistic bid. BRSIT is aiming to raise as much money possible through the sale of shares at £1000 each. The proposed community and supporter-based ownership scheme continues to gain momentum. Shortly after Rovers' relegation to The Championship 500 Rovers fans packed out King George's Hall for a presentation by BRSIT co-founder Wayne Wild. By July 2012, BRSIT was up to almost £3 million in pledged funds. I wouldn't tell anybody what to do with their money but I have pledged and BRSIT is something that I would love to see work.

Since the launch of BRSIT, corporate finance and capital raising company Seneca Partners have also been working to bring a "credible and well funded proposition" to offer Venky's a way out. Based in Haydock, Seneca Partners offers corporate finance and advisory services to individuals, entrepreneurs, corporates and investors. Rovers fan Ian Battersby is a key figure at Seneca Partners and having listened to him speak about the situation at Rovers he is clearly a knowledgeable and well informed individual. To date he is one of the few Rovers fans to have had a one-to-one with Mrs Desai. However he managed to secure a three hour meeting in India with Venky's Chairperson, I hope he is able to utilise those skills to help secure the future of Blackburn Rovers for the good of the wider community.

I have literally trawled through hundreds of hours worth of material to try and find out what is going on at Blackburn Rovers. It has been a constant struggle but I do feel I have built up a good understanding of the problems that exist. I have been strongly advised to steer clear of anything I can't prove as fact and if I don't heed this warning I can expect to end up in court. That is the level of help I have received whilst trying to piece this story together. Enough of the basic story has already been revealed to make Rovers fans' requests for more information perfectly justified. As told in their own words,

> "The trustees of the late Jack Walker, who are being professionally advised, and the club's board of directors are acutely aware of the responsibility involved in passing the club to a new owner."
> John Williams, Blackburn Rovers Chairman

> "At the request of the trustees, I was asked to assist them to find a buyer for their club."
> Jerome Anderson, Football Agent and Chairman of SEM (corporate partners to Kentaro)

> "People are crazy about football. In all these markets that I am talking about, southeast market, Middle East market and even in the European market, it is a very famous game and I feel that the Venky's brand will get an immediate recognition if we take over this club. This is the main reason, why we are doing this."
> Mrs Desai, Venky's Chairperson and Co-Owner of Blackburn Rovers

> "Every project is different, but you can measure success pretty easily. Basically, is the client happy with what's coming out at the bottom line?"
> Phillipp Huber, Chairman of Kentaro (the company advising Venky's)

"Venky's growth from next to nothing is another story of the explosion of entrepreneurship which is turning India into a global power. Britain was the pioneer in world economic dominance. We exported far more goods than we imported, then used the surplus to invest abroad. India, among others, is now returning the compliment – and we should welcome it."
Jack Straw, Former Home Secretary and MP for Blackburn

"I didn't really have any contact with the owners. I spoke with them once on the phone."
Sam Allardyce, Ex-Blackburn Rovers Manager (sacked by Venky's within one month)

"A trusted little bird told me two months ago what was going to happen. He said that the club would be taken over by an Indian company and that Sam would be pushed aside, to be replaced by the coach Steve Kean."
Andy Cole, Former Blackburn Rovers player – also coached by Steve Kean at Fulham

"You've got that issue at Blackburn of an agent involved and deciding the future of the club, Jerome Anderson, he couldn't pick his nose. It's baffling and it's a serious threat to how clubs get run and how they conduct themselves."
Fergie, Manchester United Manager

"We entered last year's January transfer window and I received a call from the owner of the club

saying 'We have one or two issues causing us concern. Would you be kind enough to help us through this difficult period?' So I basically slept at the training ground for the month of January and helped the club in so many areas."
Jerome Anderson, Football Agent and Chairman of SEM (Corporate partners to Kentaro)

"If I was an outsider and I wasn't involved in it, I would go, well that – exactly that – well that looks a bit contrived, that looks a bit cosy."
Steve Kean, Blackburn Rovers manager and SEM client on his promotion

"We feel that Myles Anderson is a player with great potential as a late developer. He could become something of a Chris Smalling."
Steve Kean, Blackburn Rovers manager and SEM client on Jerome Anderson's son

"It is not just simple bids, you have things like passports to check, things like who actually owns the player fully. These type of things have to be checked to make sure things are fit and proper."
Steve Kean, Blackburn Rovers manager and SEM client on transfers

"You can measure results in different ways – your points, your improvement, or the price that everyone is worth."
Steve Kean, Blackburn Rover manager and SEM client on results

"We do know that a few people have been generating thousands of mails demanding the ousting of current manager Steve Kean, who is a brilliant manager."
Balaji Rao, Venky's Managing Director and Co-Owner of Blackburn Rovers

"We are bottom of the league, have just gone out of the Carling Cup to a Championship club and the majority of Kean's signings to date have struggled to adjust to life in the Premier League. If Venky's do not remove the manager now, the question needs to be asked why?"
Glen Mullan, Blackburn Rovers fan

"Contractual issues have not allowed me to be selected. It is about contractually a few more games would give me a longer contract and obviously there are decisions to be made there."
Jason Roberts, Blackburn Rovers

"I hope I can still win the fans over and I can only do that by winning games."
Steve Kean, Blackburn Rover manager and SEM client

"In the case of Steve Kean, when the supporters react that way you say to yourself there's something wrong with society. Every manager knows it's a results industry."
Fergie, Manchester United manager

"Blackburn Rovers FC are at the heart of the local community. The club is vital to the area's well

being. We are just concerned that their future is safeguarded."
Kate Hollern, Leader of Blackburn with Darwen Borough Council

I've never really had any dealings with the owners. There's so many financial directors, sporting directors and god-knows-what directors at that club. It's a shame the way it has gone. I'm glad I'm out of there."
Keith Andrews, Blackburn Rovers

"If Steve Kean keeps Blackburn up but doesn't win Manager of the Year there is only one course of action open to the man who does. Decline it, on the grounds that the adversity Kean has overcome, and the manner in which he has overcome it, has done more for their profession's reputation than one man winning any amount of trophies could ever achieve."
Brian Reade, The Daily Mirror

"Not even an attempt. Friedel and Yak could have played cards."
Michel Salgado, Blackburn Rovers, on crucial game in which Rovers had zero shots

"Blackburn fans deserve relegation because they didn't support their club."
Numpties, Twitter

"We have rules, quite strict rules. They have passed all the ownership tests that we apply - in terms of the

legality of their ownership, funding and right to own a football club. But clearly, when it came to the decision-making and performance of the club, this season it has not been enough to keep them in the league. You can't possibly expect us to be sitting in our office in London and be running clubs. We just don't run clubs at all. We put in place a framework of rules but the owners themselves run clubs."
Richard Scudamore, Chief Executive of the Premier League

"I know you've been negative Andy – but I would rather be positive. I'm positive. You've been negative all season."
Steve Kean, Blackburn Rovers' manager and SEM client on relegation

"As fans and people of the town who care about the future of our club we need to pull together, support the efforts of all those who are trying to bring about influence and change and through their efforts give us back the club we love and can once again be proud of."
Cllr Maureen Bateson MBE, Ewood Ward Councillor

"The continuing support of BSkyB for Premier League football is significant beyond the revenues delivered; the longevity and quality of their commitment has done much for the English game as a whole. We are very happy to see this relationship maintained for another three seasons."

Richard Scudamore, Chief Executive of the Premier League on the £3billion TV deal

"I do believe football can and should be a force for good in the lives of those who play and watch it, not a playground for global business."
David Conn, The Guardian

"If they have got money they don't offend me."
Alan Nixon, The Daily Mirror on the 2012 takeover at Reading

The story of the last two years at Blackburn Rovers does not look good. What makes it worse is that I fear that we are only actually seeing the tip of the iceberg. I would have liked to have been able to include more detailed testimonies from the many names that have featured in the story. Believe me it has not been through a lack of effort on my part. Football is a closed shop. You only have to look at the difficulty BRSIT and BRFC Action Group have had trying to get ex-Rovers players to publicly support the fans' cause. Simon Garner, a true Rovers legend, was the first to stick his head above the parapet and to date few have followed his lead. I know there is more to come out of this story but if anyone else wants to have a try at getting the information from the people that can provide it feel free to go insane just like I have. To me it appears that the rewards for keeping quiet are greater than the rewards for speaking out. Michel Salgado, Keith Andrews, Christopher Samba, El-Hadji Diouf and Nicola Kalinic have all been publicly critical of the new order at Blackburn Rovers. It is good to see them come forward and add to Rovers fans' understanding of what is going on. Every bit of information helps build a picture. I now want to see Mrs Desai, Steve Kean, Jerome Anderson, Paul Agnew, John Williams, Tom Finn, Martin Goodman, David Brown, Paul Egerton-Vernon, Paul Hunt, Robert Coar and the people at Kentaro answer some questions. I am not talking about the sort of questions Sky's Rob Wooton was asking Jerome Anderson or the *Daily Mail*'s Matt Lawton was asking Steve Kean, I mean proper questions that can clear up what has happened at Blackburn Rovers. I still can't work out who is actually advising Venky's on football matters. By their own admission they were reliant on the advice and assistance of Kentaro and SEM before, during and immediately after the takeover – when did this stop, if indeed it has, and who then stepped in to fill in the gaps? It is so frustrating when previous employees of the club come out and say they have signed a non-disclosure agreement or fob fans off with feeble statements like "it's in the past." It may be in the past if you have landed another top job in another part of the country or you are still receiving a big wage from the club but it is very much in the present for Rovers fans and people who live in Blackburn. Personally, if this story was following me around every day I would want to bury the rumours once and for all. I don't see how those involved can expect to be taken seriously until they come forward and answer the questions the fans need answers to. It is all too easy to blame the eccentric Indian chicken farmers who live on another continent. Venky's are far from blameless but there are so many others who have contributed to the rapid decline of Blackburn Rovers

Football Club. If it wasn't Venky's causing the problems I don't see that Lawrence Bassini, Ahsan Ali Syed and Saurin Shah would have been any better. Why were these people considered suitable potential buyers for a Premier League football club? Why did the Premier League allow a football agent to play such a prominent role in advising Venky's before, during and after the takeover process? Why doesn't John Williams speak out about what is going on at Blackburn Rovers? What action was taken regarding Gael Givet's claims that he was forced to give £50,000 to an unlicensed agent? Why has the spotlight been turned on good, honest fans? Why have the club signed players who are clearly not of Premier League pedigree? Who is the real decision maker at Blackburn Rovers? Why is SEM client Steve Kean still the manager despite 18 months of failure? I could fill 100 pages with questions. It is time that those involved came forward and answered them. I don't want to be a part of football's sordid private members club. It is not my intention to try and name and shame people just for the fun of it. My aim is absolutely clear. When I hand over my wage to watch football I want to be able to believe in what I am paying for. For the "Premier League product" to work it has got to be believable that the game of football is more important than money. I just don't believe it anymore. The people at Sky continue to tell us that we are watching the biggest and the best but I am fed up of humouring the lie. The games may be fast and furious but if you watch replays of pre-1992 *Match of the Day* and *The Big Match* and you will see that they always have been. The people at the Premier League didn't invent football; they just found a way of making vast sums of money out of it. The pitches are greener, the hot dogs are bigger and the players are fitter but at what price? Top level football has completely lost its way and I am one of thousands of football fans that can't take it anymore. Whatever has been going on at Blackburn Rovers over the last 18 months, winning games has quite clearly not been the priority. That is abundantly clear and for anyone to deny it would be an insult to the intelligence of football fans. We are the ones paying for all this and that appears to have been forgotten. If the people involved in Blackburn Rovers and the Premier League wish to be taken seriously they need to move quickly to address the issues that are being raised here or risk losing all credibility.

Commercialism, greed and self-interest are destroying English football. I suspected as much when I started writing this book and I am now absolutely convinced of it.

Things will only change if people challenge how the game is being run and then do something about it. I think it is great that these various Rovers supporters groups have emerged and I can see that progress being made. This is not just about our club and I think the part of the role of these groups should be to assist supporters of other clubs when required. I know that the Liverpool supporters group The Spirit of Shankly has been a great help to the BRFC Action Group. I hope that this is something we see replicated across other groups of fans in 2012/13. I am just a normal football fan with a wife and a kid, who goes to work and tries to make my £15,000 a year stretch as far as possible. The battle against corporate greed in football can't be won by individuals. It would be good to see Rovers fans marching with fans of other clubs next season.

Carlos Tevez, a player who is paid around £1 million a month, was able to call upon the help of his union, the Professional Footballer's Association, when his employer alleged that he refused to come off the bench in a UEFA Champion's League game. When Steve Kean was criticised by Rovers fans the League Manager's Association grouped together to defend him. Who co-ordinates the frustrations of football fans when we feel aggrieved? Since the problems started at Rovers I have become aware of the Football Supporters' Federation. The group actively campaigns to ensure the rights of football fans and again I would urge people to take a look at the work they do and to get involved. The Football Supporters' Federation has been closely monitoring the progress of the Culture, Media and Sport Select Committee's work to ensure effective football governance. The Culture, Media and Sport Select Committee are proposing:

- Ownership rules overseen by the FA
- A professional club licensing regime overseen by the the FA
- Reform of the FA Board to bring in more independent directors
- A recognition that debt-financed takeovers have no benefits for supporters
- Measures to promote and simplify supporter ownership

I would suggest that there are far more problems in football than those listed above and as is usually the case I would like to see more done and quicker. When you have things like the Football Creditors rule (the law that ensures other clubs owed transfer fees and players' wages are paid before all other creditors) and the widely criticised Fit and Proper Person's Test in a world where £3 billion will shortly be divvied out to the same old faces, ineffective governance is clearly a major part of the problem. It is still debatable how many of football's problems will be solved by the introduction of UEFA Financial Fair Play rules (in which clubs in European competition have to break even) and I will wait to see how the clubs involved approach it.

I am not the only one that can see similarities between what has happened at Rovers and the recent takeover at Reading. Majority shareholder Anton Zingarevich said of a meeting with Premier League Chief Executive Richard Scudamore shortly after the takeover,

> "The impression I got was that Scudamore and the Premier League were concerned about the Blackburn experience. They wanted to know whether an agent had any control over Reading. I was able to explain to Scudamore what I was trying to achieve. Then he felt more comfortable and we got along."

I will be keeping a close eye on what goes on at Reading over the next two years and football fans should be ready to work in unison if certain standards aren't met.

As long as the game's governing bodies continue to allow our national league to be a grossly under-regulated private members club it is a cancer that will not go away. This is not just a problem that affects Blackburn Rovers. It is a problem that affects every single club in the country. Football fans cannot allow this to happen. "Arte et Labore" (meaning skill and hard work) is the club motto that has seen Blackburn Rovers Football Club through 137 years of highs, lows and everything in between. In those 137 years the club has faced many challenges. The current challenge is the biggest to date. It will take skill, hard work and the help of true football fans everywhere to overcome the threat posed by all those who put individual gain before entire communities. Rovers fans have shown that it is a fight we can win.

Lightning Source UK Ltd.
Milton Keynes UK
UKOW04f0625181213

223244UK00001B/3/P